THE HACKER'S HANDBOOK III

THE HACKER'S HANDBOOK III

HUGO CORNWALL

CENTURY
LONDON MELBOURNE AUCKLAND JOHANNESBURG

First published in 1985 as *The Hacker's Handbook,*
revised editions 1986, 1988, by Century Hutchinson Ltd,
62-65 Chandos Place, London WC2N 4NW

Century Hutchinson Australia (Pty) Ltd
88-91 Albion Street, Surry Hills,
NSW 2010, Australia

Century Hutchinson New Zealand Ltd
191 Archers Road, Glenfield,
Auckland 10, New Zealand

Century Hutchinson South Africa (Pty) Ltd
PO Box 337, Bergvlei 2012, South Africa

Reprinted 1988 (three times)

Set in Times by Avocet Marketing Services, Bicester, Oxon
Printed and bound in Great Britain by
Anchor Brendon Ltd, Tiptree, Essex

British Library Cataloguing in Publication Data
Cornwall, Hugo
The hacker's handbook III.
1. Computers—Access control
I. Title
005.8   QA76.9.A25

ISBN 0-7126-1147-9

Contents

Preface to Third Edition

The original *Hacker's Handbook* had quite modest expectations. It was written because, halfway through 1984, it had become apparent that there was a growing interest in the exploration, from the comfort of the homely personal computer, of the world of large mainframes and the data networks that connected them to each other. The same questions were coming up over and over again in magazines and hobbyist bulletin boards. Why not, the publishers and I asked ourselves, produce a book to satisfy this demand? At the same time, I and a number of other hackers were concerned to make sure that those who were going to play around with other people's machines understood the fundamental ethics of hacking and, without being too pompous about it, I thought I could do that in the course of the book.

During 1985 the original *Hacker's Handbook* went through a remarkable number of reprints and a fresh edition appeared just under a year after the first. By 1988 rather a lot of things have changed. In 1984 the home computers most likely to be owned by the book's British readers would have been the Sinclair Spectrum or the Acorn/BBC Model B. Increasingly, one must expect that the domestic market is using clones of the IBM PC or, if they have come to computing via word–processing machines, the Amstrad. PCW 8256 or 8512, or perhaps an icon–based machine like the Apple Mac or Atari ST family. These machines simply have much more power and many more features than their predecessors of three or so years previously. Among other things, the disc drive is no longer a luxury and very few people have to rely on cassette players for program and data storage. The software such computers can support is much more sophisticated.

Again on the equipment front, the typical modem was an unsophisticated device which required the user to lever a telephone handset into some rubber cups in order to make a connection to the outside world. Today's modems are not only directly connected to the telephone system, they have a large range of functions which can be called into play and which increase their versatility and value. They are also much more affordable.

The world outside the home computer has also changed. Electronic publishing was still a tentative, self–apologetic industry in 1984; now it is operating with vigour and there are many more and many different systems and services to be explored. There has been an astonishing growth in the range of electronic services available for customers of all kinds to use; some represent substantial publishing activities, others allow large companies to work ever more closely with their branches and men in the field, or to communicate more effectively with retailers. The keen competition to sell new financial services has made banks and building societies place even more of their future hopes in communications technology. Electronic mail systems are now serious commercial enterprises. At the same time, the range of network facilities – the railway lines or roads along which data can travel from one remote location to another – has been considerably extended both in terms of sophistication and the number of people who expect to use it.

In 1984 a British home computer's first use of an external service would almost certainly have been Prestel; now it could be any of up to ten useful information and electronic mail facilities. Prestel itself has been overtaken in the size of its user base by Telecom Gold. In what is now the second extensive rewrite (and hence the Third Edition) I am taking the opportunity to give new readers the chance to appreciate the world of hacking in terms of the equipment and experiences of the late- rather than the mid-1980s.

Perceptions about hacking have altered as well. In 1984 the word was only beginning to shade over from its original meaning as 'computer enthusiast' into the more specialist 'network adventurer'. However, in the last couple of years, sections of the popular press have begun to equate 'hacker' with 'computer criminal' or 'computer fraudster'. This has never been my definition. At the same time, the authorities seem to have homed in on hacking – in the sense of unauthorized entry into a computer system – as the most serious aspect of computer crime. That this is in defiance of all the research work and statistics doesn't seem to bother them. Computer crime is most typically and frequently committed by an employee of the victim. Accordingly I am taking the opportunity to explain more clearly what I regard as the purpose of, and limitations on, hacking.

In 1984 I thought I was writing for a knowledgeable elite; the first print was 5000 copies and if the book had only sold that number I guess that both the publisher and author would have felt that things had gone 'alright'. In the UK alone, ten times that number have already been sold and there have also been overseas editions. As it happens, I firmly reject accusations that the book has caused any substantive harm, but obviously knowledge of the existence of a wider readership has made me assume less about people's sense of how to behave responsibly.

There has also been a change in my personal circumstances: I now earn a good part of my living from advising on computer security and systems integrity. Since hacking in the way I describe it is such a small part of the overall range of risks faced by companies through their computer systems, there is very little conflict between those activities and the authorship of this book. However I now receive a large amount of confidential material in the course of my work. I must be explicit about the simple rule I have always adopted in deciding what to include: the confidentiality of information given to me in the course of work is paramount, just as I have always respected the confidences of hackers. But anything which has already been uncovered by hackers and enjoyed circulation among them is fair game for repetition here.

The aims remain the same. The book is an accessible introduction to the techniques of making a micro speak to the outside world, a rapid survey of the sorts of information and data out there waiting to be siphoned through a domestic machine and a scene-setter for those seduced by the sport of hacking. It is *not* the last word in hacking. No such book could ever exist because new 'last words' are being uttered all the time; indeed that is one of the many attractions of the sport.

Literary detectives who possess either of the previous editions of *The Hacker's Handbook* will have little difficulty in recognizing whole sections in this new edition, though I hope they will also identify the many new features and details. While re-writing the book I have taken the opportunity to update every aspect of those earlier editions that have proved worth retaining, in some cases considerably expanding on what had previously only been hinted at; I have replaced certain material that originally had to be omitted for legal reasons and have included some completely new descriptions of major hacks that have either come to light recently or where, for one reason or another, it is now safe to offer a report.

As with the original book, various people helped me on various aspects of this book; they will all remain unnamed – they know who they are and that they have my thanks.

Hugo Cornwall
London, October 1987

Introduction

The word 'hacker' is now used in three different but loosely associated ways: in its original meaning, at least as far as the computer industry is concerned, a hacker is merely a computer enthusiast of any kind, one who loves working with the beasties for their own sake, as opposed to operating them in order to enrich a company or research project – or to play games. In the compressed shorthand language of newspaper and TV news headlines, a 'hacker' has sometimes become synonymous with 'computer criminal'.

This book uses the word in a more restricted sense: hacking is a recreational and educational sport; it consists of attempting to make unofficial entry into computers and to explore what is there. The sport's aims and purposes have been widely misunderstood; most hackers are *not* interested in perpetrating massive frauds, modifying their personal banking, taxation and employee records or inducing one world superpower into inadvertently commencing Armageddon in the mistaken belief that another superpower is about to attack it.

Every hacker I have ever come across has been quite clear where the fun lies: it is in developing an understanding of a system and finally producing the skills and tools to command it. In the vast majority of cases the processes of 'getting in' and exploring the architecture of the operating system and applications is much more satisfying than what is in the end discovered from protected data files. In this respect the hacker is the direct descendant of the phone phreaks of fifteen years ago; phone phreaking became interesting as intra-national and international subscriber trunk dialling was introduced – when the London-based phreak finally chained his way through to Hawaii he usually had no one there to speak to – except the local weather service or American Express office to confirm that the desired target had indeed been hit.

Interestingly enough, one of the earliest of the present generation of hackers, Susan Headley, only 17 when she began her exploits in California in 1977, chose as her target the local phone company and, with the information extracted from her hacks, ran all over the telephone network. In one of the many interviews which she has given since, she has explained what attracted her: it was a sense of power. Orthodox computer designers have to be among the intellectual elite of our time; and here was a 17–year–old blonde, hitherto heavily into rock musicians, showing their work up. She 'retired' four years later when a boyfriend started developing schemes to shut down part of the phone system. Last heard of, after giving evidence to a committee of the US Congress, she was working on a 'government project'.

There is also a strong affinity with program copy-protection crunchers. As is well-known, much commercial software for micros is sold in a form to prevent obvious casual copying, say by loading a cassette, cartridge or disk into memory and then executing a 'save' on to a fresh blank disk. Copy-protection devices vary greatly in their methodology and sophistication and there are those who, without any commercial desire, enjoy nothing so much as defeating them. Every computer buff has met at least one cruncher with a vast store of commercial programs, all of which have somehow had the protection removed – and perhaps the main title subtly altered to show the cruncher's technical skills – but which are then never actually *used* at all.

But there is also a strong link with 'hacking' in that earlier sense as it existed around Massachusetts Institute of Technology at the end of the 1950s and again in the Bay Area to the south-west of San Francisco in what was becoming known as Silicon Valley in the early 1970s. It is in the existence of this link that one can find some justification for the positive benefits of hacking as a sporting activity to counter-balance the ugly stories of vandalism and invasions of privacy.

On a warm Friday afternoon in the late autumn of 1986 I was being driven in a shaking RV – recreational vehicle – past the Silicon Valley townships of San Mateo, Palo Alto, Cupertino and Sunnyvale up into the redwood-forested hills towards a prototypical American Holiday Camp. I was on my way to the Hackers 2.0 Conference, a follow-up of the first Hackercon which had been a class reunion for a group of people, some of whom had known each other for nearly fifteen years, and who were linked by their enthusiasms for stretching ever further the possibilities of computer technologies.

Among the just-under 200 attendees were people who had invented computer languages (Charles H. Moore and FORTH); those who had designed computers (the original Osborne transportable, the Apple Mac); those whose animations simulating satellite movements around distant planets for NASA have become part of the way in which most of us imagine space; those who had been members of the original Xerox team that invented the icons and pull-down menus now used in GEM, on the Apple Mac and other machines; and those who had written some of the best-selling computer games ever and who had met each other either at MIT or at the Homebrew Computing Club, from whose deliberations sprang the realisation of the personal computer.

One of the many interesting aspects of the meeting was how much all these pioneers had depended on borrowing equipment and facilities on an unofficial basis; and how they had used the resources of their employees and of the US government to experiment, explore and make contact with each other. It is salutary to realize how many of the features now taken for granted in modern computing originated, not from the big computer companies, universities or government-sponsored research organizations, but from the eccentric pre-occupations of rebels. We all assume today that computers are 'interactive', in other words, if we sit down at a keyboard and type something, the computer will reply, if only to the effect that it doesn't understand what is wanted.

The typical computer of the early 1960s didn't do that; it was simply a sophisticated processing or calculating machine: you gave it a pile of instructions and pile of data (pile here isn't just a colourful metaphor – you literally presented the machines with stacks of cards with holes strategically punched in them) and told the machine to 'run'. At the end, you had some results, either in the form of new punch-cards which you could examine with the aid of a special reader or as a printout. The machine in the meantime had switched itself off. The hackers had wanted to talk to the machine direct and get an immediate reply and they wrote the tools that would let them do so. They invented 'silly' exercises – getting the machine to draw pictures on a cathode ray tube, playing tunes through a tinny loudspeaker.

Later, they discovered how to set up computer bulletin boards, hijacking parts of mainframes for the purpose. Initially they wanted to keep in touch with each other, but later, in a rush of idealism, they tried providing mail and contact services for a wider community in Berkeley, California. The basic ideas can be seen in all commercial electronic mail services.

The personal computer was not invented by IBM, Sperry, Burroughs, companies of the early 1970s. The microprocessors upon which they were based were designed for industrial process control – for machine tools, to give intelligence to airplane landing gear, to traffic lights and so on. It was the hackers – and you can follow the same personalities through this history – who realized that these new chips, together with the memory chips that were becoming available, meant that the home-brew computer was achievable.

This first generation of hackers also included hooligans. Among the attendees at Hackers 2.0 was Cap'n Crunch. Back in 1972 the magazine *Esquire* produced a legendary article, reprinted all over the world – my copy comes from the London *Sunday Telegraph magazine* – about phone phreaks. Cap'n Crunch, John T. Draper, was one of its stars. He designed the infamous blue boxes – tone generators which mimicked the command tones used within the US telephone system for call-routing. Armed with these, you could telephone around the world for free. Later, he was to go to prison several times for his excesses. But he was also one of the earlier employees at Apple Computer.

Technological hooliganism is one of the routes by which technology advances.

Perhaps I should tell you what you can reasonably expect from this handbook: hacking is an activity like few others – it sometimes steers close to the edge of what is acceptable to conventionality and the law, it is seldom encouraged and, in its full extent, so vast that no individual or group, short of an organization like GCHQ or NSA can hope to grasp a fraction of the possibilities. So, this is not one of those books with titles like *Games Programming with the 6502* where, if the book is any good, you are any good, and given a bit of time and enthusiasm, you will emerge with some mastery of the subject-matter.

The aim of this handbook is to give you some grasp of methodology, help you develop the appropriate attitudes and skills, provide essential background and some referencing material – and point you in the right directions for more knowledge.

Up to a point, each chapter may be read by itself; it is a handbook and I have made extensive use of appendices which contain material of use long after the main body of the text has been read.

It is one of the characteristics of hacking anecdotes, like those relating to espionage exploits, that almost no one closely involved has much stake in the truth; victims want to describe damage as minimal and perpetrators like to paint themselves as heroes while carefully disguising sources and methods. In addition, journalists who cover such stories are not always sufficiently competent to write accurately, or even to know when they are being hood-winked. (A note for journalists: any hacker who offers to break into a system on demand is conning you – the most you can expect is a repeat performance for your benefit of what a hacker has previously succeeded in doing. Getting to the 'front page' of a service or network need not imply that everything within that service can be accessed. Being able to retrieve confidential information, perhaps credit ratings, does not mean that the hacker would also be able to *alter* that data. Remember the first rule of good reporting: be sceptical.) This edition includes details of the most famous hack-that-never-was; the Great Satellite Moving Caper.

So far as possible, I have tried to verify each story that appears in these pages, but despite what magazine articles have sought to suggest, it is the case that hackers work in isolated groups. A book which came out shortly after mine was called *Out of the Inner Circle* and many people persist in the view that somewhere, rather like the Holy Grail, this Inner Circle of hackers of superhuman power actually exists. (To be fair to the author of the book, Bill Landreth, and his friends, their choice of name was deliberately a bit jokey). The truth is that, at various times, groups of people with similar interests do come together and produce serendipi-tous results.

One such recent British example went, during 1984, under the name Penzance. Slightly disguised, some Penzance material appears in Chapter 5. Penzance was a veritable hothouse of talent; its members perpetrated many of the headline-grabbing events of recent years. Penzance has changed its name several times since and, looking at what remains of it, it is obvious that it is no longer the focal information exchange it once was.

Some hackers have retired, others have moved on and new ones are arriving. The new hackers often don't know the old. I am never surprised when a completely new group suddenly emerges and pulls off some startling stunt. I do not mind admitting that my sources on some of the important hacks of recent years are more remote than I would like. In these cases, my accounts are of events and methods which, in all the circumstances, I believe are true. I welcome notes of correction.

Experienced hackers may identify one or two curious gaps in the range of coverage, or less than full explanations: you can choose any combination of the following explanations without causing me any worry – first, I may be ignorant and incompetent; second, much of the fun of hacking is making your own discoveries and I wouldn't want to spoil that; third, maybe there are a few areas which really are best left alone.

Ninety-five per cent of the material is applicable to readers in all countries; however, the author is British and so are most of his experiences.

The pleasures of hacking are possible at almost any level of computer competence beyond rank beginner and with quite minimal equipment. It is quite difficult to describe the joy of using the world's cheapest micro, some clever firmware, a home-brew acoustic coupler and find that, courtesy of a friendly remote Prime or VAX, you can be playing with the fashionable multitasking operating system, Unix.

The assumptions I have made about you as a reader are that you own a modest personal computer, a modem and some communications software which you know, roughly, how to use. (If you are not confident yet, practise logging on to a few hobbyist bulletin boards.) For more advanced hacking, better equipment helps; but, just as very tasty photographs can be taken with snapshot cameras, do not believe that the computer equivalent of a Hasselblad with a trolley-load of accessories is essential.

Since you may at this point be suspicious that I have vast technical resources at my disposal, let me describe the kit that was used for most of my network adventures. For the first five years, at the centre was a battered old Apple II+, its lid off most of the time to draw away the heat from the many boards cramming the expansion slots.

I still use an industry standard dot matrix printer, famous equally for the variety of type founts possible and the paper-handling path which regularly skews off.

I have several large boxes crammed with software as I collect comms and utilities software in particular like a deranged philatelist, but I use one or two packages almost exclusively.

Modems – well at this point the set-up does become unconventional: by the phone point are jack sockets for the now almost-obsolete BT 95A and BT 96A, the current BT 600 and a North American modular jack. Somewhere around, I have two acoustic couplers, devices for plunging telephone handsets into so that the computer can talk down the line, at the operating speeds of 300/300 and 75/1200 respectively, and three heavy mushroom-coloured 'shoe-boxes' representing British Telecom modem technology of seven or more years ago and operating at various speeds and combinations of duplex/half-duplex. Whereas the acoustic coupler connects my computer to the line by audio, the modem links up at electrical level and is more accurate and free from error.

At the moment, I use an IBM PC clone upon which I run an adapted version of Procomm. Procomm is an excellent 'shareware' package obtainable for the cost of the disk upon which it is recorded; the version I have includes an untidily added-on facility for UK standard videotex for Prestel and its cousins.

I have lots of other packages I have hardly touched since first receiving them. I have rationalized my modem collection down to two: a 'smart' modem utilising the AMD9170 chip (see Chapter 3 and Appendix V) and a secondhand 1200/1200 full duplex machine.

My equipment for radio hacking is described in Chapter 9. I have access to other equipment in my work and through friends, but that's what I used most of the time.

Behind me is my other important bit of kit: a filing cabinet. Hacking is *not* an activity confined to sitting at keyboards and watching screens. All good hackers retain formidable collections of articles, promotional material and documentation. Read on and you will see why.

1985 was the year in which hackers had to think carefully about the ethics of hacking. Up till then, hacking's elite quality, it seemed to many of us, provided sufficient control to prevent matters getting out-of-hand. However, the number of copies sold of the first *Hacker's Handbook* is evidence (though not, I think, the cause) that there are many more would-be hackers than I ever thought likely. During 1986 the British authorities showed how far they were willing to go in order to track down hackers who had caused embarrassment. In 1987 they found that the law is not prepared to find all kinds of hacking illegal. Read Chapter 8 to see what happened. These factors, if nothing else, persuade me that rather more should be said both about the morality of hacking and the legal position.

I personally have always been quite sure about how far I was prepared to go in pursuing the hacking sport. For me, hacking is not, and never has been, an all-consuming activity. It is simply a natural extension of my fascination with computers, networks, and new developments in technology. I want to know and experience the new before anybody else. Popping into people's computers to see what they are doing has always seemed to me little different from viewing those same machines on an exhibition stand or at a 'proper' demonstration, except that, using my way, I can explore and test from the comfort of my own home. Breaking into areas where I was supposed to be forbidden has always been part of testing the capability of a machine and its operators. But causing damage, wilfully or inadvertently, has never been part of this. Hackers like me – and the majority are – *admire* the machines that are our targets.

Until quite recently, therefore, it never occurred to me to issue lectures on hacker behaviour. However, the small incidence of electronic vandalism from the hacking fraternity cannot be ignored and every hacker who boasts about his (or her) activities, in 'safe' environments like bulletin boards and computer clubs or more widely, should think carefully about the consequences. Although I have had some extraordinary letters from readers – one exhorted me to use my talents to investigate the links between Denis Thatcher and the Falklands Island Company – I am not aware that any hacker has so far been approached by master criminals or terrorists. My guess is that extortionists and the like prefer to pressurize those whom they can easily understand.

Nevertheless, I suppose hackers should be cautious. A group of US hackers, annoyed that a *Newsweek* journalist called Richard Sandza had betrayed what they regarded as confidences in the course of writing articles about the bulletin board movement, decided to exact revenge. They accessed credit information about him from the computer-based resources of TRW – see Chapter 4 – and then posted the details on bulletin boards across the country. Journalists do behave appallingly on occasion, but I think the hackers should have restrained themselves.

To those who argue that a *Hacker's Handbook* must be giving guidance to potential criminals, I have three things to say.

First, few people object to the sports of clay-pigeon shooting or archery although rifles, pistols and cross-bows have no 'real' purpose other than to kill things – just as such sports are valid and satisfying in themselves, so hacking is quite sufficiently fulfilling without wreaking damage or violating people's privacy.

Second, real hacking is rather more difficult than is often shown in the movies and on TV.

Last, there is the evidence of the number of hacking incidents reported in the twelve months before the book was first published and in subsequent periods of twelve months after publication: I have taken particular care to accumulate all reports of hacking and there appears to have been a distinct falling off. There could be a variety of reasons for this: more failures of detection, less interest from the news media, more caution being taken by perpetrators, more anticipation and care being shown by potential victims, and so on. Whatever else has happened, despite the number of copies sold, *Hacker's Handbook* has not led to more detected hacking.

The sport of hacking should only be indulged by those who are aware that they may find themselves inadvertently in breach of aspects of the law. Hacking itself is not against the law; indeed it would be quite difficult to provide a good legal definition – how, for example, do you separate the hacker from someone who has forgotten a legitimately owned password and attempts to recall it by successive tries at the keyboard? And how do you separate the hacker from the type of hacker who starts with a legitimate entry to a system but then is able to move beyond those areas where the computer owners intended users to travel because the system was badly set up?

Certain hacker-related activities may be illegal – phone phreaks were prosecuted for theft of electricity and, by extension, hackers could be charged with theft of cpu time or connect time. There could also be theft of copyright material on a database service – though this is likely to be a civil rather than criminal matter. The amounts of money involved here are likely to be small. An hour's illegal use of even the most highly priced database service would cost, at usual rates, just over £100 – not a large crime by most standards. Any damage deliberately caused would be regarded as criminal damage.

Hackers of the radio waves should be aware of the Wireless Telegraphy Acts, the Telecommunications Act and the Interception of Communications Act. This last Act also applies to any form of phone-tapping.

Nevertheless, there are plenty of types of hacking which do not appear to be illegal. Providing you don't forge an 'instrument' – like a magnetic card – the simple use of someone else's password apparently is not forgery; however, if you use such a password on a commercial database or electronic mail service so as to get a 'benefit', for example information that you would otherwise have to pay for, then that would be Deception under the Theft Acts.

If you hack into a database containing personal information, you may be the cause of getting the database *owner* into trouble. Under the Eighth Principle of the Data Protection Act, 1985, and the many similar world–wide items of legislation, the database owner now has a duty to prevent unauthorized disclosure and has to pay compensation to those individuals whose details he has allowed to leak out.

It may be special pleading but I believe that too much effort for too little result is currently being expended by the authorities in trying to prosecute hackers. Most hacking offences are of the same order of moral turpitude as parking on double yellow lines. The substantive damage some recent hacks have caused has been to the credibility of the victims – and sometimes those victims have made the damage worse by ostentatiously drawing attention to it.

In fact, real computer fraud is exceptionally difficult to investigate and even more difficult to bring to the courts because of sheer technical complexity; chasing hackers gives the authorities the illusion that they are doing something about computer crime, of which hacking is such a small part both in absolute numbers and measured by money involved. But if you are a hacker, be careful – to be the object of a prosecution, even an unsuccessful one, may be much more than you are willing to pay for a minor hobby.

1 First Principles

The first hack I ever did was executed at an exhibition stand run by BT's then rather new Prestel service, the world's first mass market electronic publishing medium. Earlier, in an adjacent conference hall, an enthusiastic speaker had demonstrated viewdata's potential worldwide spread by logging on to Viditel, the infant Dutch service. (The word viewdata has now been superseded by 'videotex'.) He had had, as so often happens in these circumstances, difficulty in logging on first time. He was using one of those sets that displays auto-dialled telephone numbers so that was how I found the number to call. By the time he had finished his third unsuccessful log-on attempt I (and presumably several others) had all the pass numbers.

While the BT staff were busy with other visitors to their stand, I picked out for myself a relatively neglected viewdata set. I knew that it was possible to by-pass the auto-dialler with its pre-programmed phone numbers in this particular model simply by picking up the the phone adjacent to it, dialling my preferred number, waiting for the whistle, and then hitting the keyboard button labelled 'viewdata'. I dialled Holland, performed my little by-pass trick and watched Viditel write itself on the screen. The pass numbers were accepted first time and, courtesy of... no, I'll spare them embarrassment... I had only lack of fluency in Dutch to restrain my explorations. Fortunately the first BT executive to spot what I had done was amused as well...

Most hackers seem to have started in a similar way. Essentially you rely on the foolishness and inadequate sense of security of computer salesmen, operators, programmers and designers.

For a number of years I was a hacker without realizing it. My original basic motive was that I wanted to look at remote databases without having a salesperson guiding my fingers. A skilled demonstrator can dazzle you with flashy features and stop you seeing how limited or clumsy the service actually is. Many people would have thought my level of interest rather technical: I wanted to see how quickly the remote computer responded to

1

my requests, how easy the instructions were to follow, how complete were the information and facilities offered. I have always been seduced by the vision of the universal electronic information service and I wanted to be among the first to use it.

So I began to collect phone numbers and passwords; when I didn't have a legitimate password, I 'invented' or discovered one. I thought of these episodes as country walks across a landscape of computer networks. The owners of these services, by and large, were anxious to acquire customers and, so I told myself, rather like farmers who don't mind careful ramblers, polite network adventurers like me were tolerated. After all, if I liked a service I would be likely to talk about it to potential customers.

In the early days of the computer clubs, the sort that met after hours in the local polytechnic, I began to find people who had similarly acquired lists of interesting phone numbers – only their preoccupations were not always the same as mine. There were those who sought facilities for playing with advanced languages of the type that could not be placed on micros, or those who wanted to locate the 'big' games that had to live on big machines if they were to run.

It wasn't really until late 1982 that anyone I knew used the word 'hacker' in its modern context. Up till then, hackers were American computer buffs who messed around on mainframes or had built their own home computers in garages. Quite suddenly, no one knew where from, 'hacker' had a new and specific meaning. At about the same time, it became evident that there were network explorers whose main interest was, not the remote computers themselves, but the defeat of entry validation procedures.

Then came the bulletin boards, and with them the Hacker's SIGs (special interest groups) and for the first time I became aware just how many people seemed to have acquired the same curious interests as I had.

In the Introduction to this book I referred to the pursuit as a sport and like most sports it is both relatively pointless and filled with rules, written or otherwise, which have to be obeyed if the activity is to mean anything. Just as rugby football is not just about forcing a ball down one end of a field, so hacking is not just about using any means to secure access to a computer.

On this basis opening private correspondence to secure a password on a public access service like Prestel and then running around the system building up someone's bill is not what hackers call hacking. The critical element must be the use of skill in some shape or form.

Contrary to what is often thought, hacking is not a new pursuit. I was certainly no pioneer. Hacking, both in the particular sense used in this book's title and in the wider definition adopted by a particular generation of computer pioneers, started in the early 1960s when the first 'serious' time-share computers started to appear at university sites. Very early on, 'unofficial' areas of the memory started to appear, first as mere noticeboards and scratchpads for private programming experiments, then, as locations for games. Where, and how, do you think the early Space Invaders, Lunar Landers and Adventure Games were created? Perhaps tech-hacking – the mischievous manipulation of technology – goes back even further. One of the old favourites of US campus life was to rewire the control panels of elevators (lifts) in high-rise buildings, so that a request for the third floor resulted in the occupants being whizzed to the twenty-third.

Towards the end of the 60s, when the first experimental networks arrived on the scene, particularly the legendary ARPAnet (Advanced Research Projects Agency network) opened up, the computer hackers skipped out of their own local computers, along the packet-switched high-grade communications lines, and into the other machines on the net.

But all these hackers were privileged individuals – they were at a university or research resource, and they were able to borrow terminals to work with. But by 1974 there was at least one well-established 'teenage hacker' story: a fifteen-year-old Londoner with no special training achieved an extensive penetration of a time-sharing bureau using many of the classic techniques that will be described later in this book. It was not until nine or ten years later, however, that such events became international news.

What has changed now, of course, is the wide availability of home computers – and the modems to go with them, the growth of public-access networking of computers, and the enormous quantity and variety of computers that can be accessed.

Hackers vary considerably in their native computer skills; a basic knowledge of how data is held on computers and can be transferred from one to another is essential; determination, alertness, opportunism, the abilities to analyse and synthesize, the collection of relevant helpful data – and luck, the pre-requisites of any intelligence officer – are equally important. If you can write quick effective programs in either a high-level language or machine code, well, it helps. A knowledge of on-line query procedures is helpful and the ability to work in one or more popular mainframe and mini operating systems could put you in the big league. But many of these skills can be acquired as you go on; indeed one of the aims of hacking is to get hands-on experience of computer facilities that could not possibly be placed on a mere stand-alone home computer.

The materials and information you need to hack are all around you... only they are seldom marked as such. Remember that a large proportion of what is passed off as 'secret intelligence' is openly available, if only you know where to look, and appreciate what you find.

At one time or another, hacking will test everything you know about computers and communications. You will discover your abilities increase in fits and starts and you must be prepared for long periods when nothing new appears to happen.

Popular films and TV series have built up a mythology of what hackers can do and with what degree of ease. My personal delight in such Dream Factory output is in compiling a list of all the mistakes in each such episode. Anyone who has ever tried to move a graphics game from one micro to an almost-similar competitor will know already that the chances of getting a home micro to display the North Atlantic Strategic Situation as it would be viewed from the President's Command Post are slim even if appropriate telephone numbers and passwords were available.

Less immediately obvious is the fact that most home micros talk to the outside world through limited but convenient asynchronous protocols, effectively denying direct access to the mainframe products of the world's undisputed leading computer manufacturer, which favours synchronous protocols. And home micro displays are memory-mapped, not vector-traced, and so on.

Nevertheless it is astonishingly easy to get remarkable results – and, thanks to the protocol transformation facilities of PADs in PSS networks (of which much more later), you *can* get into large IBM devices.

The cheapest hacking kit I have ever used consisted of a Sinclair ZX81 (*the* product of 1981), 16 K RAMpack, a clever firmware accessory and an acoustic coupler. Total cost, just over £100. The ZX81's touch-membrane keyboard was one liability, so were the uncertainties of the various connectors. Much of the cleverness of the firmware was devoted to overcoming the native drawbacks of the ZX81's inner configuration – the facts that it didn't readily send and receive characters in the industry-standard ASCII code , that the output port was designed more for instant access to the Z80's main logic rather than to use industry-standard serial port protocols and to rectify the limited screen display.

Yet this kit was capable of adjusting to most bulletin boards; could get into most dial-up 300/300 asynchronous ports, reconfiguring for word-length and parity if needed; could have accessed a PSS PAD and hence got into a huge range of computers not normally available to micro-owners; and, with another modem, could have got into viewdata services. You could print out pages on the ZX 'tin-foil' printer.

The disadvantages of this kit were all in convenience, not in facilities. For the real cheapskate, it is now practical to acquire kit even more cheaply. Perfectly usable micros of the 1978 generation, complete with good keyboard, cassette drive or even discs, can be purchased secondhand for £30 or £40 and old acoustic modems sell for less than £10. Chapter 3 describes the sort of kit most hackers use.

It is even possible to hack with no equipment at all; all major banks now have a network of 'hole in the wall' cash machines – ATMs or Automatic Teller Machines, as they are officially known. Major building societies have their own networks. These machines have had faults in software design and the hackers who played around with them used no more equipment than their fingers and brains. More about this later.

Though I have no intention of writing at length about hacking etiquette, it is worth one paragraph: lovers of fresh-air walks obey the Country Code, involving such items as closing gates behind one and avoiding damage to crops and livestock. Something very similar ought to guide your rambles into other people's computers: the safest thing to do is simply to browse, enjoy and learn; don't manipulate files unless you are sure a back-up exists; don't crash operating systems; don't lock legitimate users out from access; watch who you give information to; if you really discover something confidential, keep it to yourself. In fact, think carefully who you tell about *any* hacking success.

Hacking in the form described in this book rarely causes much *direct* damage; however publicity can cause the hacked computer's owners to suffer severe loss in credibility. Talking to journalists, particularly those on the tabloid press, may be appealing to the immature hacker's ego but the real damage an over-sensationalised account of your exploits can cause should never be underestimated. It should go without saying that hackers are not interested in fraud. Finally, just as any rambler who ventured across a field guarded by barbed wire and dotted with notices warning about the Official Secrets Acts would deserve most that happened thereafter, there are a few hacking projects which should never be attempted.

On the converse side, I and many hackers I know are convinced of one thing: we receive more than a little help from the system managers of the computers we attack. In the case of computers owned by universities and polytechnics, there is little doubt that a number of them are viewed like academic libraries – strictly speaking they are for the student population, but if an outsider seriously thirsty for knowledge shows up, they aren't turned away. As for other computers, a number of us are almost sure we have been used as a cheap means to test a system's defences... someone releases a phone number and low-level password to hackers (there are plenty of ways) and watches what happens over the next few weeks while the computer files themselves are empty of sensitive data. Then, when the results have been noted, the phone numbers and passwords are changed, the security improved etc. ... much easier on data processing budgets than employing programmers at £250/man/day or more. Certainly the Pentagon has been known to form 'Tiger Units' of US Army computer specialists to pinpoint weaknesses in systems security.

Two spectacular hacks of recent years have captured the public imagination: the first, the Great Prince Philip Prestel Hack, which from every point-of-view – technical, social and legal, hacking history – is likely to be regarded as 'important'. An account appears in chapter 8. The second was spectacular because it was carried out on live national television. It occurred on 2 October 1983 during a follow-up to the BBC's successful Computer Literacy series. It's worth reporting here, because it neatly illustrates the essence of hacking as a sport ... skill with systems, careful research, maximum impact with minimum real harm, and humour.

The TV presenter, John Coll, was trying to show off the Telecom Gold electronic mail service. Coll had hitherto never liked long passwords and, in the context of the tight timing and pressures of live TV, a two-letter password seemed a good idea at the time. On Telecom Gold, it is only the password that is truly confidential, system and account numbers, as well as phone numbers to log on to the system, are easily obtainable. The BBC's account number, extensively publicized, was OWL001, the owl being the 'logo' for the TV series as well as the BBC computer.

The hacker, who appeared on a subsequent programme as a 'former hacker' and who talked about his activities in general, but did not openly acknowledge his responsibility for the BBC act, managed to seize control of Coll's mailbox and superimpose a message of his own:

Computer Security Error. Illegal access. I hope your television PROGRAMME runs as smoothly as my PRO-GRAM worked out your passwords! Nothing is secure!

Hackers' Song

Put another password in,
Bomb it out and try again
Try to get past logging in,
We're hacking, hacking, hacking.

Try his first wife's maiden name,
This is more than just a game,
It's real fun, but just the same,
It's hacking, hacking, hacking.

The Nutcracker (Hackers UK)

HI THERE, OWLETS, FROM OZ AND YUG (OLIVER AND GUY)

After the hack a number of stories about how it had been carried out, and by whom, circulated – it was suggested that the hackers had crashed through to the operating system of the Prime computers upon which the Dialcom electronic mail software resided. It was also suggested that the BBC had arranged the whole thing as a stunt or alternatively, that some BBC employees had fixed it up without telling their colleagues.

Getting to the truth of a legend in such cases is almost always impossible. No one involved has a stake in the truth. British Telecom, with a strong commitment to get Gold accepted in the business community, was anxious to suggest that only the dirtiest of dirty tricks could remove the inherent confidentiality of their electronic mail service. Naturally the British Broadcasting Corporation rejected any possibility that it would connive in an irresponsible cheap stunt. But the hacker had no great stake in the truth either – he had sources and contacts to protect, and his image in the hacker community to bolster. In fact, the hacker involved, who has since gone on to write both highly successful computer games and artful firmware for specialist modems, took advantage of a weakness in the way in which the Dialcom software used by Telecom Gold sat on the operating system. Never expect *any* hacking anecdote to be completely truthful.

2 Computer-to-Computer Communications

Services intended for access by microcomputers are nowadays usually presented in a very user-friendly fashion: pop in your software disc or firmware, check the connections, dial the telephone number, listen for the tone... and there you are. Hackers, interested in venturing where they are not invited, enjoy no such luxury. They may want to access older services which preceded the modern 'human interface'; they are very likely to travel along paths intended, not for ordinary customers, but for engineers or salesmen; they could be utilizing facilities that were part of a computer's commissioning process and have hardly been used since.

So the hacker needs a greater knowledge of data-comms technology than more passive computer users and, because of its growth pattern and the fact that many interesting installations still use yesterday's solutions, some feeling for the history of the technology is pretty essential.

Getting one computer to talk to another some distance away means accepting a number of limiting factors:

1 Although computers can send out several bits of information at once, the ribbon cable necessary to do this is not economical at any great length, particularly if the information is to be sent out over a network – each wire in the ribbon would need switching separately, thus making exchanges prohibitively expensive. So bits must be transmitted one at at time, or serially.

2 Since you will be using, in the first instance, wires and networks already installed – in the form of the telephone and telex networks – you must accept that the limited bandwidth of these facilities will restrict the rate at which data can be sent. The data will pass through long lengths of wire, frequently being re-amplified, undergoing degradation as it passes through dirty switches and relays in a multiplicity of exchanges.

3 Data must be easily capable of accurate recovery at the far end.

4 Sending and receiving computers must be synchronized in their working.

5 The mode in which data is transmitted must be one understood by all computers; accepting a standard protocol may mean adopting the speed and efficiency of the slowest.

The present 'universal' standard for data transmission, as used by microcomputers and many other services, uses agreed tones to signify binary 0 and binary 1, the ASCII character set (also known as International Alphabet No. 5) and an asynchronous protocol whereby the transmitting computer and the receiving computer are locked in step every time a character is sent, and not just at the beginning of a transmission stream. Like nearly all standards, it is highly arbitrary in its decisions and derives its importance simply from the fact of being generally accepted. Like many standards too, there are a number of subtle and important variations.

To see how the standard works, how it came about and the reasons for the variations, we need to look back a little into history.

The Growth of Telegraphy

The essential techniques of sending data along wires have a history of 150 years, and some of the common terminology of modern data transmission goes right back to the first experiments.

The earliest form of telegraphy, itself the earliest form of electrical message sending, used the remote actuation of electrical relays to leave marks on a strip of paper. The letters of the alphabet were defined by the patterns of 'mark' and 'space'. The terms have come through to the present, to signify binary conditions of '1' and '0' respectively. The first reliable machine for sending letters and figures by this method dates from 1840.

The direct successor of that machine, using remarkably unchanged electro-mechanical technology and a 5-bit alphabetic code, is still in wide use today, as the telex/teleprinter/teletype. The mark and space have been replaced by holes punched in paper-tape, larger holes for mark, smaller ones for space. The code is called Baudot, after its inventor. Synchronization between sending and receiving stations is carried out by beginning each *letter* with a 'start' bit (a space) and concluding it with a 'stop' bit (mark). The 'idle' state of a circuit is thus 'mark'. In effect, therefore, each letter requires the transmission of 7 bits:

. * * . . . * (letter A: . = space; * = mark   )

of which the first . is the start bit, the last * is the stop bit and * * . . . is the code for A.

It is the principal means for sending text messages around the world and the way in which news reports are distributed globally. And, until Third-World countries are rich enough to afford more advanced devices, the technology will survive.

Early computer communications

When, 110 years after the first such machines came on line, the need arose to address computers remotely, telegraphy was the obvious way to do so. No one expected computers in the early 1950s to give instant results; jobs were assembled in batches, often fed in by means of paper-tape (another borrowing from telex, still in use) and then run. The instant calculation and collation of data was then considered quite miraculous. So the first use of data communications was almost exclusively to ensure that the machine was fed with up-to-date information, not for the machine to send the results out to those who might want it; they could wait for the 'printout' in due course, borne to them with considerable solemnity by the computer experts.

Typical communications speeds were 50 or 75 bits/s. (It is here we must introduce the distinction between bits/sec and baud rate which many people who ought to know better seem to believe are one and the same thing: the baud is the measure of speed of data transmission: specifically, it refers to the number of signal level changes per second. At lower speeds bits/s and baud rate are identical, but at higher speeds bits are communicated by methods other than varying the signal level, typically by detection of the phase-state of a signal. Thus, 1200 bits/s full duplex is actually achieved by a 600 baud signal using 4 phase angles. We'll examine this later.)

These early computers were, of course, in today's jargon, single-user/single-task; programs were fed by direct machine coding. In the very earliest computers, 'programming' meant making adjustments to wiring, using a grid of sockets and a series of connectors with jacks at either end, rather like a primitive telephone exchange. Gradually, over the next fifteen years, computers spawned multi-user capabilities by means of time-sharing techniques and their human interface became more 'user-friendly'. With these facilities grew the demand for remote access to computers and modern data communications began.

Even at the very end of the 1960s when I had my own very first encounter with a computer, the links with telegraphy were still obvious. As a result of happenstance I was in a government-run research facility to the south-west of London and the program I was to use was located on a computer just to the north of Central London; I was sat down in front of a battered teletype – capitals and figures only, and requiring not inconsiderable physical force from my smallish fingers to actuate the keys of my choice. Being a teletype, and outputting on to a paper roll, mistakes could not as readily be erased as on a VDU, and since the sole form of error reporting consisted of a solitary ?, the episode was more frustrating than thrilling. VDUs and good keyboards were then far too expensive for 'ordinary' use.

The telephone network
But by that time all sorts of changes in data-comms were taking place. The telex and telegraphy network, originally so important, had long been overtaken by voice-grade telephone circuits (Bell's invention dates from 1876). For computer communication, mark and space could be indicated by different audio tones rather than different voltage conditions. Data traffic on a a telex line can only operate in one direction at a time, but, by selecting different pairs of tones, both 'transmitter' and 'receiver' could speak simultaneously – so that in fact, one has to talk about 'originate' and 'answer' instead.

Improved electrical circuit design meant that higher speeds than 50 or 75 bits/s became possible; there was a move to 110 bits/s, then 300 and, so far as ordinary telephone circuits are concerned, 2400 bits/s is now regarded as the top limit. Special techniques are required to achieve this speed.

The 'start' and 'stop' method of synchronizing the near and far end of a communications circuit at the beginning of each individual letter has been retained, but the common use of the 5-bit Baudot code has been replaced by a 7-bit extended code called

ASCII which allows for many more characters, 128 in fact.*

Lastly, to reduce errors in transmission due to noise in the telephone line and circuitry, each letter can be checked by the use of a further bit (the parity bit), which adds up all the bits in the main character and then, depending on whether the result is odd or even, adds a binary 0 or binary 1.

The full modern transmission of a letter in this system, in this case, K, therefore, looks like this:

```
TIME
INTERVAL   9  0  1  2  3  4  5  6  7  8  9
NUMBER
```

```
LINE
CONDITION
```

```
BINARY   STOP START  1  0  0  1  0  1  1  0
DIGIT
```

The first 0 is the start bit; then follows 7 bits of the actual letter code (1001011); then the parity bit; then the final 1 is the stop code.

This system, asynchronous, start-stop, ASCII (the common name for the alphabetic code) is the basis for nearly all micro-based communications. The key variations relate to:

bit-length: you can have 7 or 8 databits. †

parity: it can be even or odd, or entirely absent. †

*Users of the IBM PC and its close compatibles will know that it can use 256 characters, the first 128 of which are standard ASCII, and the remainder are used for less common variations in a number of foreign languages, accents, umlauts, cedillas, etc. and for some graphics. You need 8 binary digits to cover all of these, of course.

† There are no 'obvious explanations' for the variations commonly found: most electronic mail services and viewdata transmit 7 databits, even parity and 1 stop bit; most hobbyist bulletin boards transmit 8 data bits, odd or no parity and 1 stop bit. These variants are sometimes written in a shorthand form: '7e1' means '7 bits, even parity, 1 stop bit', '8n1' means '8 bits, no parity, 1 stop bit' and so on. 7-bit transmission will cover most forms of text-matter, but if you wish to send machine code or other program material, or text prepared with a wordprocessor like Wordstar which uses hidden codes for formatting, then you must use 8-bit transmission protocols. Terminal emulator software – see chapter 3 – allows users to adjust for these differing requirements.

tones: the tones used to signify binary 0 and binary 1, and which computer is in 'originate' and which in 'answer', can vary according to the speed of the transmission and also whether the service is used in North America or the rest of the world. Briefly, most of the world uses tones and standards laid down by the Geneva-based organization, CCITT, a specialized agency of the International Telecommunications Union; whereas in the United States and most parts of Canada, tones determined by the telephone utility, colloquially known as Ma Bell, are adopted.

The following table gives the standards and tones in common use.

Service Designator	Speed	Duplex	Transmit 0	1	Receive 0	1	Answer
V.21 orig	300^a	full	1180	980	1850	1650	—
V.21 ans	300^a	full	1850	1650	1180	980	2100
V.23 (1)	600	half	1700	1300	1700	1300	2100
V.23 (2)	1200	f/h^b	2100	1300	2100	1300	2100
V.23 back	75	f/h^b	450	390	450	390	—
Bell 103 orig	300^a	full	1070	1270	2025	2225	—
Bell 103 ans	300^a	full	2025	2225	1070	1270	2225
Bell 202	1200	half	2200	1200	2200	1200	2025
V.22/212A	1200	full	*see below*				
V.22 *bis*	2400	full	*see below*				

^{a}any speed up to 300 bits/s can also include 75 and 110 bits/s services.
^{b}service can either be half-duplex at 1200 bits/s or asymmetrical full duplex, with 75 bits/s originate and 1200 bits/s receive (commonly used as viewdata user) or 1200 transmit and 75 receive (viewdata host).

Higher Speeds
1200 bits/s is usually regarded as the fastest speed possible on an ordinary voice-grade telephone line. Beyond this, noise on the line due to the switching circuits at the various telephone exchanges, poor cabling etc., make accurate transmission difficult. However, 2400 bits/s is becoming more common and indeed is the standard speed of teletex, the high-speed version of telex.

Transmission at these higher speeds uses different signalling techniques from those hitherto described. Simple tone detection circuits cannot switch on and off sufficiently rapidly to be reliable so another method of detecting individual 'bits' has to be employed. The way it is done is by using *phase detection*. The rate of signalling doesn't go up – it stays at 600 baud but each signal is modulated at origin by phase and then demodulated in the same way at the far end. Two channels are used, high and low (what else?), so that you can achieve bi-directional or duplex communication.

The tones are:

Originate	(*low channel*1)	1200 Hz
Answer	(*high channel*)	2400 Hz

and they are the same for the European CCITT V.22 standard and for the Bell equivalent, Bell 212A. V.22 *bis* is the variant for 2400 bits/s full duplex transmission; there is no equivalent Bell term.

The speed differences are obtained in this way:

600 bits/s (V.22)   Each bit encoded as a phase change from the previous phase. There are two possible symbols which consist of one of two phase angles; each symbol conveys 1 bit of information.

1200 bits/s (V.22 and Bell 212A)   Differential phase shift keying is used to give 4 possible symbols which consist of one of four phase angles. Each symbol coveys 2 bits of information to enable a 600 baud signal rate to handle 1200 bits.

2400 bits/s (V.22 bis)   Quadrature amplitude modulation is used to give 16 possible symbols which consist of 12 phase angles and 3 levels of amplitude. Each symbol conveys 4 bits of information to enable a 600 baud signal rate to handle 2400 bits.

It is the requirement for much more sophisticated modulation and demodulation techniques that has up till now kept the cost of higher speed modems out of the hands of home enthusiasts.

Where higher speeds are essential, leased circuits, not available via dial-up, become essential. The leased circuit is paid for on a fixed charge, not a charge based on time-connected. Such circuits can be 'conditioned', by using special amplifiers etc., to support the higher data rate.

For really high-speed transmissions, however, pairs of copper cable are inadequate. Medium speed is obtainable by the use of coaxial cable (a little like that used for TV antenna hook-ups) which have a very broad bandwidth. Imposing several different channels on one cable length is called multiplexing and, depending on the application, the various channels can either carry several different computer conversations simultaneously or can send several bits of one computer conversation in parallel, just as though there were a ribbon cable between the two participating computers. Either way, what happens is that each binary 0 or binary 1 is given not an audio tone but a radio frequency tone.

Error Correction

At higher speeds it becomes increasingly important to use transmission protocols that include error correction. Error correction techniques usually consist of dividing the transmission stream into a series of blocks which can be checked, one at a time, by the receiving computer. The 'parity' system mentioned above is one example but obviously a crude one. The difficulty is that the more secure an error correction protocol becomes, the greater becomes the overhead in terms of numbers of bits transmitted to send just one character from one computer to another. Thus, in the typical 300 bit situation, the actual letter is defined by 7 bits, 'start' and 'stop' account for another 2, and the check takes a further 1–10 in all. After a while, what you gain in the speed with which each actual *bit* is transmitted, you lose because so many bits have to be sent to ensure that a single *character* is accurately received!

Parity checking has its limitations: it will pick up only one error per character; if there are two or more then the error gets 'printed', in other words, an inaccurate character is received as valid. There are a large number of error correction protocols, though as mentioned above, the principle is nearly always the same: the originating computer divides the character stream to be sent into a series of blocks, say 128 bits or alternative base 8 or base 16 figure. The value of each bit in the block is then put through a short mathematical process (typically adding) and the result, known as a 'checksum', is placed at the end of the block. The block is then sent down the line.

The receiving computer accepts the 128 bits and the checksum and stores them in a temporary buffer; here the mathematical process is quickly repeated. If the addition (or whatever) agrees with the checksum, the 128 bits are released to the receiving computer's user and a quick acknowledgement of correct reception is sent back to the originating computer, which then prepares the next block, and so on until the entire file has been sent. If the receiving computer gets a garbled block, then it is retransmitted as necessary.

So much for the principles: unfortunately there are a large number of implementations of this basic idea. The variations depend on: size of block transmitted, checksum method, form of acknowledgement and number of unsuccessful tries permitted before transmission is aborted. Here are some of the more common error correction protocols:

ARQ   This is sometimes implemented in *hardware* in 1200 full duplex modems. Sending and receiving computers use no error correction protocol but the modems, one at each end, introduce error correction 'transparently', in other words, they take care of the checking without either of the computers being aware of what is happening.

Xmodem (sometimes called Christiansen, after its deviser)   This protocol started out among hobbyists who wished to transfer files between each other. Christiansen made his software public domain, so that users didn't need to pay for its use, and this has contributed to its popularity. Xmodem is often to be found on bulletin boards and versions have been implemented for most of the popular families of computers like C/PM and MSDOS. You may have difficulty in getting a copy if your computer was primarily for the 'home' market and does not run one of the well-known operating systems.

There are two variants of Xmodem, the more recent of which has an option giving a higher degree of protection using CRC – cyclical redundancy checking – so be warned! Some software will automatically check to see which variant of Xmodem is being used. Xmodem can only be used on systems that allow 8-bit data transmission. There are a number of Xmodem variants which allow for 7-bit transfers, or for groups of files to be specified (Xmodem itself allows only one file transfer per session); these variants are described in Appendix IX.

Kermit   This has the distinction of being implemented on

more computers, particularly mainframes, than any other. It was devised at Columbia University, New York, and versions are now available for very many of the current generation of micros: the IBM PC, Apple II and Mac, the BBC and CP/M machines. Contact the User Groups for copies which are free, though you will have to pay for the disk media. Among the big machines that carry Kermit are DEC 10s and 20s, DEC VAX and PDP-11 and the IBM 370 series under VM and CMS.*

CET Telesoftware   This is to be found on videotex (viewdata) systems – see Chapter 8 for more – and is used to transfer programs in the videotex page format. The checksum is based on the entire videotex page and not on small blocks. This is because the smallest element a videotex host can retransmit is an entire page. This is one of the features that makes telesoftware downloading rather tiresome – one slight error and over 8 kbits must be retransmitted each time at 1200 bits/s! And the retransmission request goes back to the host at only 75 bits/s!

EPAD   EPAD is used in connection with packet-switched services – see Chapter 7. If you have an ordinary micro and wish to use a service operating on PSS, you must dial into a device called a PAD, packet-assembler/disassembler, which transforms material from your machine into the packets required for the packet-switching service, and vice versa. The trouble is that, whilst PSS and its cousins use error correction during their high-speed international journeys, until recently there was no error correction between the PAD and the end-user's computer. EPAD was introduced to overcome this difficulty.

There are many many other error correction protocols. Broadcast teletext services like Ceefax and Oracle use parity for the contents of the pages but the more reliable Hamming Codes for the page and line numbers. (See page 167.) Some of the (rather expensive) terminal emulator software packages available for micros have their own proprietary products – Crosstalk, BSTAM, Move-It, Datatalk are all different. They all work, but

---

* Kermit, and some less common file transfer protocols are explained in more detail in Appendix IX.

only when computers at both ends of the transmission line are using them.

Fortunately the two public-domain protocols, Xmodem and Kermit, are being included in commercial packages as a free extra and their importance can only grow.

Synchronous Protocols

In the asynchronous protocols so far described, transmitting and receiving computers are kept in step with each other every time a character is sent, via the 'start' and 'stop' bits. In synchronous comms, the locking together is done merely at the start of each block of transmission by the sending of a special code (often SYN). The SYN code starts a clock (a timed train of pulses) in the receiver and it is this that ensures that binary 0s and 1s originating at the transmitter are correctly interpreted by the receiver. Clearly the displacement of even one binary digit can cause havoc.

A variety of synchronous protocols exist – the length of block sent each time, the form of checking that takes place, the form of acknowledgement, and so on. A synchronous protocol is not only a function of the modem, which has to have a suitable clock, but also of the software and firmware in the computers. Because asynchronous protocols transmit so many 'extra' bits in order to avoid error, savings in transmission time under synchronous systems often exceed 20–30 per cent. The disadvantage of synchronous protocols lie in increased hardware costs. Error correction is built into synchronous protocols.

One other complication exists: most asynchronous protocols use the ASCII code to define characters. IBM (Big Blue), the biggest enthusiast of synchronous comms, has its own binary code to define characters. (But the IBM PC uses a variant of ASCII – see above page 13.) In Appendix IV you will find an explanation and a comparison with ASCII.

The best-known IBM protocol that is sent along phone-lines is BSC; other IBM protocols use coaxial cable between terminal and mainframe. The hacker, wishing to come to terms with synchronous comms, has two choices: the more expensive is to purchase a protocol converter board. These are principally available for the IBM PC, which has been increasingly marketed for the 'executive workstation' audience where the ability to interface to a company's existing (IBM) mainframe is a key feature. The family of IBM PCs announced in April 1987 as replacements for their 1981 ancestors tend to have synchronous facilities built in. The alternative is to see whether the target mainframe has a port on to a packet-switched service; in that event, the hacker can use ordinary asynchronous equipment and protocols – the local PAD (packet assembler/disassembler) will carry out the necessary transformations.

Networks
Which brings us neatly to the world of high-speed digital networks using packet-switching. All the computer communications so far described have taken place either on the phone (voice-grade) network or on the telex network.

In Chapter 7 we will look at packet-switching and the opportunities offered by international data networks.

We must now specify hackers' equipment in more detail.

3 Hackers' Equipment

You can hack with almost any microcomputer capable of talking to the outside world via a serial port and a modem. In fact, you don't even need a micro; my first hack was with a perfectly ordinary viewdata terminal.

What follows in this chapter, therefore, is a description of the elements of a system I like to think of as optimum for straight-forward asynchronous ASCII and Baudot communications. What is at issue is convenience as much as anything. With kit like this, you will be able to get through most dial-up ports and into packet-switching through a PAD (packet assembler/disassembler port). It will not get you into IBM networks because these use different and incompatible protocols; we will return to the matter of the IBM world in Chapter 10. In other words, given a bit of money, a bit of knowledge, a bit of help from friends and a bit of luck, what is described is the sort of equipment most hackers have at their command.

You will find few products on the market labelled 'for hackers'; you must select those items that appear to have 'legitimate' but interesting functions and see if they can be bent to the hacker's purposes. The various sections within this chapter highlight the sort of facilities you need; before lashing out on some new software or hardware, try to get hold of as much publicity and documentation material as possible to see how adaptable the products are. In a few cases, it is worth looking at the second-hand market, particularly for modems, cables and test equipment.

Although it is by no means essential, an ability to solder a few connections and scrabble among the circuit diagrams of 'official' products often yield unexpectedly rewarding results.

The computer
Almost any popular microcomputer will do; hacking does not call upon enormous reserves of computer power. Nearly every-thing you hack will come to you in alphanumeric form, not

graphics. The computer you already have will almost certainly have the essential qualities. However the very cheapest micros, like the ZX81, while usable, require much more work on the part of the operator/hacker, and give him or her far less in the way of instant facilities. (In fact, as the ZX81 doesn't use ASCII internally, but a Sinclair-developed variant, you will need a software or firmware fix for that, before you even think of hooking it up to a modem.)

Most professional data services assume the user is viewing on an 80-column screen; ideally the hacker's computer should be capable of doing that as well, otherwise the display will be full of awkward line breaks. Terminal emulator software (see below) can sometimes provide a 'fix'.

One or two disc drives are pretty helpful, because you will want to be able to save the results of your network adventures as quickly and efficiently as possible. Most terminal emulators use the computer's free memory (i.e. all that not required to support the operating system and the emulator software itself) as store for the received data, but once the buffer is full, you will begin to lose the earliest items. You can, of course, try to save to cassette, but normally that is a slow and tedious process.

An alternative storage method is to save to a printer, printing the received data stream not only to the computer screen, but also on a dot matrix printer. However, most of the more popular (and cheaper) printers do not work sufficiently fast. You may find you lose characters at the beginning of each line. Moreover, if you print everything in real-time, you'll include all your mistakes, false starts, etc., and in the process use masses of paper.

So, if you can save to disc regularly, you can review each hack afterwards at your leisure and, using a screen editor or word processor, save or print out only those items of real interest.

The computer must have a serial port, either called that or marked RS232C (or its slight variant RS434) or V.24, which is the official designator of RS232C used outside the US, though not often marked as such on micros.

Serial Ports

Originally, the very cheapest micros, like the ZX81, Spectrum, VIC20, did not have RS232C ports, though add-on boards are available. Some of the older personal computers, like the Apple, the original Pet, the TRS-80, etc., were sold without serial ports, though standard boards are available for all of these. When the

IBM PC was first introduced you had to buy boards for video display, parallel printer and serial port – an act of folly not repeated by the various clones that appeared afterwards. The Amstrad PCW 8256 and 8512 are sold as word-processors though they are, of course, also CP/M personal computers. Their only connection to the outside world is the non-standard printer port (where the supplied matrix printer is fitted). However you can buy an interface box for around £60 which contains both a regular Centronics port for linking to regular printers and also a RS232C serial port. (Amstrad PCW users have a choice of software specially for their machine, but any CP/M comms software will work.)

You are probably aware that the RS232C standard has a large number of variants and that not all computers (or add-on boards) that claim to have a RS232C port can actually talk into a modem.

Historically, RS232C/V.24 is supposed to cover all aspects of serial communication and includes printers and dumb terminals as well as computers. The RS232C standard specifies electrical and physical requirements. Everything is pumped through a 25-pin D-shaped connector, each pin of which has some function in some implementation. But in most cases, nearly all the pins are ignored. In practice, only three connections are absolutely essential for computer to modem communication:

Pin 7   signal ground
Pin 2   characters leaving the computer
Pin 3   characters arriving at the computer

The remaining connections are for such purposes as feeding power to an external device, switching the external device on or off, exchanging status and timing signals, monitoring the state of the line, etc. Some computers, their associated firmware and particular software packages require one or other of these status signals to go 'high' or 'low' in particular circumstances, or the program hangs. On the IBM PC, for example, pin 5 (clear to send), pin 6 (data set ready) and pin 20 (data terminal ready) are often all used. If you are using an auto-answer modem – one which will intercept an inward phone call automatically, then you must also have a properly functioning pin 22 (ring indicator). Check your documentation if you have trouble. A fuller explanation of RS232C appears in Appendix VI.

Some RS232C implementations on microcomputers or add-on

boards are there simply to support printers with serial interfaces, but they can often be modified to talk into modems. The critical two lines are those serving Pins 2 and 3.

A computer serving a modem needs a cable in which Pin 2 on the computer is linked to Pin 2 on the modem.

A computer serving a printer, etc., needs a cable in which Pin 3 on the computer is linked to Pin 2 on the printer and Pin 3 on the printer is linked to Pin 2 on the computer.

If two computers are linked together directly, without a modem, then Pin 2 on computer A must be linked to Pin 3 on computer B and Pin 3 on computer B linked to Pin 2 on computer A: this arrangement is sometimes called a 'null modem' or a 'null modem cable'.

There are historic 'explanations' for these arrangements, depending on who you think is sending and who is receiving. Forget about them, they are confusing – the above three cases are all you need to know about in practice.

One difficulty that frequently arises with newer or portable computers is that some manufacturers have abandoned the traditional 25-way D-connector, largely on the grounds of bulk, cost and redundancy. Some European computer and peripheral companies favour connectors based on the DIN series (invented in Germany) while others use D-connectors with fewer pin-outs, usually 9. You will find this on the IBM PC AT and the Apple Mac. Sometimes too you will see that male (pins sticking out) and sometimes female (holes) 25-pin D-connectors are required – you'll require a gadget called a gender-changer to make them talk to each other.* *There is no standardization.* Even if you see two physically similar connectors on two devices which appear to mate together, regard them with suspicion. In each case, you must determine the equivalents of:

Characters leaving computer (Pin 2)
Characters arriving at computer (Pin 3)
Signal ground (Pin 7)

---

* Just to make life even more confusing, IBM PC compatibles use 25-pin D-connectors for both the serial interface and the parallel printer. The IBM serial connector on the chassis is male – pins sticking out.

You can usually set the speed of the port from the computer's operating system and/or from Basic. There is no standard way of doing this, you must check your handbook and manuals. In an MS-DOS machine you either use a program called SETIO.EXE or the MODE COM: command. Most RS232C ports can handle the following speeds:

75, 110, 300, 600, 1200, 2400, 4800, 9600

and sometimes 50 and 19200 bits/s as well.

In some older machines (or if separate serial boards are used) these speeds are selectable in hardware by appropriate wiring of a chip called a baud-rate generator. Many modern computers let you select speed in hardware by means of a DIL switch. The higher speeds are used either for driving printers or for direct computer-to-computer or computer-to-peripheral connections. The normal maximum speed for transmitting along phone lines is 1200 bits/s, though 2400 bits/s is beginning to appear.

Depending on how your computer has been set up, you may be able to control the speed from the keyboard – a bit of firmware in the computer will accept micro-instructions to flip transistor switches controlling the wiring of the baud-rate generator. Alternatively the speeds may be set in pure software, the micro deciding at what speed to feed information into the the serial port.

In most popular micro implementations the RS232C cannot support *split-speed* working, i.e. different speeds for receive and transmit. If you set the port up for 1200 bits/s, it has to be 1200 receive and transmit. This is a nuisance in Europe, where 75/1200 is in common use both for viewdata systems and for some on-line services. The usual way round is to have special terminal emulator software, which requires the RS232C hardware to operate at 1200/1200 and then slows down (usually the micro's transmit path) to 75 bits/s in software by means of a timing loop. An alternative method relies on a special modem, which accepts data from the computer at 1200/1200 and then performs the slowing-down to 75 bits/s in its own internal firmware. Such modems are commonly available in the UK, because of the requirement of many people to access Prestel and similar viewdata services.

Software: Terminal Emulators
We all need a quest in life; sometimes I think mine is to search for

the perfect software package to make micros talk to the outside world. As in all such quests, the goal is only occasionally approached but never reached, if only because the process of the quest causes one to redefine what one is looking for.

These items of software are sometimes called communications packages or asynchronous comms packages, and sometimes terminal emulators, on the grounds that the software can make the micro appear to be a variety of different computer terminals. Until quite recently, most on-line computer services assumed that they were being examined through 'dumb' terminals – simply a keyboard and a screen, with no attendant processing or storage power (except perhaps a printer). With the arrival of PCs all this is slowly changing, so that the remote computer has to do no more than provide relatively raw data and all the formatting and on-screen presentation is done by the user's own computer. Terminal emulator software is a sort of halfway house between 'dumb' terminals and PCs with considerable local processing power.

Given the habit of manufacturers of mainframe and mini-computers to make their products as incompatible with those of their competitors as possible (to maximize their profits), many slight variants on the 'dumb' computer terminal exist – hence the availability of terminal emulators to provide, in one software package, a way of mimicking all the popular types.

Basic software to get a computer to talk through its RS232C port, and to take in data sent to it, is relatively trivial, though some programming effort is required to take care of the condition when the receiving computer is being sent data at a faster rate than it can handle – the transmitting computer must be told to wait. However, what the hacker needs is software that will make his computer assume a number of different personalities upon command, will store data as it is collected, and print it out.

Two philosophies of presenting such software to the user exist: first, one which gives the naive user a simple menu which says, in effect, 'press a key to connect to database' and then performs everything smoothly, without distracting menus. Such programs need an 'install' procedure, which requires some knowledge, but most 'ordinary' users never see this. Normally, this is a philo-sophy of software writing I very much admire.

However, as a hacker, you will want the precise opposite. The second approach to terminal emulator software allows you to reconfigure your computer as you go on – there is plenty of on-screen help in the form of menus allowing you to turn on and off local echo, set parity bits, show non-visible control codes, etc. In a typical hack, you may have only vague information about the target computer and much of the 'fun' to be obtained from the sport of hacking is seeing how quickly you can work out what the remote computer wants to 'see' – and how to make your machine respond.

Given the numbers of popular computers on the market, and the numbers of terminal emulators for each one, it is difficult to make a series of specific recommendations. What follows therefore, is a list of the sort of facilities you should look for:

On-line help You must be able to change the software characteristics while on-line – no separate 'install' routine. You should be able to call up 'help' menus instantly, with simple commands, while holding on to the line.

Text buffer The received data should be capable of going into the computer's free memory automatically so that you can view it later off-line. The size of the buffer will depend on the amount of memory left after the computer has used up the space required for its operating system and the terminal software. If the terminal software includes special graphics as in Apple Visiterm or some of the ROM packs used with the BBC, the buffer space may be relatively small. MS-DOS computers like the IBM PC often have memories of 640k, ten times the size available to the earlier gneration of machines with processors like the Z80 or 6502, where the maximum memory size was 64k. The buffer space on MS-DOS (and 68000) machines is thus sufficient to hold 50 per cent more than the entire contents of this book. The software should tell you how much buffer space you have used, how much you have left, at any one time. A useful adjunct is an *auto log* facility which saves the text to disc. You can't use this facility if your sole means of saving data is a cassette drive. A number of associated software commands should let you turn on and off the buffer store, let you clear the buffer store, or view the buffer. You should also be able to print the buffer to a 'line' printer (dot-matrix or daisy wheel or thermal image). Some terminal emulators even include a simple line editor, so that you can delete or adjust the buffer before printing. (I use a terminal emulator which saves text files in a form which can be accessed by my word-processor and use that before printing out.)

Half/full duplex (echo on/off)   Most remote services use an echoing protocol: this means that when the user sends a character to the host computer, the host immediately sends back the same character to the user's computer, by way of confirmation. What the user sees on his computer screen, therefore, has been generated, not locally by his direct action on the keyboard, but remotely by the host computer. (One effect of this is that there may sometimes be a perceptible delay between keystroke and display of a letter, particularly if you are using a packet-switched connection – if the telephone line is noisy, the display may appear corrupt.) This echoing protocol is known as full duplex, because both the user's computer and the host are in communication simultaneously.

However, use of full duplex/echo is not universal and all terminal emulators allow you to switch on and off the facility. If, for example, you are talking into a half-duplex system (i.e. no echo), your screen would appear totally blank. In these circumstances, it is best if your software reproduces on the screen your keystrokes. You will also need local echo on if you are conversing, computer-to-computer, with a friend. However, if you have your computer set for half-duplex and the host computer is actually operating in full duplex, each letter will appear *twice* – once from the keyboard and once, echoing from the host, ggiivviinngg tthhiiss ssoorrtt ooff eeffffeecctt.

Your terminal emulator needs to be able to toggle between the two states.

Data format/parity setting   In a typical asynchronous protocol, each character is surrounded by bits to show when it starts, when it ends, and to signify whether a checksum performed on its binary equivalent comes out even or odd. The character itself is described, typically, in 7 bits and the other bits, start, stop and parity, bringing the number up to 10. (See Chapter 2.)

However this is merely one, very common, form and many systems use subtle variants – the ideal terminal emulator software will let you try out these variants *while you are still on line*. Typical variants should include:

Word length	Parity	No. stop bits
7	even	2
7	odd	2
7	even	1
7	odd	1
8	none	2
8	none	1
8	even	1
8	odd	1

Show Control Characters This is a software switch to display characters not normally part of the text that is meant to be read but which nevertheless are sent by the host computer to carry out display functions, operate protocols, etc. With the switch on, you will see line feeds displayed as ^J, a back-space as ^H, etc, see Appendix IV for the usual equivalents. On IBM PC-type machines you may find yourself getting the 'graphics' characters: the ENQ or ^E character (ASCII 005) will appear as a spade ♠.

Using this device properly, if you are unable to get the text stream to display properly on your screen, may work out what exactly is being sent from the host, and modify your local software accordingly. Control-show is also useful for spotting 'funnies' in passwords and log-on procedures – a common trick is to include ^H (backspace) in the middle of a log-on so that part of the full password is overwritten. For normal reading of text, you have Control-show switched off, as it makes normal reading difficult.

Keyboard macros This is the term for the preformatting of a log-on procedure, passwords, etc. Typical connecting procedures to PSS, Telecom Gold, US services like Dialog, The Source, CompuServe, Dow Jones, etc., are relatively complicated compared with using a local hobbyist bulletin board or calling up Prestel. Typically the user must first connect to a packet switched service like PSS, or, in the USA, Telenet or Tymnet, specify an 'address' for the host required (a long string of letters and numbers) and then, when the desired service or 'host' is on line, enter password(s) to be fully admitted. The password itself may be in several parts.

The value of the 'macro' is that you can type all this junk in once and then send off the entire stream any time you wish by means of a simple command. Most terminal emulators that have this feature allow you to preformat several such macros.

From the hacker's point of view, the best type of macro facility is one that can be itself addressed and altered in software: supposing you have only part of a password: write a little routine which successively tries *all* the unknowns; you can then let the computer attempt penetration automatically. (You'll have to read the emulator's manual carefully to see if it has software-addressable macros: the only people who need them are hackers, and, as we have often observed, very few out-and-out hacker products exist!)

Auto-dial   Some modems contain programmable auto-diallers so that frequently called services can be dialled from a single keyboard command.

Again the advantage to the hacker is obvious – a partly known telephone number can be located by writing some simple software routine to test the variables. This particular trick is one of the few items that the movie *WarGames* got right. A particularly slick implementation of this type of hacker program is called Cat-Scan and was written for the Apple II and the Novation Cat Modem*. However, not all auto-dial facilities are equally useful. Some included in US-originated communications software and terminal emulators are for specific 'smart' modems, of which more later. There is often no way of altering the software to work with other equipment. In general, each modem that contains an auto-dialler has its own way of requiring instructions to be sent to it, though some standardization around the 'Hayes' protocols is beginning to appear (see Appendix V). If an auto-dialling facility is important to you, check that your software is configurable to your choice of auto-dial modem.

Another hazard is that certain auto-diallers only operate on the multi-frequency tones method ('touch-tone') of dialling used in large parts of the United States and only very slowly being introduced in other countries. The system widely used in the UK is called 'pulse' dialling. Touch-tone dialling is much more rapid than pulse dialling, of course. Finally, on the subject of US-originated software, some packages will only accept phone numbers in the standard North American format of: 3-digit area code, 3-digit local code, 4-digit subscriber code. In the UK and

---

* For more on hackers' programs, see page 31.

Europe the phone number formats vary quite considerably. Make sure that any auto-dial facility you use actually operates on your phone system.

Auto-answer If your modem can answer the telephone, it is useful to have software that takes advantage of it. Strictly speaking, hackers don't need such a facility, but with this feature you can, for example, use a computer in your office or at a friend's to call your own. Any auto-answer facility should enable you to set your own password, of course – hackers don't like being hacked! Terminal packages will only have fairly crude auto-answer facilities. Procomm, for the IBM PC, gives you two levels of password in auto-answer mode: the first lets callers leave you messages; the second gives them access to your entire machine. If you want more, you must purchase bulletin board software.

Re-assign keyboard A related problem is that some home micro keyboards may not be able to generate all the required characters the remote service wishes to see. The normal way to generate an ASCII character not available from the keyboard is from Basic, by using a 'Print CHR$(*n*)' type command. This may not be possible when on-line to a remote computer, where everything is needed in immediate mode. Hence the requirement for a software facility to re-assign any little-used key to send the desired 'missing' feature. Typical requirements are BREAK, ESC, RETURN (when part of a string as opposed to being the end of a command), etc. When re-assigning a series of keys, you must make sure you don't interfere with the essential functioning of the terminal emulator. For example, if you designate the sequence $\langle$ ctrl $\rangle$ S to mean 'send a DC1 character to the host', the chances are you will stop the host from sending anything to you, because $\langle$ ctrl $\rangle$ S is a common command (sometimes called XOF) to call for a pause – incidentally, you can end the pause by hitting $\langle$ ctrl $\rangle$ Q.

Some of the more advanced comms packages have a 'keyboard translate' function which allows the user to manipulate both outgoing and incoming characters and translate them to any other designated character, or strip them out altogether. For example, if you were trying to receive a videotex service on a computer that couldn't handle all the special block graphics, you could set up a table so that all the graphics characters were removed before reaching your screen.

Appendix IV gives a list of the full ASCII implementation and the usual 'special' codes as they apply to computer-to-computer communications.

File protocols   When computers are sending large files to each other, a further layer of protocol, beyond that defining individual letters, is necessary. For example, if your computer is automatically saving to disk at regular intervals as the buffer fills up, it may be necessary to be able to tell the host to stop sending for a period, until the save is complete. On older time-share services, where the typical terminal is a teletypewriter, the terminal is in constant danger of being unable mechanically to keep up with the host computer's output. For this reason, many host computers use one of two well-known protocols which require the regular exchange of special control characters for host and user to tell each other all is well. The two protocols are:

Stop/start   The receiving computer can at any time send to the host a Stop ($\langle$ ctrl $\rangle$ S) signal, followed by, when it is ready a Start ($\langle$ ctrl $\rangle$ Q).

EOB/ACK   The sending computer divides its file into blocks (of any convenient length); after each block is sent, an EOB (end of block) character is sent (see ASCII table, Appendix IV). The user's computer must then respond with an ACK (acknowlege) character.

These protocols can be used individually, together or not at all. You may be able to to use the 'show control codes' option to check whether either of the protocols are in use. Alternatively, if you have hooked on to a service which, for no apparent reason, seems to stop in its tracks, you could try ending an ACK or start ($\langle$ ctrl $\rangle$ F or $\langle$ ctrl $\rangle$ S) and see if you can get things moving.

File transmission   All terminal emulators assume you will want to send, as well as receive, text files. Thus, in addition to the protocol settings already mentioned, there may be additional ones for that purpose, e.g. the Xmodem protocol very popular on bulletin boards. Hackers, of course, usually don't want to place files *on* remote computers. An associated facility is the ability to send non-ASCII (usually machine-code) files. Don't buy packages with error correction protocols specific to only one software producer. Kermit, the most widely implemented mainframe error correction protocol, is available from user groups.

File transmission protocols in frequent use appear in Appendix IX.

Specific terminal emulation Some software has pre-formatted sets of characteristics to mimic popular commercial 'dumb' terminals. For example, with a ROM costing under £60 fitted to a BBC micro, you can obtain almost all of the features of DEC's VT100 terminal, which until recently was regarded as something of an industry-standard, costing just under £1000. Other popular terminals are the VT52 and some Tektronix models, the latter for graphics display. ANSI have produced a 'standard' specification which permits 'cursor addressing' – i.e. the terminal will print at specific locations on the screen without the transmitting computer having to send lots of line feeds and spaces. The cursor is located by a series of short commands beginning with an ⟨ esc ⟩ character.

Baudot characters The Baudot code, or International Telegraphic Code No. 2, is the 5-bit code used in telex and telegraphy – and in many wire-based news services. A few terminal emulators include it as an option – and it is useful if you are attempting to hack such services. Most software intended for use on radio link-ups (see Chapter 9) operates primarily in Baudot, with ASCII as an option.

Viewdata emulation This gives you the full, or almost full, graphics and text characters of UK-standard viewdata. Viewdata TV sets and adapters use a special character-generator chip and a few, mostly British-manufactured, micros use that chip also – the Acorn Atom was one example. The BBC has a teletext mode which adopts the same display. But for most micros, viewdata emulation is a matter of using high-res graphics to mimic the qualities of the real thing, or to strip out most of the graphics. Viewdata works on a screen of 40 characters by 24 rows and as some popular home micros have 'native' displays smaller than that, some considerable fiddling is necessary to get them to handle viewdata at all.

On the IBM PC with the standard Color Graphics Adapter (CGA), for example, you can normally only get an approximation of the graphics characters or fewer colours than the seven viewdata actually uses: to get the full effect you either need a special graphics board like the EGA or a special replacement chip for the normal board – which then prevents you from getting the full graphics display of normal IBM PC programs. During the 'install' process you should find the name of the graphics adapter your machine possesses. UK software usually has a facility for the Amstrad 1512 which is non-standard.

In some emulators, the option is referred to as Prestel or Micronet – they are all the same thing. Micronet-type software usually has additional facilities for fetching down telesoftware programs (see Chapter 8).

Viewdata emulators must attend not only to the graphics presentation, but also to split-speed operation: the traditional speeds are 1200 receive from host, 75 transmit to host, though it is becoming common now to offer 300/300 and 1200/1200 full duplex ports as well. US users of such services may get them via a packet-switched network, in which case they will receive it either at 1200/1200 full duplex or at 300/300.

Integrated terminal emulators offering both 'ordinary' asynchronous emulation and viewdata emulation are still rare, though becoming more common: until recently, I have had to use completely different and non-compatible bits of software on my own home set-up.

The biggest users of videotex these days are the French (see Chapter 8). French videotex uses different protocols from the UK standards and you will need specialized comms software to receive it properly. In North America, the videotex standard is different again – NAPLPS. Software packages for the IBM PC are available.

Command files The most sophisticated of comms packages include a miniature programming language so that you set up a whole series of commands to place the entire process under remote control. For example, you could arrange for your computer to 'wake up' in the middle of the night (when call costs are low and telephone lines uncongested), get it to autodial into a remote service (trying several times if necessary), log in with appropriate passwords, receive back appropriate responses from the distant host, see if there are any messages, or execute a

```
BPARFEDSGIEECL        G1a       C  Op  MMain Index

WZI,,,,,,,,,,,,,,,,,,,,,,,,,,,,,,,,,,,,  WJDI FOCUS`W=\ UU QJGYOU'RE IN FOCUS
  BNow you can find...Christmas feature,  Bsnooker latest,IV guide...all at on
 IZ,,,,,,,,,,,,,,,,,,,,,,,,,,,,,,,,,,,,,    'ZU AGRICULTURE
     21 BUSINESS
     22 EDUCATION
     23 HOME BANKING
     24 MICROCOMPUTING
     25 TELESHOPPING
     26 TRAVEL
   IZ,,,,,,,,,,,,,,,,,,,,,,,,,,,,,,,,,,,   5 MESSAGE. SERVICESBMailbox.Telex L)
   6 NEWS, WEATHER, LEISURE. SPORT
  TIZ,,,,,,,,,,,,,,,,,,,,,,,,,,,,,,,,,,,   7 A-Z INDEXESBto information & IPs
    8 CUSTOMER GUIDEBAll about Prestel
    9 WHAI'S NEW       AJC17th DECEMBER
  IZ ,,,,,,,,,,,,,,,,,,,,,:.   ,,,.,,,,,,
```

```
              P R E S T E L        1a          Op

              Main Index

              1 FOCUS           YOU'RE IN FOCUS

              Now you can find...Christmas feature,
              snooker latest,TV guide...all at once

                 20 AGRICULTURE
                 21 BUSINESS
                 22 EDUCATION
                 23 HOME BANKING
                 24 MICROCOMPUTING
                 25 TELESHOPPING
                 26 TRAVEL

              5 MESSAGE SERVICES Mailbox,Telex Link

              6 NEWS, WEATHER, LEISURE, SPORT

              7 A-Z INDEXES to information & IPs

              8 CUSTOMER GUIDE All about Prestel

              9 WHAT'S NEW        17th DECEMBER
```

Screen formatting. The first image is what Prestel looks like viewed on a dumb terminal with various colour and format attributes appearing as ASCII characters. The second is the same page viewed via a videotex emulator.

download or upload of files, and then exit gracefully from the host.

Operating system gateway This gives you access to your computer's operating system without leaving the comms program environment – so that you can look at directories, change discs, view files, etc. It is useful on MS-DOS-type computers.

Modems

Every account of what a modem is and does begins with the classic explanation of the derivation of the term: let this be no exception. Modem is a contraction of modulator-demodulator.

A modem taking instructions from a computer (pin 2 on RS232C), converts the binary 0s and 1s into specific single tones, according to which 'standard' is being used. In RS232C/V.24, binary 0 (ON) appears as positive volts and binary 1 (OFF) appears as negative volts. The tones are then fed, either acoustically via the telephone mouth-piece, into the telephone line, or electrically, by generating the electrical equivalent direct onto the line. This is the modulating process.

In the demodulating stage, the equipment sits on the phone line listening for occurrences of pre-selected tones (again according to whichever 'standard' is in operation) and, when it hears one, it delivers a binary 0 or binary 1 in the form of positive or negative voltage pulses into pin 3 of the computer's serial port.

This explanation holds true for modems operating at up to 1200 bits/s; above this speed, the modem must be able to originate tones, and detect them according to *phase* as well, but since higher-speed working is unusual in dial-up ports – the hacker's special interest – we can leave this matter to one side.

The modem is a relatively simple bit of kit: on the transmit side it consists of a series of oscillators acting as tone generators and on receive, it has a series of narrow band-pass filters. Designers of modems must ensure that unwanted tones do not leak into the telephone line (exchanges and amplifiers used by telephone companies are sometimes remotely controlled by the injection of specific tones) and also that, on the receive side, only the distinct tones used for communications are 'interpreted' into binary 0s or 1s. The other engineering requirements are that unwanted electrical currents do not wander down the telephone cable (to the possible risk of phone company employees) or back into the user's computer.

When I started out, the only UK source of low-speed modems was British Telecom. The situation is much easier now, but de-regulation of 'telephone line attachments', which include modems, is still, as I write, so recent, that the ordinary customer can easily become confused. Moreover, modems offering exactly the same service can vary in price by over 300 per cent. Strictly speaking, all modems connected to the phone line should be officially approved by BABT or other appropriate regulatory authority.

At 300 bits/s, you have the option of using direct-connect modems which are plugged into the phone line via a standard phone socket, or using an acoustic coupler in which you place the telephone hand-set. Acoustic couplers are inherently prone to interference from room-noise but are useful for quick lash-ups and portable operation. Many acoustic couplers operate only in 'originate' mode, not in' answer'. Newer commercial direct-connect modems are cheaper than acoustic couplers.

At higher speeds acoustic coupling is not recommended, though a 75/1200 acoustic coupler produced in association with the Prestel Micronet service is not too bad, and is now exchanged on the secondhand market very cheaply indeed.

I prefer modems that have proper status lights – power-on, line-seized, transmit and receive indicators. A small loudspeaker across the line also provides useful guidance, but the connection must be made properly: in some cases the loudpseaker can behave like a microphone and feed interference *into* the line! Hackers need to know what is going on more than most users.

Modern modem design is greatly aided by a wonder chip called the AMD 7910. This contains nearly all the facilities to modulate and demodulate the tones associated with the popular speed services both in the CCITT and Bell standards. The only omission – not always made clear in the advertisements – are services using 1200/1200 full-duplex, i.e. V.22 and Bell 212A.

Building a modem is now largely a question of adding a few peripheral components, some switches and indicator lights, and a box. In deciding which 'world standard' modem to purchase, hackers should consider the following features:

1 *Status lights*   You need to be able to see what is happening on the line

2 *Auto-answer*   This enables your computer to answer the phone automatically: the modem sends a signal to the computer, usually through pin 20 of the standard D-25 connector. With auto-answer, your own computer can become a 'host' so that others can call into it. You will need bulletin-board-type software for this.

3 *Auto-dial*   A pulse dialler and associated firmware are included in some more expensive models. You should ascertain whether the auto-dialler operates on the telephone system you intend to hook the modem up to – some of the US 'smart' modems present difficulties outside the States. You will of course need software in your micro to address the firmware in the modem – and the software has to be part of your terminal emulator, otherwise you gain nothing in convenience. However, with appropriate software, you can

get your computer to try a whole bank of numbers one after the other (see page 81).

4 *D25 connector* This is the official 'approved' RS232C/V.24 physical connection – useful from the point-of-view of easy hook-up. A number of lower-cost models substitute alternative DIN connectors. You must be prepared to solder up your own cables to be sure of connecting up properly.

5 *Documentation* I always prefer items to be accompanied by proper instructions. Since hackers tend to want to use equipment in unorthodox ways, they should look for good documentation too.

6 *Hardware/software switching* Cheaper versions merely give you a switch on the front enabling you to change speeds, originate or answer mode and CCITT or Bell tones. More expensive ones – called intelligent or smart modems – feature firmware which allows your computer to send specially formatted instructions to change speed, answer the phone, hang up, dial out under program control or store a list of frequently used phone numbers. Such modems can also often read and monitor the status of a telephone call, reporting back that a connection has been made, or that a number is busy, and so on.

  The drawback is that you must have terminal emulator software capable of using all these functions. Until recently, there has been no standard instruction set. You can even find the situation where software and modem firmware conflict – for example, one viewdata emulator package I rather like uses ⟨ esc ⟩ as a prefix to most of its major commands. And ⟨ esc ⟩ is also used as a prefix for an intelligent modem I had for a while. However, a standard based on those devised in the States by the D.C. Hayes company is now emerging. The Hayes modem protocols have become rather like the Epson codes for dot-matrix printers. All Hayes commands to the modem begin with the prefix AT. You can find the common AT commands in Appendix V.

7 If you have a PC-clone you can also decide whether to have a modem on a card which fits inside one of the slots or a stand-alone box. The stand-alone can be used with most other computers, but the in-built machine removes clutter and wiring from your desk. Modems-on-a-card of course

don't have status lights, but some of them contain small loudspeakers so that you can monitor events that way.

A word on build-your-own modems. A number of popular electronics magazines and mail-order houses have offered modem designs. Such modems are not likely to be approved for direct connection to the public telephone network. However, most of them work. If you are uncertain of your kit-constructing skills, though, remember badly built modems can be dangerous both to your computer and to the telephone network.

The cheapest way of getting on-line is to purchase second-hand 'professional' equipment. British Telecom markets the UK services under the name of Datel – details are given in Appendix V. The same appendix gives the type numbers of the BT modems that are often available on the secondhand market

If you pick up secondhand older-style BT equipment, you need to know the following: BT's system of connecting modems to the line were either to hard-wire the junction box (the two outer-wires are the ones you usually need), a 4-ring plug and associated socket (type 95A) for most modems, a 5-ring plug and associated socket (type 96A) for Prestel applications – no, the fifth ring isn't used. All modern equipment has a modular jack called type 600. The USA also has a modular jack, but, of course, it is not compatible.

Test Equipment
Various items of useful test equipment occasionally appear on the secondhand market – via mail-order, in computer junk shops, in the flea-market section of exhibitions and via computer clubs.

It is worth searching out a cable 'break-out' box or a switchable RS232C cable. These let you restrap a RS232C cable without getting a soldering iron – the various lines are brought out onto an accessible matrix and you use small connectors to make (or break) the links you require; alternatively you have to toggle a series of small switches. It is useful if you have an 'unknown' modem, or an unusually configured computer.

Related to this, there is a RS232C/V.24 analyser – which gives LED status lights for each of the important lines, so you can see what is happening. Usually the lights will be different colours depending on the direction of the data flow (i.e. transmit or receive).

Lastly, if you are a very rich and enthusiastic hacker, you can buy a protocol analyser. This is usually a portable device with a

VDU, full keyboard, and some very clever firmware which examines the telephone line or RS232C port and carries out tests to see which of several popular data comms protocols is in use. Hewlett Packard do a nice range. Protocol analysers will handle synchronous transmissions as well as asynchronous. Cost: £1500 and up... and up... and up.

4 Targets: What You Can Find on Mainframes

Wherever hackers gather, talk soon moves from past achievements and adventures to speculation about what new territory
might be explored. It says much about the compartmentalization
of computer specialities in general and the isolation of micro-
owners from mainstream activities in particular that a great deal
of this discussion is like that of navigators in the days before
Columbus; the charts are unreliable, full of blank spaces and
confounded with myth. Over the last few years, since this book
first appeared, many more services have appeared. The process
of charting the variety of computer services becomes more and
more difficult.

In this chapter I attempt to provide a series of notes on the
main types of services potentially available on dial-up and give
some idea of the sorts of protocols and conventions employed.
The idea is to give voyagers an outline atlas of what is interesting
and possible – and what is not.

On-Line Hosts
On-line services were the first form of electronic publishing; a
series of big storage computers – and on occasion, associated
dedicated networks – act as hosts to a group of individual
databases by providing not only mass data storage and the
appropriate 'search language' to access it, but also the means for
registering, logging and billing users. Typically users access the
on-line hosts via a phone number which links into a public data
network using packet switching; there is more on these networks
in Chapter 7.

The on-line business began relatively by accident; large
corporations and institutions involved in complicated technological developments found that their libraries simply couldn't keep
track of the publication of relevant new scientific papers and
decided to maintain indices of the papers by name, author,
subject-matter, and so on, on computer. One of the first of these

was the armaments and aircraft company, Lockheed Corporation.

In time the scope of these indices expanded and developed and outsiders – sub-contractors, research agencies, universities, government employees, etc., were granted access. Other organizations with similar information-handling requirements asked if space could be found on the computer for their needs. Eventually Lockheed – and others – recognized the beginnings of a quite separate business; in Lockheed's case it led to the foundation of Dialog which today acts as host and marketing agent for over 300 separate databases. A cut-down version of Dialog, marketed under the name Knowledge Index, is available at tariff levels affordable by the private user. It currently contains about 60 databases and is accessible outside normal office hours. Other on-line hosts include BRS (Bibliographic Retrieval Services), Comshare (used for sophisticated financial modelling), DataStar, Blaise (British Library), F.T. Profile, I.P. Sharp (owned by Reuters), and Euronet-Diane.

On-line services, particularly the older ones, are not especially user-friendly by modern standards. They were set up at a time when both core and storage memory was expensive and the search languages tend to be abbreviated and formal. Typically they are used, not by the eventual customer for the information, but by professional intermediaries – librarians and the like – who have undertaken special courses. Originally on-line hosts were accessed by dumb terminals, usually teletypewriters like the Texas Whisperwriter portable with built-in acoustic modem – rather than VDUs.

The Dialog search language is fairly typical: the host sends a ? prompt. You start a search with the word 'begin' followed by a four-letter abbreviation of the section you wish to use – COMP for computers, EDUC for education, MAGA for magazines, and so on. Each section is broken down into individual databases and you must then select which one you wish to search. The command word for searching by keyword is 'find'. Dialog comes back with the number of 'hits' corresponding to your request and, when you feel you have narrowed down the search sufficiently, you can ask it to 'display' in long, medium or short formats.

Here is a typical search – the commands are abbreviated: 'b' for 'begin', 'f' for 'find', and so on.

```
b MAGA

ow in MAGAZINES (MAGA) Section
  Magazine Index (MAGA1) Database
Copyright 1984 Information Access Corp)

'f comput? and fraud
ROCESSING
                    25274   COMPUT?
                     1138   FRAUD
          S1          23    COMPUT? AND FRAUD

type 1/L/1-23
 /L/1
 920876
  Fail-safe credit cards.   (computer chips embedded in card will
prevent counterfeiting and illegal use)
  Slomski, Anita
  Consumers Digest    v24 p16(1)   May-June    1985
  CODEN: CNDGA
  SIC CODE: 6153
  DESCRIPTORS:  credit card-security measures; semiconductor
chips-usage; counterfeits and counterfeiting-prevention; credit
card fraud-prevention; smart cards-technological innovations
1/L/2
etc
```

The 'comput?' request includes a wild-card to cover computer, computers, computing and other variants. The 'S1' is the way Dialog identifies my own first search – I can refine it later. 'Type s1/L/1-23' is the command to tell Dialog to display the results of my search 1 in long format and to include items 1 through 23 (in fact, the lot).

Dialog has the usual Boolean operators – and, not, etc., but lacks some of the features found on more recently set-up systems. It won't let you work by date ranges and it won't let you specify that if two keywords are selected they must occur within a given number of words of each other.

The search language used on Profile is similar – it is used for databases like World Reporter and McCarthy's: the primary command is 'get' and you refine the search by using 'pick'. If you use 'getdate' or 'pickdate' you can search by date range. There are commands so that you can select two words for searching but require that the words appear in the same paragraph or same sentence. Since much of Profile material consists of newspaper and magazine material, you can search by headline, e.g. 'get @ headline'. You can choose to print the whole of your search by means of the command 'text' or simply see the most relevant sections: 'context'.

However, master Dialog and most other information retrieval search languages will become obvious.

Today the trend is to use 'front-end' intelligent software on an IBM PC which allows the naive user to pose his/her questions informally while offline; the software then redefines the information request into the formal language of the on-line host (the user does not witness this process) and then goes on-line via an auto-dial modem to extract the information as swiftly and efficiently as possible.

On-line services require the use of a whole series of passwords – the usual NUI and NUA for PSS (see Chapter 7); another to reach the host, yet another for the specific information service required. Charges are either for connect-time or per record retrieved, or sometimes a combination.

There are two broad categories of on-line service: *Bibliographic*, which merely indexes the *existence* of an article or book – you must then find a physical copy to read (Dialog is an example of this, though you can, at some expense, order hard copy via the system); and *Source*, which contains the article (or extract thereof) itself. *Full-text* services not only contain the complete article or book but will, if required, search the entire text (as opposed to mere keywords) to locate the desired information. One example of this is World Reporter (see below) and another example is LEXIS, a vast legal database which contains nearly all important US and English law judgments as well as statute.

For the UK-based user, the fullest catalogue of on-line services is to be found in the twice-yearly publication *Brit-Line*.

News Services

The vast majority of news services, even today, are not, in the strictest sense, computer-based, although computers play an important role in assembling the information and, depending on the nature of the newspaper or radio or TV station receiving it, its subsequent handling.

The world's big press agencies – United Press, Associated Press, Reuters, Agence France Presse, TASS, Xinhua, PAP, VoA – use telex techniques to broadcast their stories. Permanent leased telegraphy lines exist between agencies and customers and the technology is pure telex: the 5-bit Baudot code (rather than ASCII) is adopted, giving capital letters only and 'mark' and 'space' are sent by changing voltage conditions on the line rather than different audio tones. Speeds are 50 or 75 bits/s.

The user cannot interrogate the agency in any way. The stories come in a single stream which is collected on rolls of paper and then used as per the contract between agency and subscriber.

To hack a news-agency line you will need to get physically near the appropriate leased line, tap in by means of an inductive loop, and convert the changing voltage levels (±80 volts on the line) into something your RS232C port can handle. You will then need software to translate the Baudot code into the ASCII which your computer can handle internally and display on screen or print to a file. The Baudot code is given in Appendix IV.

None of this is easy and will probably involve breaches of several laws, including theft of copyright material!

However a number of news agencies also transmit services by radio, in which case the signals can be hijacked with a shortwave receiver. Chapter 9 explains.

As the world's great newspapers increasingly move to electronic means of production – journalists working at VDUs, subeditors assembling pages and direct-input into photo-typesetters – the additional cost to each newspaper of creating its own morgue is relatively slight and we can expect to see many more commercial services, provided there is not too much opposition from print unions.

In the meantime, other publishing organizations have sought to make articles – extract or complete – from leading magazines available also. The main UK example is Profile's World Reporter, owned by the *Financial Times*, which includes material from the BBC's monitoring service, the *Washington Post*, Associated Press, *The Economist*, *Sunday Telegraph*, *Financial Times*, *TASS*, *Keesings* and the *Guardian*. World Reporter gives the full text. Even in October 1984 it already held 500 million English words. You can get World Reporter via a gateway on the electronic mail service Telecom Gold. It is expensive for casual use, up to £1.50 a minute when you add in all the charges. In the US there is NEXIS, which shares resources with LEXIS. NEXIS held 16 million full text articles at that same date. A slightly less expensive service available is called Newsnet, but all these services are costly for casual use. They are accessed by dial-up using ordinary asynchronous protocols.

Many electronic newsrooms also have dial-in ports for reporters out on the job; depending on the system these ports not only allow the reporter to transmit his or her story from a portable computer, but may also, like Basys Newsfury used by Channel

Four News, let them see news agency tapes, read headlines and send electronic mail. Such systems have been the subject of considerable hacker speculation.

Financial Services

The financial world can afford more computer aids than any other non-governmental sector. The vast potential profits that can be made by trading huge blocks of currency, securities or commodities – and the extraordinary advantages that a slight 'edge' in information can bring – have meant that the City, Wall Street and the equivalents in Hong Kong, Japan and major European capitals have been in the forefront of getting the most from high-speed comms.

Ten years ago the sole form of instant financial information was the ticker tape – telegraphy technology delivering the latest share price movements in a highly abbreviated form. As with its news equivalents, these were (and are, for the services still exist) broadcast services, sent along leased telegraph lines. The user could only watch and 'interrogation' consisted of back-tracking along a tape of paper.

Extel (Exchange Telegraph) continues to use this technique for some of its services, like FNS, though it is gradually upgrading by using viewdata and intelligent terminals for the Examiner service. It also runs a dial-up Stock Exchange prices service called PriceLine: once you are logged in, the command ACT will list the most active shares of the moment.

However, it was Reuters in about 1973 that put together the first packages which gave some intelligence and 'questioning power' to the end user. Each Reuters Monitor is intelligent, containing (usually) a DEC PDP-8 series mini and some firmware which accepts and selects the stream of data from the host at the far end of the leased line, marshals interrogation requests and takes care of the local display. Information is formatted in 'pages' rather like viewdata frames, but without the colour. There is little point in eavesdropping into a Reuters line unless you know what the terminal firmware does. Reuters are constantly expanding the range of their services. A tie-up with a US company called Instinet has given the capacity to offer international automated dealing. They are also beginning to discard the old-fashioned monochrome screens in favour of full-colour, high-resolution versions which can display elaborate graphs. The growth of Reuters and its rivals is an illustration of technology creating markets – especially in international currency – where none existed before.

The first sophisticated Stock Exchange prices 'screens' used modified closed-circuit television technology. London had a system called Market Price Display Service – MPDS – which consisted of a number of TV displays of current prices services on different 'channels' which could be selected by the user. It then moved on to TOPIC, a leased line variant on viewdata technology, though with its magazine-like arrangement and auto-screen refresh, it has as much in common with teletext as Prestel.

After the London Stock Exchange's Big Bang in November 1986, methods of dealing in shares changed radically. Whereas before all deals had had to be carried out in person on the 'floor' of the Stock Exchange between brokers and jobbers, the process is now largely screen-based. Market-makers (who replace the jobbers as the people who give prices to buy or sell shares), now send their 'quotes' electronically to a Stock Exchange system called SEAQ (Stock Exchange Automated Quotes) using IBM PCs on leased lines to the Stock Exchange, or specially designed terminals. TOPIC is used to disseminate these prices to 'the market', i.e. Stock Exchange members who may wish to buy or sell for their clients. The TOPIC display shows all the 'quotes' from each market-maker who deals in that particular share and identifies the best quote at any one time. This is the display you are most likely to see in a Stock Exchange member's office.

Datastream represents a much higher level of information and display sophistication – using its £40,000 plus pa terminals you can compare historic data – price movements, movements against sector indices, etc. – and chart the results.

Some of the very largest securities houses have designed elaborate 'dealers' workstations' in which several screens and keyboards are ergonomically arranged. The dealer is able to call up SEAQ or TOPIC (or a 'massaged' version presenting just the information he requires), together with screens for background information on companies and clients.

All these services are only available via leased lines – City professionals would not tolerate the delays and uncertainties of dial-up facilities. However dial-up ports exist for demonstrations, exhibitions, engineering and as back-up or for *ad hoc* access on IBM PCS – and a lot of hacking effort has gone into tracking them down.

In the United States, in addition to Reuters, Telerate and local equivalents of official streams of Stock Exchange, over-the-counter and Commodities Markets data, there is Dow Jones, best known internationally for its market indices similar to those produced by the *Financial Times* in London. Dow Jones is in fact the owner of the *Wall Street Journal* and some influential business magazines. Its Dow Jones News/Retrieval Service is aimed at businesses and private investors. It features current share prices, deliberately delayed by 15 minutes, historic price data, which can be charted by the user's own computer (typically an Apple or IBM PC) and historic 'morgue' type company news and analysis. Extensions of the service enable customers to examine accounts of companies in which they are interested. The bulk of the information is US-based, but can be obtained worldwide via packet-switching networks. All you need are the passwords and special software.

Business Information

Business information is usually about the credit-worthiness of companies, company annual reports, trading opportunities and market research. The biggest electronic credit data resource is owned by the international company Dun & Bradstreet: during 1985–86 it spent £25 million on making its data available all over Europe, including the UK. The service, which covers more than 900,000 UK businesses is called DunsPrint and access is both on-line and via a viewdata front-end processor. One of the features is to compare a company's speed of payment with that of norms in their industry sector.

Another agency, part of Great Universal Stores, CCN Services, extensively used already by the big clearing banks and with 3000 customers accessing information via viewdata sets, has recently produced an extended electronic retrieval service of its own called Guardian Business Information. CCN's viewdata service is impressive: if you have a password, you can check someone's credit-rating (or your own) by giving *approximations* of name and address; the powerful software will select likely alternatives until you have found the person you want. Other UK credit services available electronically include UAPT InfoLink, and Jordan Information Services.

In addition, all UK companies quoted on the London Stock Exchange, and many others of any size who are not, have a report and analysis available from ICC (InterCompany Comparisons) who can be accessed via on-line dial-up (it's on Dialog), through a viewdata interface and also by Datastream customers. Dun & Bradstreet also have an on-line service called KBE covering 20,000 key British enterprises.

Prodigious quantities of credit and background data on US individuals and companies can be found on several of the major on-line hosts.

A valid phone number, passwords and extracts from the operations manual of one of the largest US services, TRW – it has credit histories on 90 million people – sat on some hackers' bulletin boards (of which much more later) for over twelve months during 1983 and 1984 before the company found out. No one knows how many times hackers accessed the service. According to the *Washington Post*, the password and manual had been obtained from a Sears Roebuck national chain store in Sacramento; some hackers claimed they were able to alter credit records, but TRW maintain that telephone access to their systems is designed for read-only operations alone, updating of files taking place solely on magnetic tape.

More likely, many of these credit databases allow the customers to send in reports of credit defaulters; strictly speaking, the credit data supply companies should check their material but often they don't: so, if you wish to give someone a lousy record, you acquire the password of a legitimate customer of one of the credit data companies and transmit your false information. In due course it could appear in the main database.

US market research and risk analysis comes from Frost & Sullivan. Risk analysis tells international businessmen which countries are politically or economically unstable – or likely to become so – and thus unsafe to do business with.

University Facilities
In complete contrast to computers that are used to store and present data are those where the value is to deliver processing power to the outside world. Paramount among these are those installed in universities and research institutes.

Although hackers frequently acquire phone numbers to enter such machines, what you can do once you are there varies enormously. There are usually tiers and banks of passwords, each allowing only limited access to the range of services. It takes considerable knowledge of the machine's operating system to break through from one to another and indeed, in some cases, the operating system is so thoroughly embedded in the mainframe's

hardware architecture that the substantial modifications necessary to permit a hacker to roam free can only be done from a few
designated terminals or by having physical access to the machine.
However the hobbyist bulletin-board system quite often provides
passwords giving access to games and the ability to write and run
programs in exotic languages – my own first hands-on experience
of Unix came in exactly this way. There are bulletin boards on
mainframes and even, in some cases, boards for hackers!

Given the nature of hacking, it is not surprising that some of
the earliest japes occurred on computers owned by universities.
Way back in the 1970s, MIT was the location of the famous
'Cookie Monster', inspired by a character in the then-popular
Rowan & Martin Laugh-In's television show. As someone worked
away at their terminal, the word 'cookie' would appear across
their screen, at first slowly wiping out the user's work. Unless the
user moved quickly, things started to speed up and the machine
would flash urgently: 'Cookie, cookie, give me a cookie'. The
whole screen would pulse with this message until, after a while,
the hacking program relented and the 'Monster' would clear the
screen, leaving the message: 'I didn't want a cookie anyway.' It
would then disappear into the computer until it snared another
unsuspecting user. You could save yourself from the Monster by
typing the word 'Cookie', to which it replied 'Thank you' and
then vanished.

In another US case, this time in 1980, two kids in Chicago,
calling themselves System Cruncher and Vladimir, entered the
computer at DePaul University and caused a system crash which
cost $22,000 to fix. They were prosecuted, given probation and
were then made a movie offer.

In the UK, many important university and research institution
computers have been linked together on two special data networks
called SERCNET and JANET. SERC is the Science and
Engineering Research Council. Although most of the computers
are individually accessible via PSS, SERCNET makes it possible
to enter one computer and pass through to others. During early
1984, SERCNET was the target of much hacker attention; a fuller
account appears in Chapter 7, but to anticipate a little, a local
entry node was discovered via one of the London University
college computers with a demonstration facility which, if asked
nicely, disgorged an operating manual and list of 'addresses'. One
of the minor joys of this list was an entry labelled 'Gateway to
Universe', pure Hitch-hiker material, concealing an extensive

long-term multi-function communications project. Eventually some hackers based at a home counties university managed to discover ways of roaming free around the network.

JANET, the Joint University Network, operates in a similar way but is not confined in its subject matter to science and engineering. The expert hackers on JANET tend to be located, as you might expect, in university computer departments. JANET was extensively penetrated during what some people chose to call The Rape of Janet in spring 1984. Details appear in Chapter 6.

Banking

Prominent among public fantasies about hackers is the one where banks are entered electronically, accounts examined and, in some, money moved from one to another. The fantasies, bolstered by under-researched low-budget movies and TV features, arise from confusing the details of several actual happenings.

Most 'remote stealing' from banks or illicit obtaining of account details touch computers only incidentally and involve straight-forward forgery, fraud, conning or bribery, on the part of, bank employees. There is *no* authentic account of a UK clearing bank suffering from a large-scale pure computer fraud (i.e. involving the internal manipulation of bank computing systems as opposed to feeding in false input); partly this is because the banks, fearful of their credibility with their customers, go to some length to conceal the crimes.

Large-scale banking frauds are invariably committed by employees or sub-contractors; from the point-of-view of the outside-based criminal, however, when you think about the effort involved, human methods are much more cost-effective. The typical banking fraud usually relies on a forged input form: the misleading instruction is accepted and then computers and networks take care of the rest. The manipulation of computer files or computer programs in the banking sector is extremely rare. Banks were among the pioneers in setting out the procedures to ensure that each change to a system has to be monitored and approved by a whole series of individuals, making the life of the lone criminal impossible. For hackers, however, the very considerable effort that has been made to provide security makes the systems a great challenge in themselves.

In the United Kingdom the banking scene is dominated by a handful of large companies with many branches. Cheque clearing and account maintenance are conducted under conditions of high security with considerable isolation of key elements; inter-bank transactions in the UK go through a scheme called CHAPS, Clearing House Automatic Payments System, which uses the X.25 packet switching protocols (see Chapter 7). The network is based on Tandem machines; half of each machine is common to the network and half unique to the bank. The encryption standard used is the US Data Encryption Standard. Certain parts of the network, relating to the en- and decryption of messages, apparently auto-destructs if tampered with. The service started early in 1984. The international equivalent is SWIFT, Society for Worldwide Interbank Financial Transactions, is also X.25-based and it handles over 750,000 messages a day and is increasing at 15 to 20 per cent a year. If you want someone's 'balance' (how much they have in their account), the easiest and most reliable way to obtain it is with a plausible call to the local branch. If you want some easy money, steal a cheque book and cheque card and practise signature imitation. Or, on a grander scale, follow the example of the £780,000 krugerand fraud in the City. Thieves intercepted a telephone call from a solicitor or bank manager to 'authenticate' forged drafts; the gold coins were then delivered to a bogus company.

In the United States, where federal law limits the size of an individual bank's operations and in international banking, direct attacks on banks have been much easier because the technology adopted is much cruder and more use is made of public phone and telex lines. One of the favourite techniques has been to send fake authorizations for money transfers. This was the approach used against the Security National Pacific Bank by Stanley Rifkin and a Russian diamond dealer in Geneva. $10.2 million moved from bank to bank across the United States and beyond. Rifkin obtained code numbers used in the bilateral Test Keys. Here the trick is to spot weaknesses in the cryptographic systems used in such authorizations. The specifications for the systems themselves are openly published and it is certainly true that one computer security expert, Leslie Goldberg, quite recently was able to take apart one scheme – proposed but not actually implemented – and show that much of the 'key' that was supposed to give high-level cryptographic security was technically redundant and could be virtually ignored. A surprisingly full account of his 'perfect' fraud appears in a 1980 issue of the journal *Computer Fraud and Security Bulletin*.

There are, however, a few areas where banking is becoming vulnerable to the less mathematically literate hacker. A number of international banks are offering their big corporation customers special facilities so that their treasury departments (that ensure, among other things that any spare million dollars are not left doing nothing overnight but are earning short-term interest) can have direct access to their account details via a PC on dial-up. A *Financial Times* survey in October 1985 identified thirteen major banking groups offering such services, many of them using the Geisco or ADP networks. Again, telebanking is now available via Prestel and some of its overseas imitators. Although such services use several layers of passwords to validate transactions, if those passwords are misacquired, since no signatures are involved, the bank account becomes vulnerable.

Finally, the networks of ATMs (hole-in-the-wall cash machines) are expanding greatly. Each network has its own characteristics and software facilities are being added all the time. Here in the UK, banks are not the only people with ATMs; some building societies have banded together to set up their own networks. As mentioned early in this book, hackers have identified a number of bugs in earlier versions of the machines. None of them, incidentally, lead directly to fraud. These machines allow card-holders to extract cash up to a finite limit each week (usually £100–250). The magnetic stripe contains the account number, validation details of the owner's PIN (Personal Identity Number), usually four digits, and a record of how much cash has been drawn that week.

The ATM is usually off-line to the bank's main computer and only goes on-line in two circumstances – first, during business hours, to respond to a customer's 'balance request' and second, outside regular hours, to take into local memory, lists of invalid cards which should not be returned to the customer and to dump out cheque book and printed statement requests. Hackers have found ways of getting more than their cash limit each week. The ATMs belonging to one clearing bank could be 'cheated' in this way: you asked for your maximum amount and then, when the transaction was almost completed, the ATM asked you 'Do you want another transaction, Yes/No?'

If you responded 'Yes' you could then ask for – and get – your credit limit again, and again, and again. The weakness in the system was that the magnetic stripe was not overwritten to show you had had a transaction till it was physically ejected from the machine. This bug has now been fixed. A related, but more bizarre bug, resided for a while on the ATMs used by that first bank's most obvious High Street rivals. In that case, you first had to exhaust your week's limit. You then asked for a further sum, say £75. The machine refused but asked if you wanted a further transaction. Then, if you slowly reduced the amounts you were asking for by £5 ... £75, £65, £60 ... and so on, down to £10, you could then tell the ATM to cancel the last £5 transaction, and the machine gave you the full £75. Some hackers firmly believe the bug was placed there by the original software writer. This bug too has now been fixed. Neither of these quirks resulted in hackers 'winning' money from the banks involved; the accounts were, in every case, properly debited. The only victory was to beat the system.

In the first two editions of this book at this point I wrote: 'For the future, I note that the cost of magnetic stripe reader/writers which interface to PCs is dropping to very low levels. I await the first inevitable news reports.' I was aware of a particular fraud that was easy to carry out, but hesitated to describe it. In autumn 1986 I was asked by the Channel 4 TV consumer advice programme *4 What It's Worth* to advise them on ATM fraud in general and in particular to assess a scheme involving forged mag stripe cards that had been uncovered in Germany. The scheme was actually more complicated than the one I had had in mind.

Briefly, the fraud (which I do not regard as a legitimate hack) consists of cloning mag stripe cards using a reader/writer add-on for a PC. You obtain from a pickpocket a legitimate ATM card together with its associated PIN. If you were to use the card itself the most you would obtain would be the maximum weekly limit which for most people in the UK is between £100 and £250. After that the mag stripe would have been overwritten and you'd have to wait till the beginning of the next week before further sums could be drawn, by which time the card would have been reported stolen and would be on a hot list.

Now, some of the data on the mag stripe is encrypted, but this needn't deter the fraudster. All you have to do is to copy exactly the contents of your legitimate stolen card (before use) on to a blank mag stripe card. Do this as many times as you like. You can then get the ATM to pay out the maximum limit every time a card is fed in.

In this simple form, the fraud will *not* work in every case all the time. ATM networks, although they look very similar, vary from one bank to another. Some banks do have main computer systems which work in realtime, i.e., if you withdraw a sum of money, your account is instantly diminished by that sum. So cloning a mag stripe card brings limited benefits: once the account is depleted, alarm bells will ring. Other bank ATM systems, as we saw above however, work on a batch basis. Here, there is no immediate check on the status of the customer's account: the decision to pay out is made, not by the bank's main computer but by the local ATM. There are checks on batch-type ATMs as these machines, *most of the time*, are connected to a central computer resource which can provide a degree of security and also give a report on the previous day's 'balance'. The fraud will work when the ATM is not connected to this secondary network. A TV researcher working for *4 What It's Worth* was able to demonstrate the fraud working, though of course any cash gained was immediately returned.

Electronic Mail
Electronic mail services work by storing messages created by subscribers until they are retrieved by their intended recipients. The ingredients of a typical system are: registration/logging on facilities, storage, search and retrieval, networking, timing and billing. Electronic mail is an easy add-on to most mainframe installations, but in recent years various organizations have sought to market services to individuals, companies and industries where electronic mail was the main purpose of the system, not an add-on.

The system software in widest use in the UK is that of ITT-Dialcom; it's the one that runs Telecom Gold. Telecom Gold had, in spring 1987, getting on for 80,000 users.

When the Dialcom/Telecom Gold service was first marketed, the assumption was made that most users would want to concentrate on a relatively narrow range of correspondents. Accordingly, the way it was sold was as a series of systems,* each run by a 'manager': someone within a company. The 'manager'

---

* Just to make life difficult, the word 'system' is used in two different ways. One refers, as mentioned above, to groups of users. But 'system' can also refer to individual computers running Dialcom software. These are always signified by a two-digit number. UK Dialcom systems are in the range 72 to 86 (with the Irish Eirmail occupying System 74), Germany is 15 and 16, and so on. The full electronic address of a Dialcom subscriber begins with the system number, followed by a colon.

was the only person who had direct contact with the electronic mail owner and he in turn was responsible for bringing individual users on to his 'system' – he could issue 'mailboxes' direct, determine tariff levels, put up general messages. Now, the strategy is moving closer to what happens in most other services, where every user has a direct relationship with the electronic mail company.

Options you can use when sending mail

At the 'Send, Read or Scan' prompt:

READ (*or* **SCAN**) **UNREAD**
READ (*or* **SCAN**) **EXPRESS**
READ (*or* **SCAN**) **UNREAD EXPRESS**
READ (*or* **SCAN**) **FILE xxxx** (*xxxx = file name*)
READ (or SCAN) 1 3 2   (*read in that order*)
READ (or SCAN) 2-6   (*read 2 to 6 incl*)
READ (or SCAN) -5   (*read up to 5 incl*)
READ (or SCAN) 6-   (*read from 6 onwards*)
Note you can abbreviate **READ** *as* **R**
                                   SCAN *as* **SC**
                                   UNREAD *as* **U**
                                   EXPRESS *as* **EX**

CRT   (*Cancels HARDCOPY prompt*)
DA d/m/y   (*R or SC items sent on date*)
DA d/m/y-   (*R or SC items sent on or after date*)
DA -d/m/y   (*R or SC items sent on or before date*)
DA d/m/y-d/m/y (*R or SC items sent on or between dates*)
DIS REF   (*display the Reference Directory – your personal list*)
DIS REF ?xxxx? (*search for string xxxx*)
DIS FILES   (*display names of filed mail*)
DELETE FI xxxx (*delete xxxx from files*)
FROM xxxx   (*R or SC anything received from name xxxx*)
HARDCOPY   (*read mail without any of the '–More–' prompts*)
HELP   (*print list of options available at this prompt*)
MORE   (*cancels the NO MORE option*)
NOMORE   (*read mail without the first '–More–' prompt*)
SU xxxx   (*R or SC items with xxxx in subject line*)
TEXT xxxx   (*R or SC items with xxxx anywhere in the text*)

At the 'Action Required' prompt:

AGAIN   (*redisplay the whole message*)
REPLY   (*key in your reply, and end it with ..SEND or .S*)
AP REPLY   (*append the original message to the reply that follows*)
FO xxx   (*forward the above message to this mailbox number, together with my comments*)
FILE xx   (*put the message in my file under the name xx*)
DEL   (*delete message from my mail*)
QUIT   (*quit back to command* **>**)

At the '–More–' prompt, all the above plus the following:

C/R	*(press Return for Enter) key to continue reading text)*
HARDCOPY	*(Read mail without further '–More–' prompts)*
NEXT	*(leave this message and go on to the next one)*
NO	*(same as above)*

Options you can use when reading mail

At the 'To:' prompt:

EX	*(EXpress: Goes right to the top of the recipient's message stack)*
CC	*(Carbon Copy: A copy goes to each person named)*
BC	*(Blind Copy: Names of people who receive blind copies are not seen by other recipients)*
AR	*(Acknowledgement Requested: You are told automatically if your message has been read)*
RR	*(Reply Requested: The person who receives this message is invited to key in a reply)*

At the 'Text:' prompt:

.T	*(gets out of File Requests; also takes you back to Action Required)*
.To xxx	*(add to the 'To:' line)*
.EX	*(express to all recipients)*
.EX xxx	*(express only to person named)*
.CC xxx	*(copy only to person named)*
.BC xxx	*(blind copy only to name)*
.DIS	*(display whole of the text)*
.DIS HE	*(display header – only the 'To:' and 'Subject:' lines)*
.DIS TO	*(display only the 'To:' line)*
.SU xxxx	*(change subject line to xxxx)*
.Q	*(quit back to command >)*
.SEND or .S	*(send message)*
.LOAD xx	*(load into text area file xx created by the System Editor)*

Other Dialcom Systems: list

Australia (Minerva)	07,08
Canada (Infotex)	20–1
Denmark (Databoks)	71
Germany (Telebox)	15–16
Hong Kong (Dialcom)	88–9
Ireland (Eirmail)	74
Israel (Goldnet)	05
Japan (KDMINC)	14
Korea (Dialcom)	52
Mexico (Telepro)	52

Netherlands (Memocom)	27
New Zealand (Starnet)	09
Puerto Rico (Dialcom)	25
Singapore (Telebox)	10–11
UK (Telecom Gold)	72–86
USA (Dialcom)	38
	41–50
	52
	57–8
	60–4
	94–5
	97–8

The services vary according to their tariff structures and levels; and also the sort of additional facilities – some offer bi-directional interfaces to telex; some contain electronic magazines, a little like videotex. Telecom Gold in particular has been building up its range of additional services. There is a home computer enthusiast's service called Microlink and there are links or gateways to some of the big information retrieval services. A gateway is a link between two large computers and a means by which a customer on one can become a user on another, but still be under the control of the first machine (for billing purposes and to ensure you don't stray!). Among the gatewayed services are Euronet-Diane, Profile/World Reporter, *Financial Times* technology newsletters, the Airline Guide, Infomatics Daily Bulletin and business-orientated services like Infocheck and Jordans. To use these you often don't need to pre-register but you get charged at a premium connect time. Such facilities are useful for very occasional use but are expensive if utilized frequently. Electronic mail is sometimes added on to existing networks – Dialog has added a feature called Dialmail; Geisco, an international networking resource for larger companies offers data transportation, databases and electronic mail – it doesn't want small users, though.

Inter-connection between the various electronic mail services is not easy; each one currently has its own format for messages and a set of internal commands. It is rather a pain if you have to use more than one, although there are bureaux that will, for a fee, collect messages sent on one service and dump them, suitably reformatted, on another. In the longer term, there is now an internationally agreed set of standards – it is called X.400 – but no large service is, at the time of writing, actually using it. Many of the large e-mail systems have however said they expect to be moving over to it.

Apart from Dialcom/Telecom Gold-type services, the basic systems tend to be quite robust and hacking is mainly concentrated on second-guessing users' IDs. Many of the systems have now sought to increase security by insisting on passwords of a certain length – and by giving users only three or four attempts at logging on before closing down the line. But increasingly their customers are using PCs and special software to automate logging-in. The software packages of course have the IDs nicely pre-stored.

The particular weakness of Dialcom derives not from the package itself, but from the way in which it has to be installed on the Prime computers upon which it runs. When you see a prompt (a $>$) on Telecom Gold, you are in fact seeing the prompt for the operating system of a Prime computer, PRIMOS: Dialcom is only *one* of a series of programs that might be available at that point. For example, you could expect to find a simple line editor, perhaps a command language (a little like BATCH in MS-DOS) and also various text files. This set-up increases the flexibility of Dialcom, but it creates risks in terms of security. If whoever set up the Prime in the first place left more facilities accessible than they should have, then a hacker has all sorts of opportunities. This is how the BBC Hack described in Chapter I was able to take place: the hacker had more programming resources than he should have had – and he took advantage.

Early in 1987 something similar happened with Eirmail, the equivalent service of the Irish PTT, when a hacker calling himself Greenbeard was able to turn himself into a system manager and start awarding free accounts to his friends. Greenbeard explained how he had done it in the RTE TV show *Zero*. Dialcom isn't particularly insecure provided it has been set up properly.

Government Computers
Among hackers themselves the richest source of fantasizing revolves around official computers like those used by the tax and national insurance authorities, the police, armed forces and intelligence agencies.

The Pentagon, in fact, was hacked in 1983 by a 19-year-old Los Angeles student, Ronald Mark Austin. Because of the techniques he used, a full account is given in the operating systems section of

Chapter 6. NASA, the Space Agency, has also acknowledged that its e-mail system has been breached and that messages and pictures of Kilroy were left as graffiti. This leaves only one outstanding mega-target, Platform, the global data network of 52 separate systems focused on the headquarters of the USA's electronic spooks, the National Security Agency at Fort Meade, Maryland. The network includes at least one Cray-1, the world's most powerful number-cruncher, and facilities provided by GCHQ at Cheltenham.

Although I know UK phone freaks who claim to have managed to appear on the internal exchanges used by Century House (MI6) and Curzon Street House (MI5) and have wandered along AUTOVON, the US secure military phone network, I am not aware of anyone bold or clever enough to have penetrated the UK's most secure computers.

Over the next few years, the UK government is due to spend £200 million on the GDN – Government Data Network – which will lead to the Home Office, Inland Revenue, Department of Health and Social Security and Customs and Excise all being on the same network. Apparently there are also to be facilities for various 'unnamed departments' – this probably means the Security Service. Already civil liberties groups are claiming that the GDN specification is a significant step towards Big Brother-type surveillance.

It must be acknowledged that in general it is far easier to obtain the information held on these machines – and lesser ones like the DVLC (vehicle licensing) and PNC (Police National Computer, also due for extensive upgrading) by human means than by hacking – bribery, conning and blackmail being the most obvious, and the methods invariably used by private detectives.

Nevertheless, there is an interesting hacker's exercise to be told in demonstrating how far it is possible to produce details from open sources of these systems, even when the details are supposed to be secret. But this relates to one of the hacker's own secret weapons – thorough research, the subject of the next chapter.

5 Hackers' Intelligence

Of all the features of hacking that mystify outsiders it is how the phone numbers that give access to the computer systems and the passwords that open the data files ever reach hackers. Of all the features of the ways in which hacking is portrayed in films, books and TV, the most misleading is the concentration on the image of the solitary genius bashing away at a keyboard trying to 'break in'.

Most actual unauthorized computer invasions are quite simple: you acquire, from someone else – we'll see how in a minute – a phone number and a password to a system; you dial up, wait for the whistle, tap out the password, browse around for a few minutes and log off. You've had some fun, perhaps, but you haven't really done anything except follow a well-marked path. This isn't hacking in any worthwhile sense. After the first edition of this book was published I received rather too many letters from would-be enthusiasts asking me to please, please send them some 'real' telephone numbers. There's as much point to this as writing to the groundsman at Wembley requesting if you can be allowed to put a soccer ball between the goal posts – the *point* of football is to score when 11 men and a referee are trying to stop you and the *point* of hacking is to find things out for yourself.

Successful hacking depends on good research. The materials of research are all around: as well as direct hacker-orientated material of the sort found on bulletin board systems and heard in quiet corners during refreshment breaks at computer clubs, huge quantities of useful literature are published daily by the marketing departments of computer companies and given away to all comers, sheaves of stationery and lorry loads of internal documentation containing important clues are left around to be picked up. It is up to the hacker to recognize this treasure for what it is, and to assemble it in a form in which it can be used.

Anyone who has ever done any intelligence work, not necessarily for a government, but for a company, or who has worked as an investigative journalist, will tell you that easily 90 per cent of the information you want is freely available and that the difficult part is recognizing and analysing it. Of the remaining 10 per cent, well over half can usually be inferred from the material you already have, because, given a desired objective, there are usually only a limited number of sensible solutions. You can go further – it is often possible to test your inferences and, having done that, develop yet further hypotheses.

So the dedicated hacker, far from spending all the time staring at a VDU and 'trying things' on the keyboard, is often to be found wandering around exhibitions, attending demonstrations, picking up literature, talking on the phone (voice-mode!) and scavenging in refuse bins.

But both for the beginner, and the dedicated hacker who wishes to consult with his colleagues, the bulletin board movement has been the single greatest source of intelligence.

Bulletin Boards

Since 1980, when good software enabling solitary micro-computers to offer a welcome to all callers first became widely available, the bulletin board movement has grown by leaps and bounds. If you haven't logged on to one already, now is the time to try. At the very least it will test out your computer, modem and software – and your skills in handling them. Current phone numbers together with system hours and comms protocol requirements are regularly published in computer mags – for UK-based readers, Peter Toothill's column in *Personal Computer World* is recommended and you will will also find some steers within the Clubspot section in Prestel Microcomputing and on Telecom Gold's Microlink; once you have got into one bulletin board, you will find details of others as most bulletin-board owners belong to an association.

Bulletin boards nearly always operate on micros; most of them are single-user systems, though in every other respect they can look like big mainframes; the first one I ever used was running on a Tandy TRS-80, a 1978–79 generation personal computer. They allow people to leave messages for each other, either privately, so that only the designated recipient can read it, or publicly, so that everyone who wants to can browse through, pick up useful information and maybe contribute as well. Bulletin boards also have text files, perhaps of news or summaries of useful information, which can either be read immediately or downloaded onto your own machine for reading and perhaps printing out later.

Often, too, you may find computer programs to download, but remember that most sophisticated programs are quite long and it can easily take over an hour to download an average program at 300 bits/s; you might do better to acquire a copy on a floppy disc. Bulletin boards also let users *upload* files as well, but the organisers may want to get to know you before letting you use that facility.

In the UK you will find two big families of bulletin board. The older generation, and by far the more numerous and useful, are ASCII-based, look like professional online services and usually run at 300 bits/s, 8 databits, no parity. Some of them can operate at higher speeds also and will detect, from the carrier tone sent by your modem, which speed to transmit in. Alternatively, you may have to send a series of carriage returns to wake up the bulletin board's modem to operate at the correct speed. After a while, you'll learn the particular software packages in use from their way of displaying prompts and the sorts of commands available – TBBS by eSoft run on TRS-80s and the IBM PC, Fido* is just on the IBM PC and there are others, not often used, for the IBM-PC as well as for CP/M machines and the old Apple. Some of the younger generation are viewdata or videotex compatible – they are like Prestel and are accessed at 75/1200 bits/s, 7 databits, even parity, which means that those with Micronet packages can use them. Because they operate on a frame-by-frame basis they are less flexible than the 300 bits/s packages. A popular videotex bulletin board package is CommunItel which runs on the BBC Model B.

Affordable multi-user bulletin boards are beginning to appear, both in ASCII format and in videotex. There are two advantages: several people can communicate with the board at the same time and those logged on can chat with each other as well as with the sysop.

Bulletin boards were originally designed for use by computer hobbyists, but in fact they can be used for almost anything. By

* One of the interesting features of Fido is that all Fido-based bulletin boards have the capacity to link together to forward on messages. Thus you can leave a message on one Fido board and, if the sysops have made previous arrangements, it can be picked up from another. What happens is that, at a suitably 'dead' time of day, Fido I can call Fido II and perform an automated file exchange. This facility is based on ideas developed for Unix–based minis called Usenet, which operates across continents. Newer versions of TBBS software have similar capabilities, but most bulletin-board networks are based on Fido.

concentrating on the file display facilities you can become a mini-electronic publisher. Some bulletin boards are used for professional purposes, such as the sharing of medical information or so that salesmen can keep in touch with their head office without recourse to the big electronic mail companies. On a less savoury note, they have also been used for sexual contacts, including child pornography.

Somewhere on most hobbyist boards you will find a series of special interest group (SIG) sections and among these, often, will be a Hacker's club. Entrance to each SIG will be at the discretion of the sysop, the bulletin-board owner. Since the BBS software allows the sysop to conceal from users the list of possible SIGs, it may not be immediately obvious whether a hacker's section exists on a particular board. Often the sysop will be anxious to form a view of a new entrant before admitting him or her to a 'sensitive' area. It has even been known for bulletin boards to carry *two* hacker sections: one, admission to which can be fairly easily obtained; and a second, the very existence of which is a tightly controlled secret, where mutually trusting initiates swap information.

The first timer, reading through a hacker's bulletin board, will find that it seems to consist of a series of discursive conversations between friends. Occasionally, someone may write up a summary for more universal consumption. You will see questions being posed... if you feel you can contribute, do so, because the whole idea is that a BBS is an information exchange. It is considered crass to appear on a board and simply ask 'Got any good numbers?'; if you do, you will not get any answers. Any questions you ask should be highly specific, show that you have already done some groundwork, and make clear that any results derived from the help you receive will be reported back to the board. Confidential notes to individuals, not for general consumption, can be sent using the E-Mail option on the bulletin board, but remember, *nothing* is hidden from the sysop.

A flavour of the type of material that can be seen on bulletin boards appears from this slightly doctored excerpt (I have removed some of the menu sequences in which the system asks what you want to do next and have deleted the identities of individuals):

Msg#: 3538 #MODEM-SPOT#
01/30/84 12:34:04 (Read 39 Times)
From: xxxxxx xxxxxxxx
To: ALL
Subj: BBC/MAPLIN MODEMS
RE THE CONNECTIONS ON THE BBC/MAPLIN MODEM SETUP, THE CTS PIN IS USEDTO
HANDSHAKE WITH THE RTS PIN E.G. ONE UNIT SENDS RTS (READY TO SEND) AND THE
SECOND UNIT REPLIES CTS (CLEAR TO SEND), USUALLY DONE BY TAKING PIN HIGH. IF
YOU STRAP IT HIGH I WOULD SUGGEST VIA A 4K7 RESISTOR TO THE VCC/+VE RAIL (5V)
IN THE EVENT OF A BUFFER OVERFLOW, THESE RTS/CTS PINS ARE TAKEN LOW AND THIS
STOPS THE DATA TRANSFER. ON A 25WAY D TYPE CONNECTOR TX DATA IS PIN 2
RX DATA IS PIN 3
RTS IS PIN 4
CTS IS PIN 5
GROUND IS PIN 7

ALL THE BEST -- ANY COMMTO xxxxxx xxxxxxxx.
(DATA COMMS ENGINEER)

Msg#: 3570 #MODEM-SPOT#
01/31/84 23:43:08 (Read 31 Times)

From: xxxx xxxxx
To: xxxxxx xxxxxxxx
Subj: REPLY TO MSG# 3538 (BBC/MAPLIN MODEMS)
ON THE BBC COMPUTER IT IS EASIER TO CONNECT THE RTS (READY TO SEND) PIN TO THE
CTS (CLEAR TO SEND) PIN. THIS OVERCOMES THE PROBLEM OF HAND SHAKING.
SINCE THE MAPLIN MODEM DOES NOT HAVE HAND SHAKING. I HAVE PUT MY RTS CTS JUMPER
INSIDE THE MODEM. MY CABLES ARE THEN STANDARD AND CAN BE USED WITH HANDSHAKERS.
REGARDS

Msg#: 3662 #HACKER'S CLUB#
02/04/84 23:37:11 (Read 41 Times)
From: xxx xxxxxxx
To: ALL
Subj: PUBLIC DATA NET
Does anyone gnow what the Public Data Net is? I appear to have access to it,&
I daren't ask what it is'
Also, can anyone tell me more about the Primenet systems... Again, I seem to
have the means, but no info. F'rinstance, I have a relative who logs on to
another Prime Both of our systems are on Primenet, is there any way we can
communicate?
More info to those who want it...

/N>ext msg, <R>eply, or <S>top?
Msg has replies, read now(Y/N)? y

Reply has been deleted

/N>ext msg, <R>eply, or <S>top?

Msg#: 3739 #HACKER'S CLUB#
02/06/84 22:39:06 (Read 15 Times)
From: xxx xxxxxxx
To: xxx xxxx
Subj: REPLY TO MSG# 3716 (PRIMENET COMMS)
Ahh, but what is the significance of the Address-does it mean a PSS number, or
some thing like that? Meanwhile, I'll get on-line (via voice-link on the phone')
to my cousin, and see what he has on it....
Msg#: 3766 #HACKER'S CLUB#
02/07/84 13:37:04 (Read 13 Times)
From: xxxxxxx xxx
To: xxxxx xxxxxxxx
Subj: REPLY TO MSG# 3701 (PUBLIC DATA NET)
Frimenet is a loal area network. I know of one in Poole, And BTGold use one
between their systems too. It is only an internal network. I suggest using PSS
to communicate between diffferent primes. Cheers.

N ext msg, R eply, or S top?

Msg#: 3799 *BBC*
02/07/84 22:09:05 (Read 4 Times)
From: xxxxx xxxxxxx
To: xxxxx xxxxxx
Subj: REPLY TO MSG# 3751 (RGB VIDEO)
The normal video output BNC can be made to produce colour video by making a
link near to the bnc socket on the pcb. details are in the advanced user guide
under the chapter on what the various links do. If you require more I will try
to help, as I have done this mod and it works fine

Msg#: 935 *EREWHON*
09/20/83 01:23:00 (Read 90 Times)
From: xxxxx xxxx
To: ALL
Subj: US PHONE FREAKING
USA Phone Freaking is done with a 2 out of 5 Code.   The tones must be with 30
Hz. and have less than 1 % Distortion.

Master Tone Frequency = 2600 Hz.
>1 = 700 & 900 Hz
>2 = 700 & 1100 Hz
>3 = 900 & 1100 Hz
>4 = 700 & 1300 Hz
>5 = 900 & 1300 Hz
>6 = 1100 & 1300 Hz
>7 = 700 & 1500 Hz
>8 = 900 & 1500 Hz
>9 ? 1100 & 1500 Hz
>0 = 1300 & 1500 Hz
>Start Key Signal = 1100 & 1700 Hz
>End Key Signal = 1300 & 1700 Hz
> Military Priority Keys 11=700 & 1700 ; 12=900 & 1700 - I don't reccomend
using these. (
The method of use will be explained in a separate note. DO NOT DISCLOSE WHERE
YOU GOT THESE FREQUENCIES TO ANYONE'

Msg#: 936 *EREWHON*
09/20/83 01:34:43 (Read 89 Times)
From: xxxxx xxxx
To: ALL
Subj: UK PHONE FREAKING

The UK system also uses a 2 out of 5 tone pattern.

The Master Frequency is 2280 Hz
>1 = 1380 & 1500 Hz
>2 = 1380 & 1620 Hz
>3 = 1500 & 1620 Hz
>4 = 1380 & 1740 Hz
>5 = 1500 & 1740 Hz
>6 = 1620 & 1740 Hz
>7 = 1380 & 1860 Hz
>8 = 1500 & 1860 Hz
>9 = 1620 & 1860 Hz
>0 = 1740 & 1860 Hz
>Start Key = 1740 & 1980 ; End Keying = 1860 & 1980 Hz
>Unused I think 11 = 1380 & 1980 ; 12 = 1500 & 1980 Hz

This is from the CCITT White Book Vol. 6 and is known as SSMF No. 3 to some
B.T. Personnel.

The 2280 Hz tone is being filtered out at many exchanges so you may need quite
a high level for it to work.

Msg#: 951 *EREWHON*
09/21/83 17:44:28 (Read 79 Times)
From: xxxxxxxxxx
To: PHONE FREAKS
Subj: NEED YOU ASK

In two other messages you will find the frequencies listed for the internal phone system controls. This note is intended to explain how the system could be operated. The central feature to realise is that (especially in the USA) the routing information in a call is not in the Dialled Code. The normal sequence of a call is that the Area Code is received while the Subscriber No. is stored for a short period. The Local Exchange reads the area code and selects the best route at that time for the call.   The call together with a new "INTERNAThe call together with a new "INTERNAL" dialling code is then sent on to the next exchange together with the subscriber number. This is repeated from area to area and group to group. The system this way provides many routes and corrects itself for failures.

The Technique.   Make a Long Distance call to a number which does not answer. Send down the Master Tone. (2600 or 22080 Hz) This will clear the line back, but leave you in the system. You may now send the "Start Key Pulse" followed by the Routing Code and the Subscriber No. Finish with the "End Keying Pulse". The system sees you as being a distant exchange requesting a route for a call.

Meanwhile back at the home base. Your local exchange will be logging you in as still ringing on the first call. There are further problems in this in both the USA and the UK as the techniques are understood and disapproved of by those in authority. You may need to have a fairly strong signal into the system to get past filters present on the line. Warning newer exchanges may link these filters to alarms. Try from a phone box or a Public Place and see what happens or who comes.

Example:- To call from within USA to UK:-
> Ring Toll Free 800 Number
> Send 2600 Hz Key Pulse
> When line goes dead you are in trunk level
> Start Pulse 182 End Pulse = White Plains N.Y. Gateway continued in next message

Msg#: 952 *EREWHON*
09/21/83 18:03:12 (Read 73 Times)
From: xxxxxxxxxxx
To: PHONE FREAKS
Subj: HOW TO DO IT PT 2

> Start Pulse 044 = United Kingdom
> 1 = Londof (Note no leading 0 please)
> 730 1234 = Harrods Department Store.

Any info on internal address codes would be appreciated from any callers.

Msg#: 1028 *EREWHON*
09/25/83 23:02:35 (Read 94 Times)
From: xxxx xx:xxxxx
To: ALL
Subj: FREEFONE PART 1

The following info comes from a leaflet entitled 'FREEFONE':

"British Telecom's recent record profits and continuing appalling service have prompted the circulation of this information. It comprises a method of making telephone calls free of charge."
.pa
Circuit Diagram:

```
                    0----o-------      -------o----0
                    :    :                    :    :
                    :    :                    :    :
                    L    o--------  --------o    P
                    I    :                    :    H
                    N    :                    :    O
                    E    o--    ------  ----o    N
                    :    :                    :    E
                    :    :                    :    :
                    I    :                    :    :
                    N    o-------   --------o    :
                    :                            :
                    :                            :
                    :                            :
                    0----------------------------0
```

```
S1 =
C1 =
D1 =
D2 =
R1 =
```

continued...

Msg#: 1029 #EREWHON#
09/25/83 23:19:17 (Read 87 Times)
From: xxxx xxxxxx
To: ALL
Subj: FREEFONE PART 2

Circuit Operation:

The circuit inhibits the charging for incoming calls only. When a phone is
answered, there is normally approx. 100mA DC loop current but only 8mA or so is
necessary to polarise the mic In the handset. Drawing only this small amount is
sufficient to fool BT's ancient 'Electric Meccano'.

It's extremely simple. When ringing, the polarity of the line reverses so D1
effectively answers the call when the handset is lifted. When the call is
established, the line polarity reverts and R1 limits the loop current while D2
is a LED to indicate the circuit is in operation. C1 ensures speECh is
unaffected. S1 returns the telephone to normal.

Local calls of unlimited length can be made free of charge. Long disTance calls
using this circuit are prone to automatic disconnection, this varies from area
to area but you will get at least 3 minutes before the line is closed down.
Further experimentation should bear fruit in this respect.

Sith the phone on the hook this circuit is completely undetectable. The swItch
should be cLosed if a call iS received from an operator, for example, or to
make an outgoing call. It has proved extremely useful, particularly for friends
phoning from payphones with jammed coin slots.

#Please DO NOT tell ANYONE where yoU found this information#

Msg#: 1194 #EREWHON#
10/07/83 04:50:34 (Read 81 Times)
From: xxxx xxxxxx
To: ALL
Subj: FREE TEST NUMBERS

Free Test Numbers
=================
Here are some no's that have been found to work:
Dial 174 <last 4 figs of your no>: this gives unobtainable then when you
replace handset the phone rings.
Dial 175 <last 4 figs of your no>: this gives 'start test...start test...',
then when you hang-up the phone rings. Pick it up and you either get dial tone
whiah indicates OK or you will get a recording i.e 'poor insulation B line'
telLing you what's wrong. If you get dial tone you can immediately dial 1305 to
do a further test which might say 'faulty dial pulses'.
Other numbers to try are 182, 184 or 185.
I have discovered my exchange (Pontybodkin) gives a test ring for 1267.
These numbers all depend on you local exchange so It pays to experiment, try
numbers starting with 1 aS thEse are all local functIons. Then when you
discover something of interest let me know on this SIG.

Msg#: 2241 #EREWHON#
12/04/83 20:48:49 (Read 65 Times)
From: SYSOP
To: SERIOUS FREAKS
Subj: USA INFO
There is a company (?) in the USA called Loopmaniacs Unlimited , PO Box 1197,
Port Townsend, WA, 98368, who publish a line of books on telephone hacking.
Some have circuits even.   Write to M. Hoy there.

One of their publcns is "Steal This Book" at $5.95 plus about $4 post. Its worth stealing, but don't show it to the customs.'

Msg#: 3266 #EREWHON#
01/22/84 06:25:01 (Read 53 Times)
From: xxx xxxxxxx
To: ALL
Subj: UNIVERSITY COMPUTERS
As already described getting onto the UCL PAD allows various calls. Via this network you can access many many university/research cl]]~puters To get a full list use CALL 40 then HELP, select GUIDE. Typing '32' at the VIEW prompt will start listing the addresses. Most of these can be used at the pad by 'CALL addr' where addr is the address. For passwords yotry DEMO, HELP etc. If you find anything interesting report it here.
HINT: To aviod the PAD hanging up at the end of each call use the LOGON command - use anything for name and pwd. This seems to do the trici.
Another number: Tel: (0235) 834531. This is another data exchange. This one's a bit harder to wake up. You must send a 'break level' to start. This can be done using software but with a maplin just momentarily pull out the RS232 conn. Then send RETURNs. To get a list od 'classes' you could use say Manchesters HELP:- CALL 1020300, user:DEMO pwd:DEMO en when you're on HELP PACX.

Msg#: 3687 #HACKER'S CLUB#
02/05/84 14:41:43 (Read 416 Times)
From: xxxx xxxxxxx
To: ALL
Subj: HACKERS NUMBERS

The following are some of the numbers collected in the Hackers SIB:
#########
Commodore BBS (Finland)   358 61 116223
#########
Gateway test   01 600 1261
PRESTEST (1200/75)   01 583 9412
Some useful PRESTEL nodes - 640..Res.D (Martlesham's experiments in Dynamic Prestel, DRCS, CEPT standards, Picture Prestel), 601 (Mailbox,Telemessaging, Telex Link - and maybe Telecom Gold), 651 (Scratchpad -always changing). Occasionally parts of 650 (IP News) are not properly CUGed off. 190 sometimes is interesting as well.
#########
These boards all specialise in lonely hearts services '
The boards with an asterisk all use BELL Tones
#Fairbanks, AK, 907-479-0315
#Burbank, CA,   213-840-8252
#Burbank, CA,   213-842-9452
#Clovis, CA,   209-298-1328
#Glendale, CA, 213-242-1882
#La Palma, CA   714-220-0239
#Hollywood, CA, 213-764-8000
#San Francisco CA 415-467-2588
#Santa Monica CA, 213-390-3239
#Sherman Oaks CA, 213-990-6830
#Tarzana , CA,   213-345-1047
#Crystal River, FL904-795-8850
#Atlanta, GA,   912-233-0863
#Hammond, IN,   219-845-4200
#Cleveland, OH, 216-932-9845
#Lynnefield, MA, 617-334-6369
#Omaha, NE,   402-571-8942
#Freehold, NJ, 201-462-0435
#New York, NY, 212-541-5975
#Cary, NC.   919-362-0676
#Newport News,VA 804-838-3973
#Vancouver, WA, 206-256-6624
Marseilles, France 33-91-91-0660
#########
Both USA nos. prefix (0101)
a) Daily X-rated Joke Service 516-922-9463

b) Auto-Biographies of young ladies who normally work in unpublishable magazines on 212-976-2727.
c)Dial a w##K: 0101,212,976,2626; 0101,212,976,2727;

Msg#: 3688 #HACKER'S CLUB#
02/05/84 14:44:51 (Read 393 Times)
From: xxxx xxxxxxx
To: ALL
Subj: HACKERS NUMBERS CONT
Hertford PDP 11/70 Haclers BBS:
Call 0707-263577 with 110 baud selected.
type: SET SPEED 300 CR
After hitting CR switch to 300 baud.
Then type: HELLO 124,4 CR
'Password: HAE4 CR>
When logged on type: COMMAND HACKER/CR
Use: BYE to log out.
#########
EUCLID   388-2333
TYPE A COUPLE OF (CR) THEN PAD (CR)
ONCE LOGGED ON TO PAD TYPE CALL 40 (CR) TRY DEMO AS A USERID WHY NOT
TRY A FEW DIFFRER DIFFERENT CALLS THIS WILL LET U LOG ON TO A WHOLE
NETWORK SYSTEM ALL OVER EUROPE'
YOU CAN ALSO USE 01-278-4355.
#########
Unknown 300 Baud   01-854 2411
01-854 2499
#########
Honeywell:From London dial the 75, else 0753(SLOUGH)
75 74199 75 76930
Type: TSS
User id: DD1003
password: Unwnown (up to 10 chars long)
Type: EXPL GAMES LIST to list gamec

To run a game type: FRN GAMES/(NAME).E for a fortran game.
Replace FRN with BRN for BASIC games.
#########
Central London Poly   01 637 7732/3/4/5
#########
PSS (300)   0753 6141
#########
Comshare (300)   01 351 2311
#########
'Money Box'   01 828 9090
#########
Imperial College   01 581 1366
01 581 1444
#########
These are most of the interesting numbers that have come up over the
last bit. If I have omitted any, please leave them in a message.

Cheers, xxxx.

Msg#: 5156 #HACKER'S CLUB#
04/15/84 08:01:11 (Read 221 Times)
From: xxxxx xxxxxxx
To: ALL
Subj: FINANCIAL DATABASES
You can get into Datastream on dial-up at 300/300 on 251 6180 -
no I don't have any passwords....you can get into Inter Company
Comparisons (ICC) company database of 60,000 companies via their
1200/75 viewdata front-end processor on 253 8788. Type #### when
asked for your company code to see a demo...

Msg#: 5195 #HACKER'S CLUB#
04/17/84 02:28:10 (Read 229 Times)
From: xxxxxxxxx xxxxxxx
To: ALL

Subj: PSS TELEX
THIS IS PROBOBLY OLD HAT BY NOW BUT IF YOU USE PSS THEN A92348###### WHERE
##=UK TELEX NO. USE CTRL/P CLR TO GET OUT AFTER MESSAGE. YOU WILL BE CHARGED
FOR USE I GESS.

Msg#: 7468 #EREWHON#
06/29/84 23:30:24 (Read 27 Times)
From: xxxxxx xxxxxx
To: PHREAKS
Subj: NEW(OLD..) INFO
TODAY I WAS LUCKY ENOUGH TO DISCOVER A PREVIOUSLY UNKNOWN CACHE OF THE AMERICAN
MAGAZINE KNOWN AS TAP. ALTHO THEYRE RATHER OUT OF DATE (1974-1981) OR SO THEY
ARE PRETTY FUNNY AND HAVE A FEW INTERESTING BITS OF INFORMATION, ESPECIALLY IF
U WANT TO SEE THE CIRCUIT DIAGRAMS OF UNTOLD AMOUNTS OF BLUE/RED/BLACK/???
BOXES THERE ARE EVEN A FEW SECTIONS ON THE UK (BUT AS I SAID ITS COMPLETELY
OUT OF DATE). IN THE FUTURE I WILL POST SOME OF THE GOOD STUFF FROM IAP ON
THIS BOARD (WHEN AND IF I CAN GET ON THIS BLOODY SYSTEM''). ALSO I MANAGED TO
FIND A HUGE BOOK PUBLISHED BY AT&T ON DISTANCE DIALING (DATED 1975). DUNNO. IF
ANYBODY'S INTERESTED THEN LEAVE A NOTE REQUESTING ANY INFO YOU'RE AFTER CHEERS
PS ANYBODY KNOW DEPRAVO THE RAT?? DOES HE STILL LIVE?

Msg#: 7852 #HACKER'S CLUB#
08/17/84 00:39:05 (Read 93 Times)
From: xxxx xxxxx
To: ALL USERS
Subj: NKABBS
NKABBS IS NOW ONLINE. FOR ATARI & OTHER MICRO USERS. OPERATING ON 300 BAUD VIA
RINGBACK SYSTEM. TIMES 2130HRS-2400HRS DAILY. TEL :0795 842324. SYSTEM UP AT
THESE TIMES ONLY UNTIL RESPONSE GROWS. ALL USERS ARE WELCOME TO LOGON.
EVENTUALLY WE WILL BE SERVING BBC.COMMDORE VIC 20/64 OWNERS.+NEWS ETC.

Msg#:8154 #EREWHON#
08/02/84 21:46:11 (Read 13 Times)
From: ANON
To: ALL
Subj: REPLY TO MSG# '1150 (PHREAK BOARDS)

[][][][][][][][][][][][][]
[] PHREAK BOARD NUMBERS []
[]   ACROSS THE U.S.   []
[][][][][][][][][][][][][]

IF YOU KNOW OF A BOARD THAT IS NOT LISTED HERE. PLEASE LET ME KNOW ABOUT IT.

JOLLY ROGER	713-468-0174	PIRATE'S BEACH	305-865-5432
PIRATE'S CHEST	617-981-1349	PIRATE'S COVE	516-698-4008
PIRATE'S DATA CENTER	213-341-3962	PIRATE'S WAREHOUSE	415-924-8338
PIRATE'S SPACE STATION	617-244-8244	PIRATE'S PORT	512-345-3752
PIRATE'S OUTHOUSE	301-299-3953	PIRATE'S NEWSTAND][	213-373-3318
PIRATE'S HANDLE][	314-434-6187	PIRATE'S GOLDMINE	617-443-7428
PIRATE'S DREAM	713-997-5067	PIRATE'S SHIP	312-445-3883
PIRATE'S TRADE	213-932-8294	PIRATE'S MOUNTAIN	213-472-4287
PIRATE'S TREK	914-634-1268	PIRATE'S TREI][	914-967-2917
PIRATE'S TREK III	914-835-3627	PIRATE'S TREI IV	714-972-1124
PIRATE-80	305-225-8059	PORT OR THIEVES	305-798-1051
SANCTUARY	201-891-9567	SECRET SERVICE	213-932-8294
SECRET SERVICE][	215-855-7913	SHERWOOD FOREST	212-896-6063
SKELETON ISLAND	804-285-0041	GALAXY ONE	215-224-0864
BOCA HARBOR	305-392-5924	R.A.G.T.I.M.E.	217-429-6310
PIRATES OF PUGET SOUND	206-783-9798	KINGDOM OF SEVEN	206-767-7777
THE INSANITARIUM	609-234-6106	THE STAR SYSTEM	516-698-7345
HAUNTED MANSION	516-367-8172	ALPHANET	203-227-2987
WASTELANDS	513-761-8250	HACKER HEAVEN	516-796-6454
PIRATE'S HARBOR	617-720-3600	PHANTOM ACCESS	814-868-1884
SKULL ISLAND	203-972-1685	THE CONNECTION	516-487-1774
THE TEMPLE	305-798-1615	THE TAVERN	516-623-9004
SIR LANCELOT'S CASTLE	914-381-2124	PIRATE'S HIDEAWAY	617-449-2808
PIRATE'S CITY	703-780-0610	PIRATE'S PILLAGE	317-743-5789
PIRATE'S GALLEY	213-796-6602	THE PARADISE ON-LINE	512-477-2672
THE PAWN SHOPPE	213-859-2735	MAD BOARD FROM MARS	213-470-5912

MISSION CONTROL	301-983-8293	NERVOUS SYSTEM	305-554-9332
BIG BLUE MONSTER	305-781-1683	DEVO	305-652-9422
THE I.C.'S SOCKET	213-541-5607	TORTURE CHAMBER	213-375-6137
THE MAGIC REALM	212-767-9046	HELL	914-835-4919
PIRATE'S BAY	415-775-2384	CRASHER BBS	415-461-8215
BEYOND BELIEF	213-377-6568	ALCATRAZ	301-881-0846
PIRATE'S TROVE	703-644-1665	THE TRADING POST	504-291-4970
CHEYANNE MOUNTAIN	303-753-1554	DEATH STAR	312-627-5138
ALAMO CITY	512-623-6123	THE CPU	313-547-7903
CROWS NEST	617-862-7037	TRADER'S INN	618-856-3321
PIRATE'S PUB][	617-891-5793	PIRATE'S PUB	617-894-7266
PIRATE'S I/O	201-543-6139	BLUEBEARDS GALLEY	213-842-0227
SOUNDCHASER	804-788-0774	MIDDLE EARTH	213-334-4323
SPLIT INFINITY	408-867-4455	EXIDY 2000	713-442-7644
CAPTAIN'S LOG	612-377-7747	SHERWOOD FOREST][	914-352-6543
THE SILMARILLION][	714-535-7527	WARLOCK'S CASTLE	618-345-6638
TWILIGHT PHONE	313-775-1649	TRON	312-675-1819
THE UNDERGROUND	707-996-2427	THE SAFEHOUSE	612-724-7066
THE INTERFACE	213-477-4605	THE GRAPE VINE	612-454-6209
THE DOC BOARD	713-471-4131	THE ARK	701-343-6426
SYSTEM SEVEN	415-232-7200	SPACE VOYAGE	713-530-5249
SHADOW WORLD	713-777-8608	OXGATE	804-898-7493
OUTER LIMITS	213-784-0204	MINES OF MORIA][	408-688-9629
METRO	313-855-6321	MERLIN'S TOWER	914-381-2374
MAGUS	703-471-0611	GREENTREE	919-282-4205
GHOST SHIP III - PENTAGON	312-627-5138	GHOST SHIP][- ARAGORNS	312-644-5165
GHOST SHIP - TARDIS	312-528-1611	GENERAL HOSPITAL	201-992-9893
DATA THIEVES	312-392-2403	DARK REALM	713-333-2309
DANGER ISLAND	409-846-2900	COSMIC VOYAGE	713-530-5249
CORRUPT COMPUTING	313-453-9183	CAMELOT	312-357-8075
THE ORACLE	305-475-9062	PIRATE'S GUILD	312-279-4399
PIRATE'S PLANET	901-756-0026	HKGES	305-676-5312
CAESER'S PALACE	305-253-9869	MINES OF MORIA	713-871-8577
CRASHER BBS	415-461-8215	A.S.C.I.I.	301-984-3772

If anybody is mad enough to actually dial up one (or more!) of these BBs please
log everything so that others may benefit from your efforts. IE- WE only have
to register once, and we find out if this board suits our interest. Good luck
and have fun! Cheers.

Msg#: 8163 #HACKER'S CLUB#
08/30/84 18:55:27 (Read 78 Times)
From: xxxxxxxx xxxxxxx
To: ALL
Subj: #####################################
NBBS East is a relatively new bulletin board running from 10pm to 1230am on
0692 630610. There are now special facilities for BBC users with colour,
graphics etc. If you call it then please try to leave some messages as more
messages mean more callers, which in turn means more messages Thanks a lot. Jon

Msg#: 8601 #HACKER'S CLUB#
09/17/84 10:52:43 (Read 57 Times)
From: xxxxx xxxxxxxx
To: xxxxx xxxxxxxx
Subj: REPLY TO MSG# 8563 (HONEYWELL)
The thing is I still (sort of) work for XXX so I don't think they would be
too pleased if I gave out numbers or anything else, and I would rather I keep my
job. Surely you don't mean MFI furniture ??

Msg#: 8683 #HACKER'S CLUB#
09/19/84 19:54:05 (Read 63 Times)
From: xxxxxx xxxxxxx xxx
To: ALL
Subj: DATA NODE
To those who have difficulty finding interesting numbers, try the UCL Data Node
on 01-388 2333   (300 baud).When you get the Which Service? prompt, type PAD
and a couple of CRs. Then, when the PAD:
prompt appears type CALL X00X00X, where is any(number orrange of numbers.
Indeed, you can try several formats and numbers until you find something
interesting. The Merlin Corn computer is 9002003. And it's difficult to trace
you through a data exchange! If anyone finds any interesting numbers, let me
know on this board, or Pretzel mailbox 012495225.

```
Msg has replies, read now(Y/N)? Y

Msg#: 9457 #HACKER'S CLUB#
10/11/84 01:52:56 (Read 15 Times)
From: xxxxxx xxxxxxxxxx
To: xxxxx xxxxxxxxxx
Subj: REPLY TO MSG# 8683 (DATA NODE)
IF YOU WANT TO KNOW MORE ABOUT THIS xxxxx PHIN PHONE xxxx xxxxxx
ON 000 0000

Msg#: 8785 #HACKER'S CLUB#
09/21/84 20:28:59 (Read 40 Times)
From: xxxx xxxxS
To: ALL
Subj: NEW NUMBER
NEW COMPUTER ON LINE TRY RINGING 960 7868 SORRY THATS 01 (IN LONDON) IN FRONT.
GOOD LUCK'
```

Please note that none of these hints, rumours, phone numbers and passwords are likely to work by the time you are reading this... however, I was both amused and alarmed to discover that three months after the first edition of this book appeared, some of the numbers *were* still operational. Here is the timetable I had worked to: material siphoned off bulletin board, August 1984; lightly edited prior to delivery to publisher, November 1984; publication, March 1985; some numbers still valid after all the publicity, May 1985! When the second edition came out, in February 1986, there were *still* a few live numbers. The lack of security consciousness of some system managers beggars belief.

Can I also resolve one puzzle which earlier readers seem to have set for themselves? No UK bulletin board that I know of has so far carried a super-SIG called Erewhon or even Nowhere. In mid-1984 the true name of the SIG was Penzance and it did include many of the best hackers around, some of them actually using their real names. I made the name alteration on the print-out using my wordprocessor's 'global change' facility so that readers got the flavour of the SIG, but not its identity. Since then, the SIG's real name has been changed several times.

In the case of the US credit agency TRW, described in the previous chapter, valid phone numbers and passwords appear to have sat openly on a number of bulletin boards for up to a year before the agency realized. The owner of one of these, MOG-UR in Los Angeles, one Tom Tcimpidis, had his equipment seized by police on the prodding of Pacific Telephone. The event caused a panic among sysops on both sides of the Atlantic and it was suggested that the sysop could be held responsible for *all* material on a board, whether or not he had placed it there – or even personally seen the material. Some sysops even considered using 'naughty word' search programs to alert them to the messages that might cause trouble. However in the end the charge against Tcimpidis was dropped through lack of evidence.

In Chapter 10 I include extracts from one of the most famous US bulletin boards: The Private Sector. This is the bulletin board that was at the centre of the Great Satellite Caper that never was. It is also the electronic facility of the hacker newsletter 2600. 2600Hz is the tone US phonephreaks must send down the line in order to toggle the exchange into accepting the supervisory tones necessary for phreaking. 2600, like its sort-of predecessor, TAP, covers both US phonephreaking as well as computer hacking.

Some university mainframes have hackers' boards hidden on them as well.

It is probably bad taste to mention it, but of course people try to hack bulletin boards as well. An early version of one of the most popular packages could be hacked simply by sending two semi-colons (;;) – when you did that, the system allowed you to become the sysop, even though you were sitting at a different computer; you could access the user file, complete with all passwords, validate or devalidate whomever you liked, destroy mail, write general notices, create whole new areas, and even access the fundamental operating system by exiting to the DOS.

Research Sources
The computer industry has found it necessary to spend vast sums on marketing its products and whilst some of that effort is devoted to 'image' and 'concept' type advertising – to making senior management comfortable with the idea of the XXX Corporation's hardware because it has 'heard' of it – much more is in the form of detailed product information.

This information surfaces in glossies, in conference papers, and in magazine journalism. Most professional computer magazines are given away on subscription to 'qualified' readers; mostly the publisher wants to know if the reader is in a position to influence a key buying decision – or is looking for a job.

I have never had any difficulty in being regarded as qualified – certainly no one ever called round to my address to check up the size of my mainframe installation or the number of employees. If in doubt, you can always call yourself a consultant. Registration is usually a matter of filling in a post-paid card. My experience is that, once you are on a few subscription lists, more magazines, unasked for, tend to arrive every week or month – together with invitations to expensive conferences in far-off climes. Do not be put off by the notion that free magazines must be garbage – in the computer industry, as in the medical world, this is absolutely not the case. Essential regular reading for hackers are *Computing, Computer Weekly, Network, Software, PC Week, PC Magazine, PC User, Datalink, Communicate, Communications Management, Datamation, Mini-Micro Systems,* and *Telecommunications.* There are plenty of others; if you are so minded, you can receive a new magazine every day of the year and be so occupied reading them that you won't have time to earn a living as well.

The articles and news items often contain information of use to hackers: who is installing what, where; what sort of facilities are being offered; what new products are appearing and what features they have. Sometimes you will find surveys of sub-sets of the computer industry. In most magazines, however, this is not all: each advertisement is coded with a number which you have to ring round on a tear-out post-paid (again!) 'bingo card': each one you mark will bring wads of useful information: be careful, however, to give just enough information about yourself to ensure that postal packets arrive and not sufficient to give the 'I was just passing in the neighbourhood and thought I would call in to see if I could help' sales rep a 'lead' he thinks he can exploit.

Another excellent source of information are exhibitions: there are the ubiquitous 'product information' sheets, of course, but also the actual machines and software to look at and, maybe play with; perhaps you can even get a full-scale demonstration and interject a few questions. The real bonus of exhibitions, of course, is that the security sense of salespersons, exhausted by performing on a stand for several days – and the almost compulsory off-hours entertainment of top clients or attempted seduction of the hired-in 'glamour' – is rather low. Passwords are often written down on paper and consulted in your full view – all you need is a quick eye and a reasonable memory.

At both exhibitions and conferences it is a good idea to be a freelance journalist. Most computer mags have relatively small full-time staff and rely on freelancers, so you won't be thought odd. And you'll have your questions answered without anyone asking 'And how soon do you think you'll be making a decision?'

Sometimes the lack of security at exhibitions and demonstrations defies belief. When ICL launched its joint venture product with Sinclair, the One-Per-Desk communicating executive work-stations, it embarked on a modest road-show to give hands-on experience to prospective purchasers. The demonstration models had been pre-loaded with phone numbers ... of senior ICL directors, of the ICL mainframe at its headquarters in Putney and various other remote services.

Now that specialist computer programmes are appearing on television, it is not unknown for telephone numbers and passwords to be broadcast to several million people at a time. During the first run of the BBC's pioneering computer literacy series which went out rather late at night I got into the habit of using my videorecorder as a time-shift device and used to view the following morning. One day, watching a section on viewdata, particularly private viewdata, I was surprised to see the telephone number and password of the Herts County Council private system being displayed on a viewdata adapter. It took but a moment to rewind the tape, inch the freeze-frame forward slowly and garner the numbers at my leisure. I abandoned the rest of the programme and rushed to my viewdata set – and marched straight into the Herts machine. Two or three days later, someone had obviously had a quiet word with them and the password was no longer valid... In the same series, BBC accountants became alarmed when the *New York Times* Information Bank (which no longer exists in that form) rang to tell them that their usage seemed to have gone up dramatically. A few days before, the Information Bank had been the featured subject. A dummy account had been set up so that the presenter could show log-on procedures in what was thought to be complete security. However, when the programme came to be taped, the dummy account failed to work. Ever-resourceful, a floor engineer got hold of the BBC's real account number and arranged for the presenter to feed it in, saving, as he hoped, the day. Neither the presenter nor the show's director realized what had happened – until the *New York Times* rang.

Beyond these open sources of information are a few murkier ones. The most important aid in tackling a 'difficult' operating system or applications program is the proper documentation. These can be obtained in a variety of ways. Sometimes a salesman may let you look at a manual while you 'help' him find the bit of information he can't remember from his sales training. Perhaps an employee can provide a 'spare', or run you a photocopy. In some cases, you may even find the manual stored electronically on the system; in which case, print it out. Another desirable document is an organization's internal phone book. It may give you the numbers for the computer ports, but, failing that, you will be able to see the *range* of numbers in use and, if you are using an auto-dial modem coupled with a search-and-try program, you will be able to define the search parameters more carefully (see the next chapter). A phone book will also reveal the names of computer managers and system engineers; perhaps they use fairly obvious passwords.

Such material can often be found in rubbish bins. Susan Headley, the Californian hacker mentioned at the beginning who later turned state's evidence to avoid sharing a prosecution with her former boyfriend (and who tends to appear rather frequently in TV documentaries about hacking), speaks of the habit of her local phone company to throw away complete system documentation even if only the smallest up-date was issued. Headley would march to the company's gates with a plastic carrier bag of aluminium cans asking if she could scavenge for more 'for charity'. She and her team always had nearly up-to-date documentation. In the UK, British Telecom is also quite careless about its internal paperwork. It never ceases to astonish me what organizations leave in refuse piles without first giving them a session with the paper-shredder. Investigative journalist Duncan Campbell says many of his best stories have been helped along with discoveries in rubbish bins.

I keep my cuttings carefully stored away in a secondhand filing cabinet; items that apply to more than one interest area are duplicated in the photocopier. You never know when you might need them.

Inference

But hackers' research doesn't rely simply on collecting vast quantities of paper against a possible use. If you decide to target on a particular computer or network, it is surprising what can be found out with just a little effort.

Does the organization that owns the system publish any information about it, in a handbook, annual report, house magazine? When was the hardware and software installed? Did any of the professional weekly computer mags write it up? What do you know about the hardware? What sorts of operating systems would you expect to see? Who supplied the software? Do you know anyone with experience of similar systems? And so on. With experience, you should be able to identify certain well-known 'host' environments.

By way of illustration, I will describe certain inferences it is reasonable to make about the principal installation used by Britain's security service, MI5. At the end, you will draw two conclusions: first, that someone seriously interested in illicitly extracting information from the computer would find the traditional techniques of espionage – suborning of MI5 employees by bribery, blackmail or appeal to ideology – infinitely easier than pure hacking; second, remarkable detail can be accumulated about machines and systems, the very existence of which is supposed to be a secret – and by using purely open sources and reasonable guesswork.

The MI5 databanks and associated networks have long been the subject of interest to civil libertarians. Few people would deny absolutely the need for an internal security service of some sort, or deny that service the benefit of the latest technology. But, civil libertarians ask, who are the legitimate targets of MI5's activities? If they are 'subversives', how do you define them? By looking at the type of computer power MI5 and its associates possess, it is possible to see if perhaps they are casting too wide a net for anyone's good. If, as has been suggested, the main installation can hold and access 20 million records, each containing 150 words, and Britain's total population including children, is 56 million, then perhaps an awful lot of individuals are being marked as 'potential subversives'.

It was to test these ideas out that two journalists, not themselves out-and-out hackers, researched the evidence upon which hackers have later built. The two writers were Duncan Campbell of the *New Statesman* and Steve Connor, first of *Computing* and more recently on the *New Scientist*.

The inferences work this way: the only computer manufacturer likely to be entrusted to supply so sensitive a customer would be British and the single candidate would be ICL. You must therefore look at their product range and decide which items would be suitable for a really large, secure, real-time database management job. In the late 1970s, the obvious path was the 2900 series, possibly doubled up and with substantive rapid-access disc stores of the type EDS200.

Checking through back issues of trade papers it is possible to see that just such a configuration, in fact a dual 2980 with a 2960 as back-up and 20 gigabytes of disc store, were ordered for classified database work by 'the Ministry of Defence'. ICL, on questioning by the journalists, confirmed that they had sold three such large systems, two abroad and one for a UK government department. Campbell and Connor were able to establish the site of the computer, in Mount Row, London W1, (it has been moved since to MI5's largest site at Curzon Street House) and, in later stories, gave more detail, this time obtained by a careful study of advertisements placed by two recruitment agencies over several years. The main computer, for example, has several minis attached to it, and at least 200 terminals. The journalists later went on to investigate details of the networks – connections between National Insurance, Department of Health, Police and Vehicle Driving Licence systems.

In fact, at a technical level, and still keeping to open sources, you can build up even more detailed speculations about the MI5 main computer. ICL's communication protocols, CO1, CO2, CO3, are published items – you can get terminal emulators to work on a PC, and both the company and its employees have published accounts of their approaches to database management systems, notably CAFS, which, incidentally, integrates software and hardware functions to an unusually high degree giving speed but also a great deal of security at fundamental operating-system level.

Researching MI5 is an extreme example of what is possible; there are few computer installations of which it is in the least difficult to assemble an almost complete picture.

6 Hackers' Techniques

The time has now come to sit at the keyboard, phone and modems at the ready, relevant research materials convenient to hand and see what you can access. In keeping with the 'handbook' nature of this publication, I have put my most solid advice in the form of a trouble-shooting appendix (I), so this chapter talks around the techniques rather than spelling them out in great detail.

Hunting Instincts
Good hacking, like birdwatching and many other pursuits, depends ultimately on raising your intellectual knowledge almost to instinctive levels. The novice twitcher will, on being told 'There's kingfisher!', roam all over the skies looking for the little bird and probably miss it. The experienced ornithologist will immediately look low over a patch of water, possibly a section shaded by trees, because kingfishers are known to gulp the sort of flies that hover over streams and ponds.

So a good deal of skilful hacking depends on knowing what to expect and how to react. The instinct takes time to grow, but the first stage in such development is the realization that you need to develop it in the first place.

Tricks with Phones
If you don't have a complete phone number for a target computer then you can get an audo-dialler and a little utility program to locate it for you. An examination of the phone numbers in the vicinity of the target machine should give you a *range* within which to search. The program then accesses the auto-dial mechanism of the modem and 'listens' for any whistles. The program should enable the phone line to be disconnected after two or three 'rings' as auto-answer modems have usually picked up by then.

Such programs and their associated hardware are a little more complicated than the popularized portrayals suggest: you must have software to run sequences of calls through your auto-dialler, the hardware must tell you whether you have scored a 'hit' with a modem or merely dialled a human being, and, since the whole point of the exercise is that it works unattended, the process must generate a list of numbers to try. In fact, you must use one of the new generation 'smart' modems which are able to read the line and send a report back up into the RS232C port of the computer. Users of such programs in the USA have considerable advantages over those in the UK. Many areas in the USA use 'touch-tone' dialling, whereas the public network in the UK still uses 'pulse'. This means that each call takes much longer to originate – and so the list of numbers that can be tried in a session is considerably reduced.

One of the best programs of this sort is Cat-Scan, which works specifically on the Apple II with the Novation Apple Cat Modem, a remarkably flexible device which was widely available at one stage in North America but never officially exported to Europe. The short documentation, reproduced here, shows what it could do:

```
=======#=======================================================
+                                                          ++
+              C A T   S C A N   4 . 0                     ++
+                    BY : THE CHIP                         ++
+          BROUGHT TO YOU BY : FEDERAL EXPRESS             ++
+                                                          ++
================================================================
This programs needs no other software loaded.

    The program CAT SCAN 4.0 is the first real hacker (that works)
to come out in a long time.  It works only for the Apple Cat, (of
course) and allows you to hack night and day in complete saftey.
What follows is a brief explanation of all the options and what
they mean in the program CAT SCAN 4.0.


HACK:

    Hack does exactly what it says - hack.  After you hit 1 you
will have a option to start at the # which you last aborted at.
    Select that or hit space.

    Hit "D" to turn off key-click.


PARMS:

    [ESC] exits any function.
    There are two parameter sections to choose. (1 and 2)   Number
one allows you to enter in the following:
```

```
1] starting number
2] ending number
3] service (y/n)
   A] service number
   B] service code
      (service can be any service with less that
      ten digits in the code)
4] area code   (800 for scanning 800's)
5] time limit
   (a good setting is 15)
```

The second enters in the following:
(pre-set values which are bilieved to be the best are listed first)
```
1] 3-way hold time
   (holds this amount between calls for people
   with three way dialing)
2] rings accepted
3] busy tones accepted
4] clicks accepteds
   (these three specify the amount of each before
   the line is hung up)
5] record busy lines
6] record lines with tones
   (longer than hex:F0)
7] record lines with carr
8] long distance dialing
   This option changes the speed of dialing.
```

LOAD, SAVE NUMBERS:

    Obviously

PRINT NUMBERS:

    This will print out numbers found according to the parameter
settings in parms 2. Each will either have a C, T or B after it
specifying what it was.

Some notes to follow:

    This is a very complicated hacker, be carefull in setting it's
parameters or you can really fuck it up. For hacking 800's, just
specify the area code as '800' and it will ad the 1 at the
beginning. Do not use a service with 1-800, cause itll fuck up
the service. LD DIALING is a important part of the hacker,
it is the little counter you see up in the left corner of the scr
if it runs out before or between clicks on the line, youll never g
any numbers recorded. That is why on long distance calls, you mi
want to bring it up a bit. The three way hold is another sensati
one. ever count is 100ms. the setting of five is near 15 second
nobody will ever need to set it over 15, unless there trying to be
extra safe in hacking gov lines or somthing.

WRITTEN BY : THE CHIP
BROUGHT TO YOU BY : FEDERAL EXPRESS
DOCS BY : THE CHIP

One of the interesting features of Apple Cat Modem was that its tones were not limited to those defined by the Bell protocols (see p. 14) but were fully programmable. Computer-using phone-phreaks soon realized that they could turn them into blue boxes for long-distance exploration of the telephone networks. The possession of such blue boxes in the USA had become illegal, but the Cat Modem and a suitable program circumvented this.

Logging On

You dial up, hear a whistle ... and the VDU stays blank. What's gone wrong? Assuming your equipment is not at fault, the answer must lie either in wrong speed setting or wrong assumed protocol. Experienced hackers listen to a whistle from an unknown computer before throwing the data button on the modem or plunging the phone handset into the rubber cups in an acoustic coupler. Different tones indicate different speeds and the trained ear can easily detect the difference – Appendix III gives the common variants.

Some modems, particularly those on mainframes but increasingly on some of the larger bulletin boards, can operate at more than one speed – the user sets it by sending the appropriate number of carriage returns. In a typical situation, the remote computer answers at 110 bits/s (for teletypewriters) and two carriage returns take it up to 300 bits/s – the normal default for asynchronous working. Some modems can sense the speed differences by the originate tone from the remote computer.

Some hosts will not respond until they receive a character from the user. Try sending a space or carriage return.

If these obvious things don't work and you continue to get no response, try altering the protocol settings (see Chapters 2 and 3). Straightforward asynchronous protocols with 7-bit ASCII, odd or even parity and surrounded by one stop and one start bit is the norm, but almost any variant is possible. A PAD on PSS (see Chapter 7) needs a ⟨ cr ⟩ ⟨ cr⟩⟨A2⟩⟨cr⟩ to wake it up and tell it to send data in the form acceptable to a dumb terminal.

Once you start getting a stream from the host, you must evaluate it to work out what to do next. Are all the lines over-writing each-other and not scrolling down the screen? Get your terminal software to insert carriage returns. Are you getting a lot of corruption? Check your phone connections and your proto-cols. Are you getting some recognizable characters, but are they jumbled up with others? Perhaps the remote computer expects to be viewed on an intelligent terminal which can accept instructions for formatting and highlighting data – like a VT52 or VT100. You will have to use a terminal emulation. The more familiar you are at this point with your terminal software (see Chapter 3) the more rapidly you will get results.

Passwords

Everyone thinks they know how to invent plausible and acceptable passwords – here are the ones that seem to come up over and over again:

HELP   TEST   TESTER   SYSTEM   SYSTEM
MANAGER   SYSMAN   SYSOP   ENGINEER   OPS
OPERATIONS   CENTRAL   DEMO   SECRET   LOVE
SEX   (plus the usual euphemisms for sexual activity)
DEMONSTRATION   AID   DISPLAY   CALL
TERMINAL   EXTERNAL   REMOTE   CHECK
NET   NETWORK   PHONE   FRED

Are you puzzled by the special inclusion of FRED? Look at your computer keyboard some time and see how easily the one-fingered typist can find those four letters!

Most systems, as delivered, contain default passwords for testing and installation purposes. They should of course be removed during commissioning, but often they are not. Bulletin boards sometimes contain 'hacker's guides' to various systems and will often include the default passwords.

If you know of individuals likely to have legitimate access to a system you should find out what you can about them to see if you can second-guess their choice of personal password. Own names or those of loved ones, or initials are the top favourites. Sometimes there is some slight anagramming and other forms of obvious jumbling. If the password is numeric, the obvious things to try are birthdays, home phone numbers, vehicle numbers, bank account numbers (as displayed on cheques) and so on. Sometimes numeric passwords are even easier to guess: I have found myself system manager of a private viewdata system simply by offering it the password 1234567890 and, as we will see later, other hackers have been astonished at the results obtained from 11111111, 22222222 (which turned up in the Prince Philip Prestel hack), or 1010101, 2020202.

It is a good idea to see if you can work on the mentality and known pre-occupations of the legitimate password holder: if he's keen on classic rock n'roll, you could try ELVIS; a gardener might choose CLEMATIS; Tolkien readers almost invariably select FRODO or BILBO; those who read Greek and Roman literature at ancient universities often assume that no one would ever guess a password like EURIPIDES; it is a definitive rule that radio amateurs never use anything other than their call-signs.

Military users like words like FEARLESS and VALIANT or TOPDOG; universities, large companies and public corporations whose various departments are known by acronyms (like the BBC) can find those initials reappearing as passwords.

Poorly set up access control systems (that's what the professionals call them) make life easy for the hacker. Many hosts show you how many characters are required for a valid password. Worse still, you may find that all the passwords on a particular system fall into a pattern or set of patterns – for example, there may be always a four-character alpha string, followed by four numbers followed by a further three characters, which are always an indicator for a particular location or office. When the original Prestel passwords were issued, those for information providers, those who had paid for space on which to edit on the service, always began with the three numbers 790 . . .; this has now been changed.

One less publicized trick is to track down the name of the top person in the organization and guess a computer identity for him or her; the hypothesis is that he/she was invited to try the computer when it was first opened and was given an 'easy' password which has neither been used since nor wiped from the user files. A related trick is to identify passwords associated with the hardware or software installer; usually the first job of a system manager on taking over a computer is to remove such IDs, but often they neglect to do so. Alternatively a service engineer may have a permanent ID so that, if the system falls over, it can be returned to full activity with the minimum delay.

Nowadays there is little difficulty in devising theoretically secure password systems and bolstering them by allowing each user only three false attempts before disconnecting the line, as does Prestel, for example. The real problem lies in getting humans to follow the appropriate procedures. Most of us can only hold a limited quantity of character and number sequences reliably in our heads. Make a log-on sequence too complicated, and users will feel compelled to write little notes to themselves, even if expressly forbidden to do so. After a while the complicated process becomes counter-productive. I have an encrypting/decrypting software package for the IBM PC. It is undoubtedly many times more secure than the famous Enigma codes of World War II and after. The trouble is that that you need up to 25 different 14-digit numbers, all different, of your specification which you and your correspondent must share if successful recovery of the original text is to take place. Unfortunately the most convenient way to store these sequences is in a separate disk file (get one character wrong and decryption is impossible) and it is all too easy to save the key file either with the enciphered stream, or with the software master, in both of which locations they are vulnerable.

Nowadays many ordinary users of remote computer services use terminal emulator software to store their passwords. It is all too easy for the hacker to make a quick copy of a 'proper' user's disk, take it away, and then examine the contents of the various log-on files – usually by going into an 'amend password' option. The way for legitimate users to obtain protection, other than the obvious one of keeping such disks secure, is to have the terminal software itself password protected, and all files encrypted until the correct password is input. But then that new password has to be committed to the owner's memory ...

Passwords can also be embedded in the firmwave of a terminal. This has been the approach used in many Prestel viewdata sets when the user can, sometimes with the help of the Prestel computer, program his or her set into an EAROM (electrically alterable read only memory). If, in the case of Prestel, the entire fourteen-digit sequence is permanently programmed in the set, that identity (and the user bill associated with it) is vulnerable to the first person who hits 'viewdata' button on the keypad. Most users only program in the first ten digits and key in the last four manually.

A skilful hacker can make a terminal disgorge its programmed ID by sticking a modem in answer mode on its back (reversing tones and, in the case of viewdata, speeds also) and sending the ASCII ENQ (ctrl–E) character, which will often cause the user's terminal to send its identity.

A more devious trick with a conventional terminal is to write a little program which overlays the usual sign-on sequence. The program captures the password as it is tapped out by the legitimate user and saves it to a file where the hacker can retrieve it later.

People reuse their passwords. The chances are that, if you obtain someone's password on one system, the same one will appear on any other system to which that individual also has access.

Programming Tricks

In most longish magazine articles about electronic crime, the writer includes a list of 'techniques' with names like Salami Trap Door and Trojan Horse. Most of these are not directly applicable to pure hacking, but refer to activities carried out by programmers interested in fraud.

The Salami technique, for example, consists of extracting tiny sums of money from a large number of bank accounts and dumping the proceeds into an account owned by the fraudsman. Typically there's an algorithm which monitors deposits which have as their last digit '8'; it then deducts '1' from that and the £1 or $1 is siphoned off.

The Trojan Horse is a more generalized technique which consists of hiding away a bit of unorthodox active code in a standard legitimate routine. The code could, for example, call a special larger routine under certain conditions and that routine could carry out a rapid fraud before wiping itself out and disappearing from the system for good.

The Trap Door is perhaps the only one of these techniques that pure hackers use. A typical case is when a hacker enters a system with a legitimate identity but is able to access and alter the user files. The hacker then creates a new identity, with extra privileges to roam over the system, and is thus able to enter it at any time as a 'super-user' or 'system manager'.

Hardware Tricks

For the hacker with some knowledge of computer hardware and general electronics, and who is prepared to mess about with circuit diagrams, a soldering iron and perhaps a voltmeter, logic probe or oscilloscope, still further possibilities open up.

One of the most useful bits of kit consists of a small cheap radio receiver (MW/AM band), a microphone and a tape recorder. Radios in the vicinity of computers, modems and telephone lines can readily pick up the chirp chirp of digital communications without the need of carrying out a physical phone 'tap'. Alternatively an inductive loop with a small low-gain amplifier in the vicinity of a telephone or line will give you a recording you can analyse later at your leisure. By identifying the pairs of tones being used, you can separate the caller and the host. By feeding the recorded tones onto an oscilloscope display you can freeze 'bits', 'characters' and 'words'; you can strip off the start and stop bits and, with the aid of an ASCII to binary table, examine what is happening. With experience it is entirely possible to identify a wide range of protocols simply from the 'look' of an oscilloscope. A cruder technique is simply to tape-record down the line and then play back sign-on sequences. The limitation is that, even if you manage to log on, you may not know what to do afterwards. A simple tape-recording of a line fed into the rubber ears of an acoustic coupler, itself linked to a micro running a terminal package, will nearly always result in a good display.

Listening on phone lines is of course a technique also used by some sophisticated robbers. In 1982 the Lloyds Bank Holborn branch was raided. The alarm did not ring because the thieves had previously recorded the 'all-clear' signal from the phone line and then, during the break-in, stuffed the recording up the line to the alarm monitoring apparatus.

Sometimes the hacker must devise ad hoc bits of hardware trickery in order to achieve his ends. Access has been obtained to a well-known financial prices service largely by stringing together a series of simple hardware skills. Here, in outline, is how it was done.

The service is available mostly on leased lines, as the normal vagaries of dial-up would be too unreliable for the City folk who are the principal customers. However, each terminal also has an associated dial-up facility, in case the leased line should go down. In addition, the same terminals can have access to Prestel. Thus the hacker thought that it should be possible to access the service with ordinary viewdata equipment instead of the special units supplied along with the annual subscription.

Obtaining the phone number was relatively easy: it was simply a matter of selecting manual dial-up from the appropriate menu, and listening to the pulses as they went through the regular phone. The next step was to obtain a password; the owners of the terminal to which he had access did not know their ID – they had no need to because it was programmed into the terminal and sent automatically. The hacker could have put a micro 'back-to-front' across the line, as explained above, and sent an ENQ to see if an ID would be sent back. Instead he tried something less obvious.

The terminal was known to be programmable, provided one

knew how and had the right type of keyboard. Engineers belonging to the service had been seen doing just that. How could the hacker acquire 'engineer' status? He produced the following hypothesis: the keyboard used by the service's customers was a simple affair, lacking many of the obvious keys used by normal terminals. The terminal itself was manufactured by the same company that produced a range of editing terminals for viewdata operators and publishers. Perhaps if one obtained a manual for the editing terminal, important clues might appear.

A suitable photocopy was obtained and, lo and behold, there were instructions for altering terminal IDs, setting auto-diallers and so on. Now to obtain a suitable keyboard. Perhaps a viewdata editing keyboard, or a general purpose ASCII keyboard with switchable baud rates?

So far, no hardware difficulties. An examination of the back of the terminal revealed that the supplied keypads used rather unusual connectors, not the 270 degree 6-pin DIN which is the Prestel standard. The hacker looked in another of his old files and discovered some literature relating to viewdata terminals. Now he knew what sort of things to expect from the strange socket at the back of the special terminal; he pushed in an unterminated plug and proceeded to test the free leads with a voltmeter against what he expected; eight minutes and some cursing later he had it worked out; five minutes after that he had built himself a little patch cord between an ASCII keyboard, set initially to 75 bits/s and then to 1200 bits/s as the most likely speeds; one minute later he found the terminal was responding as he had hoped.

Now to see if there were similarities between the programming commands in the equipment for which he had a manual and the equipment he wished to hack. Indeed there were: on the screen before him was the menu and ID and phone data he had hoped to see. The final test was to move over to a conventional Prestel set, dial up the number for the financial service and send the ID ... the hack had been successful.

The hacker himself was remarkably uninterested in the financial world and, other than describing to me how he worked his trick, has now gone in search of other targets.

The current enthusiasm among computer security experts trying to sell hi-tech goodies to the paranoid is Tempest. Tempest is the name given to a series of US standards prescribing limits for electromagnetic radiation from computer installations and peripherals. It is possible to 'read' the contents of a VDU screen up to

300 meters away by tuning a suitable TV and radio receiver to the video and synchronizing frequencies of the display tube. The VDU's image is, of course, constantly being refreshed so that it is not too difficult to recreate.

You can conduct some experiments yourself to see how it is done. The video elements of a display radiate out harmonics at frequencies between 100 MHz and 600 MHz. Take an ordinary domestic television and tune away from any broadcast signal (TV receivers in the UK cover the frequency band 470 MHz to 800 MHz) – you will see a picture of 'snow'. Now, attach a portable desk-top aerial – say with four or five elements. Aim the antenna at your 'target' VDU (not another television set). You should see the quality of the 'snow' change – become brighter.

You will get better results if you can secure a television capable of picking up Band III TV broadcasts, as used in many continental European countries as the radiation from the VDU is stronger in this part of the RF spectrum. What the TV is picking up is the video elements of the transmission. You can't resolve an image at this stage because the sync elements necessary to stabilize an image don't radiate out nearly as well.

If you take an AM (medium-wave) receiver and tune around 1570 to 1600 kHz you should hear a buzz which increases as you approach the VDU. The buzzing sound is a harmonic of the VDU's line sync. In a Tempest eavesdropping unit, the two radio detectors – TV and medium-wave radio – are linked – the pulses from the medium-wave radio synchronizing the video elements the TV picks up and thus giving a stable image on the TV screen; they can be placed on a video recorder for later examination. The image will normally appear in reverse: black letters on a lighter background; they may also show a tendency to 'swim', the result of a failure of proper line synchronization. Similar technology is used by the detector vans which occasionally roam the streets to see if you have paid your television licence.

It is also possible to 'bug' a CPU – you can try it for yourself with a small portable radio. The difficulty is interpreting in a useful way what you pick up. GCHQ at Cheltenham are believed to have solved the problem of bugging typewriters, incidentally – each letter as it is impacted onto a piece of paper makes a slightly different sound – build up a table of these sounds, get an audio tape of someone typing, or a line printer, and a relatively simple computer program (once you have cracked the sound recognition problem) will regenerate the output for you – a marvellous way of bypassing encryption devices as the printers you try to bug in this way are presumably those handling 'clear' text.

The National Security Agency first started a program to certify equipment as meeting Tempest standards as long ago as 1977, but it is only since 1985 that most civilians have become aware of the problem. Amateur eavesdropping kit could be built for around £30, though tuning up for each 'target' VDU isn't that simple outside the laboratory. Tempest eavesdropping works, but like other technologies that security consultants produce to scare potential clients such as bouncing lasers off windows to translate the vibrations of glass panes into the sounds of conversations held inside rooms, a multiplicity of practical engineering difficulties limits its use in the real world. What is also questionable is how much useful information can be obtained in this fashion – the most the technique offers is an imperfect window, one screen at a time, on what a user is viewing – and you need to get awkwardly close to the target before you get results. Spooks will do far better by more conventional hacking methods.

Operating Systems

The majority of simple home micros operate only in two modes – in Basic or machine code. Nearly all computers of a size greater than this use operating systems, essentially housekeeping routines which tell the processor where to expect instructions from, how to identify and manipulate both active and stored memory, how to keep track of drives and serial ports (and joysticks and mice), how to accept data from a keyboard, locate it on a screen, dump results to screen or printer, or disc drive, and so on.

Familiar micro-based operating systems include CP/M, MS-DOS, CP/M-86 and so on. More advanced operating systems have more facilities – the capacity to have several users all accessing the same data and programs without colliding with each other, enlarged standard utilities to make fast file creation, fast sorting and fast calculation much easier. Under simple operating systems, the programmer has comparatively few tools to help him; maybe just the Basic language which itself contains no standard procedures – almost everything must be written from new each time. But most computer programs rely, in essence, on a small set of standard modules – forms to accept data to a program, files to keep the data in, calculations to transform that data, techniques to sort the data, forms to present the data to the user upon demand, the ability to present results in various graphics, and so on.

So programs written under more advanced operating systems tend to be comparatively briefer for the same end-result than those with Basic acting not only as a language, but also as the computer's housekeeper.

When you enter a mainframe computer as an ordinary customer, you will almost certainly be located in an applications program, perhaps with the capacity to call up a limited range of other applications programs whilst staying in the one which has logged you on as user and is watching your connect-time and central processor usage.

One of the immediate aims of a serious hacker is to get out of this environment and see what other facilities might be located on the mainframe. For example, if access can be had to the user-log it becomes possible for the hacker to create a whole new status for himself, as a system manager, engineer, whatever. The new status, together with a unique new password, can have all sorts of privileges not granted to ordinary users. The hacker, having acquired the new status, logs out in his original identity and then logs back with his new one.

There is no single way to break out of an applications program into the operating system environment; people who do so, seldom manage it by chance; they tend to have had some experience of a similar mainframe. One of the corny ways is to issue a BREAK or ⟨ctrl⟩ C command and see what happens; but most applications programs concerned with logging users on to systems tend to filter out 'disturbing' commands of that sort. Sometimes it is easier to go beyond the logging-in program into another 'authorized' program and try to crash out of that. Computers tend to be at their most vulnerable when moving from one application to another – making a direct call on the operation system. The usual evidence for success is that the nature of the prompts will change. To establish where you are in the system, you should ask for a directory – DIR, LS or its obvious variants often give results. Directories may be hierarchical, as in MS-DOS version 2 and above, so that at the bottom level you simply get directories of other directories. Unix machines exhibit this trait; what you need is the *root* directory. And once you get a list of files and programs ... well, that's where the exploration really begins.

Over the years a number of instant guides to well-known operating systems have appeared on bulletin boards. The extracts

given here, which have probably had the widest currency, carry
no guarantee from me as to their reliability:

**   The basics of hacking: intro   **

The first of a set of articles: an introduction to the world of the
hacker. Basics to know before doing anything, essential to your
contin-uing career as one of the elite in * * the country...

This article, "the introduction to the world of hacking" is meant to
help you by telling you how not to get caught, what not to do on a
computer system, what type of equipment should I know about now, and
just a little on the history, past present future, of the hacker.
Welcome to the world of hacking! We, the people who live outside of
the normal rules, and have been scorned and even arrested by those
from the 'civilized world', are becomming scarcer every day. This is
due to the greater fear of what a good hacker (skill wise, no moral
judgements here) can do nowadays, thus causing anti- hacker sentiment
in the masses. Also, few hackers seem to actually know about the
computer systems they hack, or what equipment they will run into on
the front end, or what they could do wrong on a system to alert the
'higher' authorities who monitor the system.   This article is
intended to tell you about some things not to do, even before you get
on the system. We will tell you about the new wave of front end
security devices that are beginning to be used on computers. We will
attempt to instill in you a second identity, to be brought up at time
of great need, to pull you out of trouble. And, by the way, we take
no, repeat, no, responcibility for what we say in this and the
forthcoming articles.

Enough of the bullshit, on to the fun: after logging on your favorite
bbs, you see on the high access board a phone number! It says it's a
great system to "fuck around with!" This may be true, but how many
other people are going to call the same number? So: try to avoid
calling a number given to the public. This is because there are at
least every other user calling, and how many other boards will that
number spread to? If you call a number far, far away, and you
plan on going thru an extender or a re-seller, don't keep calling the
same access number (i.E. As you would if you had a hacker running),
this looks very suspicious and can make life miserable when the phone
bill comes in the mail.

Most cities have a variety of access numbers and services, so use as
many as you can. Never trust a change in the system... The 414's, the
assholes, were caught for this reason: when one of them connected to
the system, there was nothing good there. The next time, there was a
trek game stuck right in their way! They proceded to play said game
for two, say two and a half hours, while telenet was tracing them!
Nice job, don't you think? If anything looks suspicious, drop the
line   immediately!! As in, yesterday!! The point we're trying to get
accross is: if you use a little common sence, you won't get
busted.

Let the little kids who aren't smart enough to recognize a trap get
busted, it will take the heat off of the real hackers. Now, let's say
you get on a computer system... It looks great, checks out,
everything seems fine. Ok, now is when it gets more dangerous. You
have to know the computer system (see future issues of this article
for info on specific systems) to know what not to do. Basically, keep

away from any command which looks like it might delete something, copy
a new file into the account, or whatever! Always leave the account in
the same status you logged in with. Change *nothing*... If it isn't
an account with priv's, then don't try any commands that require them!
All, yes all, systems are going to be keeping log files of what users
are doing, and that will show up. It is just like dropping a
trouble-card in an ess system, after sending that nice operator a
pretty tone. Spend no excessive amounts of time on the account in one
stretch. Keep your calling to the very late night if possible, or
during business hours (believe it or not!). It so happens that there
are more users on during business hours, and it is very difficult to
read a log file with 60 users doing many commnds every minute. Try to
avoid systems where everyone knows each other, don't try to bluff.
And above all: never act like you own the system, or are the best
there is.

They always grab the people who's heads swell... There is some very
interesting front end equipment around nowadays, but first let's
define terms... By front end, we mean any device that you must pass
thru to get at the real computer. There are devices that are made to
defeat hacker programs, and just plain old multiplexers. To defeat
hacker programs, there are now devices that pick up the phone and just
sit there... This means that your device gets no carrier, thus you
think there isn't a computer on the other end. The only way around it
is to detect when it was picked up. If it pickes up after the same
number ring, then you know it is a hacker- defeater. These devices
take a multi- digit code to let you into the system. Some are, in
fact, quite sophisticated to the point where it will also limit the
user name's down, so only one name or set of names can be valid logins
after they input the code... Other devices input a number code, and
then they dial back a pre-programmed number for that code.

These systems are best to leave alone, because they know someone is
playing with their phone. You may think "but i'll just reprogram the
dial-back." Think again, how stupid that is... Then they have your
number, or a test loop if you were just a little smarter. If it's your
number, they have your balls (if male...), If its a loop, then you are
screwed again, since those loops are *monitored*. As for
multiplexers... What a plexer is supposed to do is this: the system
can accept multiple users. We have to time share, so we'll let the
front- end processor do it... Well, this is what a multiplexer does.
Usually they will ask for something like "enter class" or "line:".
Usually it is programmed for a double digit number, or a four to five
letter word. There are usually a few sets of numbers it accepts, but
those numbers also set your 300/1200 baud data type. These
multiplexers are inconvenient at best, so not to worry. A little about
the history of hacking: hacking, by our definition, means a great
knowledge of some special area. Doctors and lawyers are hackers of a
sort, by this definition. But most often, it is being used in the
computer context, and thus we have a definition of "anyone who has a
great amount of computer or telecommunications knowledge." You are
not a hacker because you have a list of codes... Hacking, by our
definition, has then been around only about 15 years. It started,
where else but, mit and colleges where they had computer science or
electrical engineering departments. Hackers have created some of the
best computer languages, the most awesome operating systems, and even
gone on to make millions.

Hacking used to have a good name, when we could honestly say "we know

what we are doing". Now it means (in the public eye): the 414's,
ron austin, the nasa hackers, the arpanet hackers... All the people
who have been caught, have done damage, and are now going to have to
face fines and sentences.   Thus we come past the moralistic crap, and
to our purpose: educate the hacker community, return to the days when
people actually knew something... program guide: three more articles
will be written in this series, at the present time. Basics of hacking
i: dec's basics of hacking ii: vax's (unix) basics of hacking iii:
data general it is impossible to write an article on ibm, since there
are so many systems and we only have info on a few... This article has
been written by: the Knights of Shadow

```
              THE BASICS OF HACKING: VAX'S AND UNIX.
                UNIX IS A TRADEMARK OF BELL LABS
                (AND YOU KNOW WHAT *THAT* MEANS)
```

WELCOME TO THE BASICS OF HACKING VAX'S AND UNIX. IN THIS ARTICLE, WE
DISCUSS THE UNIX SYSTEM THAT RUNS ON THE VARIOUS VAX SYSTEMS. IF YOU
ARE LICENCED TO BELL, THEY CAN'T MAKE MANY CHANGES.

HACKING ONTO A UNIX SYSTEM IS VERY DIFFICULT, AND IN THIS CASE, WE
ADVISE HAVING AN INSIDE SOURCE, IF POSSIBLE. THE REASON IT IS
DIFFICULT TO HACK A VAX IS THIS: MANY VAX, AFTER YOU GET A CARRIER
FROM THEM, RESPOND

=> LOGIN:

THEY GIVE YOU NO CHANCE TO SEE WHAT THE LOGIN NAME FORMAT IS. MOST
COMMONLY USED ARE SINGLE WORDS, UNDER 8 DIGITS, USUALLY THE PERSON'S
NAME. THERE IS A WAY AROUND THIS: MOST VAX HAVE AN ACCT. CALLED
'SUGGEST' FOR PEOPLE TO USE TO MAKE A SUGGESTION TO THE SYSTEM ROOT
TERMINAL. THIS IS USUALLY WATCHED BY THE SYSTEM OPERATOR, BUT AT LATE
HE IS PROBABLY AT HOME SLEEPING OR SCREWING SOMEONE'S BRAINS OUT. SO
WE CAN WRITE A PROGRAM TO SEND AT THE VAX THIS TYPE OF A MESSAGE: A
SCREEN FREEZE (CNTRL-S), SCREEN CLEAR (SYSTEM DEPENDANT), ABOUT 255
GARBAGE CHARACTERS, AND THEN A COMMAND TO CREATE A LOGIN ACCT., AFTER
WHICH YOU CLEAR THE SCREEN AGAIN, THEN UN- FREEZE THE TERMINAL. WHAT
THIS DOES: WHEN THE TERMINAL IS FROZEN, IT KEEPS A BUFFER OF WHAT IS
SENT. WELL, THE BUFFER IS ABOUT 127 CHARACTERS LONG. SO YOU OVERFLOW
IT WITH TRASH, AND THEN YOU SEND A COMMAND LINE TO CREATE AN ACCT.
(SYSTEM DEPENDANT). AFTER THIS YOU CLEAR THE BUFFER AND SCREEN AGAIN,
THEN UNFREEZE THE TERMINAL. THIS IS A BAD WAY TO DO IT, AND IT IS
MUCH NICER IF YOU JUST SEND A COMMAND TO THE TERMINAL TO SHUT THE
SYSTEM DOWN, OR WHATEVER YOU ARE AFTER... THERE IS ALWAYS, *ALWAYS* AN
ACCT. CALLED ROOT, THE MOST POWERFUL ACCT. TO BE ON, SINCE IT HAS ALL
OF THE SYSTEM FILES ON IT. IF YOU HACK YOUR WAY ONTO THIS ONE, THEN
EVERYTHING IS EASY FROM HERE ON... ON THE UNIX SYSTEM, THE ABORT KEY
IS THE CNTRL-D KEY. WATCH HOW MANY TIMES YOU HIT THIS, SINCE IT IS
ALSO A WAY TO LOG OFF THE SYSTEM!

A LITTLE ABOUT UNIX ARCHITECHTURE: THE ROOT DIRECTORY, CALLED ROOT,
IS WHERE THE SYSTEM RESIDES. AFTER THIS COME A FEW 'SUB' ROOT
DIRECTORIES, USUALLY TO GROUP THINGS (STATS HERE, PRIV STUFF HERE, THE
USER LOG HERE...). UNDER THIS COMES THE SUPERUSER (THE OPERATOR OF THE
SYSTEM), AND THEN FINALLY THE NORMAL USERS. IN THE UNIX 'SHELL'
EVERYTHING IS TREATED THE SAME. BY THIS WE MEAN: YOU CAN ACCESS A
PROGRAM THE SAME WAY YOU ACCESS A USER DIRECTORY, AND SO ON. THE WAY
THE UNIX SYSTEM WAS WRITTEN, EVERYTHING, USERS INCLUDED, ARE JUST
PROGRAMS BELONGING TO THE ROOT DIRECTORY. THOSE OF YOU WHO HACKED
ONTO THE ROOT, SMILE, SINCE YOU CAN SCREW EVERYTHING... THE MAIN LEVEL
(EXEC LEVEL) PROMPT ON THE UNIX SYSTEM IS THE $, AND IF YOU ARE ON THE
ROOT, YOU HAVE A # (SUPER-USER PROMPT). OK, A FEW BASICS FOR THE
SYSTEM... TO SEE WHERE YOU ARE, AND WHAT PATHS ARE ACTIVE IN REGUARDS
TO YOUR USER ACCOUNT, THEN TYPE

=) PWD

THIS SHOWS YOUR ACCT. SEPERATED BY A SLASH WITH ANOTHER PATHNAME
(ACCT.), POSSIBLY MANY TIMES. TO CONNECT THROUGH TO ANOTHER PATH,
OR MANY PATHS, YOU WOULD TYPE:

YOU=) PATH1/PATH2/PATH3

AND THEN YOU ARE CONNECTED ALL THE WAY FROM PATH1 TO PATH3. YOU CAN
RUN THE PROGRAMS ON ALL THE PATHS YOU ARE CONNECTED TO. IF IT DOES
NOT ALLOW YOU TO CONNECT TO A PATH, THEN YOU HAVE INSUFFICIENT PRIVS,
OR THE PATH IS CLOSED AND ARCHIVED ONTO TAPE. YOU CAN RUN PROGRAMS
THIS WAY ALSO:

YOU=) PATH1/PATH2/PATH3/PROGRAM-NAME

UNIX TREATS EVERYTHING AS A PROGRAM, AND THUS THERE A FEW COMMANDS TO
LEARN... TO SEE WHAT YOU HAVE ACCESS TO IN THE END PATH, TYPE

=) LS

FOR LIST. THIS SHOW THE PROGRAMS YOU CAN RUN. YOU CAN CONNECT TO
THE ROOT DIRECTORY AND RUN IT'S PROGRAMS WITH

=) /ROOT

BY THE WAY, MOST UNIX SYSTEMS HAVE THEIR LOG FILE ON THE ROOT, SO YOU
CAN SET UP A WATCH ON THE FILE, WAITING FOR PEOPLE TO LOG IN AND
SNATCH THEIR PASSWORD AS IT PASSES THRU THE FILE. TO CONNECT TO A
DIRECTORY, USE THE COMMAND:

=) CD PATHNAME

THIS ALLOWS YOU TO DO WHAT YOU WANT WITH THAT DIRECTORY. YOU MAY BE
ASKED FOR A PASSWORD, BUT THIS IS A GOOD WAY OF FINDING OTHER USER
NAMES TO HACK ONTO. THE WILDCARD CHARACTER IN UNIX, IF YOU WANT TO
SEARCH DOWN A PATH FOR A GAME OR SUCH, IS THE *.

=) LS /*

SHOULD SHOW YOU WHAT YOU CAN ACCESS. THE FILE TYPES ARE THE SAME AS
THEY ARE ON A DEC, SO REFER TO THAT SECTION WHEN EXAMINING FILE. TO
SEE WHAT IS IN A FILE, USE THE

=) PR FILENAME

COMMAND, FOR PRINT FILE. WE ADVISE PLAYING WITH PATHNAMES TO GET THE
HANG OF THE CONCEPT. THERE IS ON-LINE HELP AVAILABLE ON MOST SYSTEMS
WITH A 'HELP' OR A '?'. WE ADVISE YOU LOOK THRU THE HELP FILES AND PAY
ATTENTION TO ANYTHING THEY GIVE YOU ON PATHNAMES, OR THE COMMANDS FOR
THE SYSTEM. YOU CAN, AS A USER, CREATE OR DESTROY DIRECTORIES ON THE
TREE BENEATH YOU. THIS MEANS THAT ROOT CAN KILL EVERY- THING BUT ROOT,
AND YOU CAN KILL ANY THAT ARE BELOW YOU. THESE ARE THE

=) MKDIR PATHNAME
=) RMDIR PATHNAME

COMMANDS. ONCE AGAIN, YOU ARE NOT ALONE ON THE SYSTEM... TYPE

=) WHO

TO SEE WHAT OTHER USERS ARE LOGGED IN TO THE SYSTEM AT THE TIME.   IF
YOU WANT TO TALK TO THEM=) WRITE USERNAME WILL ALLOW YOU TO CHAT AT
THE SAME TIME, WITHOUT HAVING TO WORRY ABOUT THE PARSER.   TO SEND MAIL
TO A USER, SAY

=) MAIL

AND ENTER THE MAIL SUB-SYSTEM. TO SEND A MESSAGE TO ALL THE USERS
ON THE SYSTEM, SAY

=) WALL

WHICH STANDS FOR 'WRITE ALL' BY THE WAY, ON A FEW SYSTEMS, ALL YOU
HAVE TO DO IS HIT THE <RETURN> KEY TO END THE MESSAGE, BUT ON OTHERS
YOU MUST HIT THE CNTRL-D KEY. TO SEND A SINGLE MESSAGE TO A USER, SAY

=) WRITE USERNAME

THIS IS VERY HANDY AGAIN! IF YOU SEND THE SEQUENCE OF CHARACTERS
DISCUSSED AT THE VERY BEGINNING OF THIS ARTICLE, YOU CAN HAVE THE
SUPER-USER TERMINAL DO TRICKS FOR YOU AGAIN. PRIVS: IF YOU WANT
SUPER-USER PRIVS, YOU CAN EITHER LOG IN AS ROOT, OR EDIT YOUR ACCT. SO
IT CAN SAY

=) SU

THIS NOW GIVES YOU THE # PROMPT, AND ALLOWS YOU TO COMPLETELY BY-PASS
THE PROTECTION. THE WONDERFUL SECURITY CONSCIOUS DEVELOPERS AT BELL
MADE IT VERY DIFFICULT TO DO MUCH WITHOUT PRIVS, BUT ONCE YOU HAVE
THEM, THERE IS ABSOLUTELY NOTHING STOPPING YOU FROM DOING ANYTHING YOU
WANT TO. TO BRING DOWN A UNIX SYSTEM:

=) CHDIR /BIN
=) RM #

THIS WIPES OUT THE PATHNAME BIN, WHERE ALL THE SYSTEM MAINTENANCE
FILES ARE. OR TRY:

=) R -R

THIS RECURSIVELY REMOVES EVERYTHING FROM THE SYSTEM EXCEPT THE REMOVE
COMMAND ITSELF...OR TRY:

=> KILL -1,1
=> SYNC

THIS WIPES OUT THE SYSTEM DEVICES FROM OPERATION. WHEN YOU ARE FINALLY
SICK AND TIRED FROM HACKING ON THE VAX SYSTEMS, JUST HIT
YOUR CNTRL-D AND REPEAT KEY, AND YOU WILL EVENTUALLY BE LOGGED OUT.

THE REASON THIS FILE SEEMS TO BE VERY SKETCHY IS THE FACT THAT BELL
HAS 7 LICENCED VERSIONS OF UNIX OUT IN THE PUBLIC DOMAIN, AND THESE
COMMANDS ARE THOSE COMMON TO ALL OF THEM. WE RECOMMEND YOU HACK ONTO
THE ROOT OR BIN DIRECTORY, SINCE THEY HAVE THE HIGHEST LEVELS OF
PRIVS, AND THERE IS REALLY NOT MUCH YOU CAN DO (EXCEPT DEVELOPE
SOFTWARE) WITHOUT THEM.

THIS ARTICLE WRITTEN BY: THE KNIGHTS OF SHADOW

[END]/1984

```
***************************************
** The basics of hacking iii: D G   **
***************************************
```

Welcome to the basics of hacking iii: data general computers. Data
general is favored by large corporations who need to have a lot of
data on-line. The data general aos, which stands for advanced
operating system, is a version of bastardized unix. All the commands
which were in the unix article, will work on a data general.   Once
again, we have the problem of not knowing the format for the login
name on the data general you want to hack. As seems to be standard,
try names from one to 8 digits long. Data general designed the
computer to be for busi- nessmen, and is thus very simplistic, and
basically fool proof (but not damn fool proof). It follows the same
login format as the unix system: dg=> login: you=> username dg=>
password: you=> password passwords can be a maximum of 8 characters,
and they are almost always set to a default of 'aos' or 'dg'. (Any you
know about businessmen...) A word about control characters: cntrl-o
stops massive print-outs to the screen, but leaves you in whatever
mode you were. (A technical word on what this actually does: it
tells the cpu to ignore the terminal, and prints everything out to the
cpu! This is about 19200 baud, and so it seems like it just cancels.)
 Cntrl-u kills the line you are typing at the time. Now for the weird
one: cntrl-c tells the cpu to stop, and wait for another cntrl
character. To stop a program, you actually need to type cntrl-c and
then a cntrl-b. Once you get on, type 'help'. Many dg (data general)
computers are sold in a package deal, which also gets the company free
customizing. So you never know what commands there might be. So we
will follow what is known as the 'eclipse standard', or what it comes
out of the factory like. To find out the files on the directory you
are using, type => dir to run a program, just like on a dec, just type
its name. Other than this, and running other people's programs, there
really isn't a standard... *** Hark, yon other system users *** to
see who is on, type => who (and a lot of the other unix commands,
remember?). This shows the other users, what they are doing, and what
paths they are connected across. This is handy, so try a few of those
paths yourself. To send a message, say => send username this is a one

time message, just like send on the dec 10. From here on, try
commands from the other previous files and from the 'help' listing.
Superuser: if you can get privs, just say: => superuser on and you
turn those privs on! By the way, you remember that computers keep a
log of what people do? Type: => syslog /stop and it no longer records
anything you do on the system, or any of the other users. It screams
to high heaven that it was you who turned it off, but it keeps no
track of any accounts created or whatever else you may do. You can
say=> syslog /start   to turn it back on (now why would you want to
do something like that?????) To exit from the system, type=> bye and
the system will hang up on you. Most of the systems around, including
decs, vax's, and dg's, have games. These are usually located in a path
or directory of the name games or <games> or games: try looking in
them, and you may find some trek games, adventure, zork, wumpus (with
bent arrows in hand) or a multitude of others. There may also be
games called 'cb' or 'forum'. These are a sort of computer conference
call. Use them on weekends, and you can meet all sorts of interesting
people.

If you would like to see more articles on hacking (this time far more
than just the basics), or maybe articles on networks and such, then
leave us mail if we are on the system, or have the sysop search us
down. We call a lot of places, and you may just find us. This
completes the series of articles on hacking...
  These articles were: the basics of hacking: introduction the basics
of hacking i: dec's the basics of hacking ii: vax's (unix) the basics
of hacking iii: dg's This and the previous articles by: the Knights of
Shadow [end] 1984

                    RSX11M VERSION 3.X REAL TIME OPERATING SYSTEM

                       AN INTRODUCTION...........

                          BY TERMINUS (SYSOP OF METRONET)
                                        AND
                          LORD DIGITAL (CO-SYSOP AND COHORT)

                       CALL METRONET AT 301-944-3023 * 24 HOURS
                          'THE INTELLIGENT PHREAKS CHOICE'

OTHER SYSTEMS MAY DISPLX^"!%M
FILE ONLY IF THEY RETAIN THE CREDITS.
ORIGINALLY DISPLAYED ON METRONET (THE SYSTEM FOR THE 80'S AND BEYOND).

DESCRIPTION:

RSX11M IS A DISK-BASED REAL TIME OPERATING SYSTEM WHICH RUNS ON ANY PDP11
PROCESSOR EXCEPT THE PDP11/03 OR THE LSI-11.IT PROVIDES AN ENVIRONMENT FOR
THE EXECUTION OF MULTIPLE REAL TIME TASKS (PROGRAM IMAGES) USING A PRIORITY
STRUCTURED EVENT DRIVEN SCHEDU+KK
MECHANISM.SYSTEM GENERATION ALLOWS THE
USER TO CONFIGURE THE SOFTWARE FOR SYSTEMS RANGING IN SIZE FROM SMALL 16K
WORD SYSTEMS TO 1920K WORD SYSTEMS.
RSX11M CAN BE GENERATED AS EITHER A MAPPED OR UNMAPPED SYSTEM,DEPENDING ON

WHETHER THE HARDWARE CONFIGURATION INCLUDES A KT11 MEMORY MANAGEMENT UNIT.
IF THE CONFIGURATION DOES NOT INCLUDE HARDWARE MEMORY MANAGEMENT THE SYSTEM
CAN SUPPORT BETWEEN 16K AND 28K WORDS OF MEMORY.IF THE CONFIGURATION INCLUDES
HARDWARE MEMORY MANAGEMENT,THE SYSTEM CAN SUPPORT BETWEEN 24K AND 124K WORDS
OF MEMORY ON PROCESSORS OTHER THAN THE PDP11/70,OR BETWEEN 64K WORDS AND 1920
K WORDS ON THE PDP11/70.
MEMORY IS LOGICALLY DIVIDED INTO PARTITIONS INTO WHICH TASKS ARE LOADED AND
EXECUTED.ACTIVITY IN A PARTITION CAN BE EITHER USER CONTROLLED OR SYSTEM-
CONTROLLED,THE USER DETERMINES THE PLACEMENT OF TASKS IN THE FORMER,AND THE
SYSTEM CONTROLS THE PLACEMENT OF TASKS IN THE LATTER.AUTOMATIC MEMORY COM-
PACTION MINIMIZES ANY FRAGMENTATION OF A SYSTEM CONTROLLED PARTITION.UNMAPPED
SYSTEMS SUPPORT ONLY USER CONTROLLED PARTITIONS.MAPPED SYSTEMS SUPPORT BOTH
USER CONTROLLED AND SYSTEM CONTROLLED PARTITIONS.
REAL TIME INTERRUPT RESPONSE IS PROVIDED BY THE SYSTEM'S TASK SCHEDULING MECH-
ANISM WHICH RECOGNIZES 250 SOFTWARE PRIORITY LEVELS.THE USER SPECIFIED TASK
PRIORITY DETERMINES THE TASK'S ELIGIBILITY TO EXECUTE.A TASK CAN BE FIXED
IN A PARTITION TO ENSURE IMMEDIATE EXECUTION WHEN IT IS ACTIVATED,OR IT CAN
RESIDE ON DISK WHILE IT IS DORMANT TO MAKE MEMORY AVAILABLE TO OTHER TASKS.
TASK CHECKPOINTING ENABLES TASKS TO BE DISPLACED FROM A PARTITION TO ENABLE A
HIGHER PRIORITY NON-RESIDENT TASK TO EXECUTE.
RSX11M OFFERS COMPLETE PROGRAM DEVELOPMENT FACILITIES AS WELL AS A REAL TIME
RESPONSE RUN-TIME SYSTEM.PROGRAM DEVELOPMENT AND REAL TIME TASKS CAN EXECUTE
CONCURRENTLY IN SYSTEMS WITH AT LEAST 24K WORDS OF MEMORY.THE SYSTEM'S SOFT-
WARE PRIORITY LEVELS ENABLE THE USER TO COMPILE/ASSEMBLE,DEBUG AND INSTALL
TASKS WITHOUT AFFECTING REAL TIME TASK RESPONSE.
TASKS CAN BE WRITTEN IN MACRO-11 ASSEMBLY LANGUAGE,AND OPTIONALLY FORTRAN IV,
FORTRAN IV PLUS,COBOL 11,AND BASIC.SHAREABLE LIBRARIES AND SYSTEM SUPPORT FOR
USER CREATED LIBRARIES ARE PROVIDED.A TEXT EDITOR,UTILITIES,SYMBOL CROSS REF-
ERENCE AND TASK MEMORY DUMP FACILITY IS PROVIDED TO ASSIST TASK DEVELOPMENT
AND CHECK OUT.
THE RSX11M FILE SYSTEM PROVIDES AUTOMATIC SPACE ALLOCATION AND FILE STRUCTURES
AND FILE STRUCTURES FOR ALL BLOCK-STRUCTURED DEVICES.FEATURES INCLUDE:

* SEQUENTIAL,RANDOM,AND RELATIVE (WITH RMS 11) FILE ORANIZATIONS.
* FILE PROTECTION
* DEVICE INDEPENDENCE AND LOGICAL DEVICE ASSIGNMENT.

DURING SYSTEM GENERATION THE USER CAN SELECT A MINIMUM 2K WORD VERSION OF THE
FILE SYSTEM TO CONSERVE SPACE.ON SYSTEMS WITH OTHER THAN THE MINIMUM 2K WORD
VERSION OF THE FILE SYSTEM,MULTI HEADER FILE SUPPORT IS PROVIDED.IT ENABLES
FILE SIZE TO BE LIMITED ONLY BY THE CAPACITY OF THE VOLUME ON WHICH IT RESIDES
(USUALLY SYSTEMS HAVE MULTIPLE 160 OR 300 MBYTE CDC DRIVES).
INDIRECT COMMAND FILE SUPPORT PROVIDES BATCH LIKE FACILITIES.A TERMINAL USER
CAN CREATE A FILE CONTAINING SYSTEM COMMANDS.THE SYSTEM CAN THEN BE INSTRUCTED
TO EXECUTE THE COMMANDS IN THE FILE WITHOUT OPERATOR INTERVENTION.THE INDIRECT
COMMAND FILE PROCESSOR CAN BE EXECUTING COMMAND FILES CONCURRENT WITH REAL
TIME TASK EXECUTION.

RSX11M VERSION 3.X TUTORIAL
BY
TERMINUS AND LORD DIGITAL

CALL METRONET AT 301-944-3023 * 24 HOURS

'THE INTELLIGENT PHREAKS CHOICE'

USER IDENTIFICATION CODE

THE PURPOSE OF USER IDENTIFICATION CODES (UIC) IS TO PROVIDE A METHOD THROUGH
WHICH FILES CAN BE ALLOCATED,LOCATED AND MAINTAINED ON A DEVICE.ON A RANDOM
ACCESS DEVICE THERE ARE USER FILE DIRECTORIES (UFD) IN WHICH FILES ARE CATA-
LOGUED.A PARTICULAR UFD IS REFERENCED BY SPECIFYING THE ASSOCIATED UIC.UICS
ARE OF THE FORM: [GROUP,MEMBER]
THE GROUP NUMBER IDENTIFIES THE GROUPS OF DIRECTORIES.THE MEMBER NUMBER IS
USED TO IDENTIFY A SPECIFIC MEMBER OF A PARTICULAR GROUP.THE CONVENTIONS ARE:

1. GROUP NUMBERS BETWEEN 0 AND 7 (OCTAL) ARE RESERVED FOR ACCESS BY
   THE 'SYSTEM OPERATOR'.USERS ASSIGNED A GROUP NUMBER IN THIS RANGE
   ARE THEREFORE REFERRED TO AS 'PRIVELEGED USERS'.
2. THE UIC [0,0] IS RESERVED FOR THE SYSTEM DIRECTORY.THE ASSOCIATED
   UFD CONTAINS A DIRECTORY OF ALL UFD'S ON THE DEVICE.THIS UFD IS
   THEREFORE THE MASTER FILE DIRECTORY (MFD).
3. NO USER CAN BE ASSIGNED THE UIC [0,0].

COMMON UIC'S ON RSX11M VERSION 3.X

```
0,0   MASTER FILE DIRECTORY
1,1   SYSTEM LIBRARIES
1,2   STARTUP AND HELP FILES
1,3   LOST FILE DIRECTORY
1,6   ERROR LOGGING FILES
1,54  DEC SYSTEM TASKS
7,2   ERROR MESSAGE FILES
7,3   QUEUE MANAGER FILES
```

WELL,LETS START GETTING SPECIFIC....

FILETYPES

```
.CMD   INDIRECT COMMAND FILE (EDITED AND CREATED BY THE EDITOR)
.DAT   DATA FILE
.DOC   DOCUMENT FILE
.HLP   HELP FILE
.LST   LIST FILE (GENERATED BY THE MACRO-11 ASSEMBLER)
.MAC   MACRO-11 SOURCE FILE (ASSEMBLER)
.MAP   TASK MAP FILE
.MLB   MACRO LIBRARY FILE (USED BY BIGMAC.TSK)
.MSG   MESSAGE FILE
.OBJ   COMPILED TASK OBJECT FILE
.OLB   OBJECT LIBRARY FILE (USED BY BIGTKB.TSK)
.PMD   POST MORTUM OR SNAPSHOT DUMP FILE (CORE DUMP)
.SML   SYSTEM MACRO LIBRARY FILE
.STB   TASK SYMBOL TABLE FILE
.SYS   BOOTABLE OPERATING SYSTEM FILE
.TMP   TEMPORARY FILE
.TSK   TASK OR DRIVER IMAGE FILE
.TXT   TEXT FILE
```

FILE SPECIFICATION DEFAULTS

] FIELD	]	DEFAULT	]
] DDNN:	] SY:		]
] [GGG,MMM]	] THE UIC WITH WHICH YOU LOGGED ON,OR A UIC DETERMINED BY		]
]	] THE MCR COMMAND SET /UIC=[GGG,MMM]		]
] FILENAME	] NO DEFAULT		]
] FILETYPE	] DEPENDS ON THE COMMAND STRING IN WHICH THE FILE SPECIFIER		]
]	] APPEARS.		]
] VERSION	] FOR INPUT FILES,THE HIGHEST EXISTING VERSION.FOR OUTPUT		]
]	] FILES,THE HIGHEST EXISTING VERSION + 1.NOTE THAT SOME CMDS		]
]	] REQUIRE AN EXPLICIT VERSION NUMBER.		]

WILDCARDS (AN ASTERISK CONVENTION)

] DDNN:	] CANNOT BE WILDCARDED.MUST BE SPECIFIED OR DEFAULT TO SY:	]
] [GGG,MMM]	] ALL UIC'S ON THE SPECIFIED OR DEFAULT DEVICE EXCEPT [0,0]	]
] FILENAME	] ALL FILENAMES WITH THE SPECIFIED,DEFAULTED OR WILDCARDED	]
]	] UIC,TYPE AND VERSION.	]
] FILETYPE	] ALL FILETYPES WITH THE SPECIFIED,DEFAULTED OR WILDCARDED	]
]	] UIC,NAME AND VERSION.	]
] VERSION	] ALL VERSIONS OF THE SPECIFIED,DEFAULTED OR WILDCARDED UICS	]
]	] NAMES,AND TYPES.	]

FILE SPECIFIERS

        DDNN:[GROUP,MEMBER]FILENAME.FILETYPE;VERSION/SW.../SUBSW...

WHERE:
        DDNN: IS THE PHYSICAL DEVICE NAME ON WHICH THE VOLUME CONTAINING
        THE DESIRED FILE IS MOUNTED.FOR EXAMPLE,DM1: OR DQ1:.THE NAME
        CONSISTS OF TWO ASCII CHARACTERS FOLLOWED BY AN OPTIONAL ONE OR
        TWO OCTAL UNIT NUMBER AND A COLON.
        (NOTE: IN MOST CASES,IF A UNIT NUMBER IS NOT GIVEN,IT WILL DEFAULT
        TO 0.)
                DD - 2 ALPHA CHARACTERS
                NN - 2 OCTAL NUMBERS - RAK

IS (0-77)
                : - REQUIRED WHEN DEVICE IS SPECIFIED

        [GROUP,MEMBER] IS THE GROUP NUMBER AND MEMBER NUMBER ASSOCIATED WITH
        THE USER FILE DIRECTORY (UFD) CONTAINING THE DESIRED FILE.

                [- REQUIRED WHEN UIC SPECIFIED
                GROUP - OCTAL NUMBER - RANGE IS (0-377)
                MEMBER - OCTAL NUMBER - RANGE IS (0-377)

```
        ]         - REQUIRED WHEN UIC SPECIFIED

FILENAME IS THE NAME OF THE FILE.

        FILENAME - ALPHANUMERIC CHARACTERS - MAXIMUM IS 9

.FILETYPE IS THE FILETYPE OF THE FILE.THE FILETYPE IS A CONVENIENT
MEANS OF DISTINGUISHING DIFFERENT FORMS OF THE SAME FILE.FOR EXAMPLE,
A FORTRAN SOURCE PROGRAM MIGHT BE NAMED COMP.FTN,THE OBJECT FILE FOR
THE SAME PROGRAM MIGHT BE NAMED COMP.OBJ AND THE RUNNABLE CODE FOR THE
PROGRAM MIGHT BE NAMED COMP.TSK.

        .         - REQUIRED WHEN FILETYPE SPECIFIED
        FILETYPE - ALPHANUMERIC CHARACTERS - MAXIMUM IS 3

;VERSION IS AN OCTAL NUMBER THAT SPECIFIES DIFFERENT VERSIONS OF THE
SAME FILE.FOR EXAMPLE,WHEN A FILE IS CREATED,IT IS ASSIGNED A VERSION
NUMBER OF 1 BY DEFAULT.THEREAFTER,EACH TIME THE FILE IS OPENED,THE FILE
CONTROL SYSTEM (FCS) - F11ACP.TSK - CREATES A NEW FILE WITH THE SAME
FILENAME.FILETYPE AND A VERSION NUMBER INCREMENTED BY 1.

        ;         - REQUIRED WHEN VERSION IS SPECIFIED
        VERSION - OCTAL NUMBERS - RANGE IS (1-77777)

/SW.../SUBSW... DISCUSSED LATER

A PROGRAM PERFORMS I/O ON LOGICAL UNIT NUMBERS (LUNS) WHICH THE PROGRAMMER OR
AN OPERATOR SUBSEQUENTLY ASSIGNS TO SPECIFIC DEVICES BEFORE THE PROGRAM WILL
ACTIVELY USE THE LUNS.ALSO,IN RSX11M A CONNECTED DEVICE IS INOPERABLE UNLESS
THERE IS A RESIDENT I/O DRIVER FOR THE DEVICE TYPE.AN I/O DRIVER PERFORMS
THE FUNCTIONS THAT ENABLE PHYSICAL I/O OPERATIONS TO OCCUR.RSX11M RECOGNIZES
TWO TYPES OF I/O DEVICES:
        1. PHYSICAL DEVICE NAMES - NAMES ASSOCIATED WITH A HARDWARE CONTROLLER
        2. PSEUDO - DEVICE NAMES - NAMES OT ASSOCIATED WITH ANY PHYSICAL DE-
           VICE UNTIL THEY ARE ASSOCIATED TO A PHYSICAL DEVICE.
```

NAME	MFGR	PHYSICAL DEVICE
DB	DIVA	COMPUTROLLER V CONTROLLER
DK	DEC	RK11 CONTROLLER
DM	SI	MODEL 4500 CONTROLLER
DP	SI	MODEL 9500 CONTROLLER
DQ	SI	MODEL 9500 CONTROLLER WITH SHARED COMPUTER OPTION
DX	DEC	RX11 CONTROLLER
FX	SMS	FT0100D FLOPPY CONTROLLER
LP	VERSATEC	CONTROLLER AND PRINTER/PLOTTER
LT	TI	MODEL 810 LINE PRINTER
MT		MAGTAPE CONTROLLER
		(DEC TMI CONTROLLER)
		(WP WESTERN PERIPHERALS)
		(CIPHER MAGTAPE CONTROLLER)
PP	DEC	PC11 PAPER TAPE PUNCH
PR	DEC	PC11/PR11 PAPER TAPE READER
TT		ANY TERMINAL CONNECTED
XL	DEC	DL11-E ASYNCHRONOUS COMMUNICATIONS LINE INTERFACE

```
LOGICAL DEVICES ARE SYSTEM GENERATION (SYSGEN) OPTIONS OF RSX11M THAT ALLOW
THE USER TO ASSIGN LOGICAL NAMES TO PHYSICAL DEVICES BY MEANS OF THE MCR
COMMAND 'ASN'.
```

CODE	DEVICE FUNCTION
LB	SYSTEM LIBRARY.DISK CONTAINING SYSTEM LIBRARIES
SD	DISK WHICH CONTAINS ALL FILES NECESSARY FOR NORMAL SYSTEM USE
SY	SYSTEM DEFAULT DEVICE CONTAINING ALL TASKS AND FILES WHICH DO NOT NEED TO BE ACCESSED FOR WRITE FUNCTIONS DURING NORMAL SYSTEM OPERATION.
CO	CONSOLE OUTPUT DEVICE,DEVICE TO WHICH SYSTEM ERROR MESSAGES ARE SENT. THIS IS NORMALLY 'RED'IRECTED TO TT0:
CL	CONSOLE LISTING DEVICE.DEVICE WHICH RECIEVES ALL I/O FOR DEFAULT LUN 6 THIS IS NORMALLY 'RED'IRECTED TO TT0:
TI	TERMINAL INPUT DEVICE,TERMINAL FROM WHICH A TASK WAS REQUESTED.

NULL DEVICE

NL	THE BIT BUCKET

RSTS Systems

So, you've decided that you'd like to try to down an RSTS system? Well, here's a beginner's guide:

The RSTS system has two parts, the Priviledged accounts, and the User accounts. The Priviledged accounts start with a 1 In the format [1,1], [1,10], etc. T o show the Priv. accounts we'll just use the wildcard [1, *].)

The priviledged accounts are what every RSTS user would love to have, because if you have a priviledged account you have COMPLETE control of the whole s ystem. How can I get a [1,*] account? you may ask....We ll, it takes A LOT of hard work. guessing is the general ru le. for instance, when you first log in there will be a # sign: # (You type a [1,*] account, lik e) 1,2 It will then say Password: (You then type anything up to 6 letters/numbers Upper Case only) ABCDEF

If it says ?Invalid Password, try again ' then you've not done it YET...Keep trying.

Ok, we'll assume you've succeeded. You are now in the priviledged account of an RSTS system. The first thing you should do is kick everyone else off the system (Well, maybe just the other P riviledged users)....You do this with the Utility Program.

PUT KILL (here you type the Job # of the user you'd like to get ut of your way). If the system won't let you, you'll have to look for the UTILTY program. Search for it by typing DIR [1,*]UTILTY.* Now, you've found it and kicked off all the important people (If you want you can leave the ot her people on, but it's important to remove all other [1,*] users, even the detached ones). To find out who 's who on the system type SYS/P- That will print out all the priviledged users). Or type SYS to se Everyone.

Next on your agenda is to get all the passwords (Of Course). Do this by run$MONEY (If it isn't there, search for it with DIR[1,*]MONEY.* and r un it using the account where you gound it instead o f the $)

There will be a few questions, like Reset? and Disk? Here's the Important answers. Disk? SY (You want the system password) Reset? No (You want to leave eve rything as it is) passwords? YES (You want the pas swords Frinted) There are others but they aren't important, just hit a C/R. There is ONE more,

t will say s omething like Output status to? KB: (This is i
mportant, you want to see it, not send it elsewhere).

Ok, now you've got all the passw ords in your hands. Your
ext step is to make sure the next time you come you can get in
ain. This is the h ard part. First, in order to make sure tha t
o one will disturb you, you use the UTILTY program to make it so
o one can login. Type UT SET NO LOGINS. (also you can type UT
ELP if you need help on the program) Next you have to Change the
OGI N program....I'm sorry, but this part is fuzzy, Personnally
I've never gotten this far. Theorectically he re's what you
o: Find out where the program is, type DIR [1,*]LOGIN.* If
here is LOGIN.BAS a nyplace, get into that account (Using your
asswo rd list, and typing HELLO and the account you'd l ike to
nter). On the DIR of the program there is a date (Like
1-Jan-80). To make it look good you type UTDATE (and the date
f the program). Next, you make it easy for yourself to a ccess
he program. You type PIP (And the account and name of the
rogram you atre changeing) <60>=(ag ain the name of the
rogram). Now what you do is OLD the progr am. Type OLD (Name of
he program) Now that is all theoretical. If anyone runs into
roblems, tell me about it and I'll see if I can either figure it
ut or get someone else to.

Next thing you want to do is LIST the program and find
ut where The input of the Account # is. To get this far you have
o knwo a lot a bout programming and what to look for... Here is
enerally the idea, an i dea is all it is, because I have not
een able to field te st it yet: Add a conditional so that if you
ype in a code word and an account # it will respond wi th the
assword. This will take a while to look for, and a few minutes
o change, but you can do it, you've got that RSTS system in your
ack pocket.

Let's say you've (Someho w) been able to change the
rogram. The next thing yo u want to do is replace it, so put it
ack wher e you got it (SAVE Prog-name), and the put it back to
he Prot Level (The # in the <## #> signs) by typing PIP (Prog
ame)<232>=Pr ogname (Note, in all of this, don't use the ()'s
they are just used by me to show you what goes where). Now
ou've gotten this far, what do you do? I say, experiment! Look
at all the progr ams, since you have Privilged status you can
nalyz e every program. Look around forthe LOG program, and find
ut what you can do to that. The last thing to do bef ore you
eave is to set the date back to what it was using
he UTILTY program again UT DATE (and the current date).

HACKING THE HP2000

PREFACE

The purpose of this tutorial is to give potential hackers useful
information about Hewlett-Packard's HP2000 systems. The following
notation will be used throughout this tutorial:
<CR> - carriage return, RETURN, ENTER, etc.
^C - a control character (control-C in example)
CAPITAL LETTERS - computer output & user input

SYSTEM INFORMATION
Each HP2000 system can support upto 32 users in a Timeshared BASIC
TSB) environment.   The systems usually run a version of Hewlett
Packard's Timeshared/BASIC 2000 (various Levels).

LOGON PROCEDURE
Once connected to a HP2000, type a numeral followed by a <CR>.   The
system should then respond with: PLEASE LOG IN. If it does not
immediately respond keep on trying this procedure until it does (they
tend to be slow to respond).
User ID: The user id consists of a letter followed by 3 digits, eg,
A241.
Password: The passwords are from 1 to 6 printing and/or non-printing
          (control) characters. The following characters will NOT be
          found in any passwords so don't bother trying them: line
          delete (^X), null (^@), return (^M), linefeed (^J), X-OFF
          (^S), rubout, comma (^L), space (^`), back arrow (<-), &
          underscore (_). HP also suggests that ^E
          is not used in passwords (but I have seen it done!).

The logon format is: HELLO-A123,PASSWD
           Where: HELLO is the login command. It may be
                   abbreviated to HEL. A123 is the user id &
                   PASSWD is the password.
The system will respond with either ILLEGAL FORMAT or ILLEGAL ACCESS
depending upon whether you screwed up the syntax or it is an invalid
user id or password. The messages: PLEASE LOG IN, ILLEGAL FORMAT, &
ILLEGAL ACCESS also help you identify HP2000 systems.

The system may also respond with ALL PORTS ARE BUSY NOW - PLEASE TRY
AGAIN LATER or a similar message. One other possibility is NO TIME
LEFT which means that they have used up their time limit without
paying.
Unlike other systems where you have a certain amount of tries to
login, the HP2000 system gives you a certain time limit to logon
before it dumps you. The system default is 120 seconds (2 minutes).
The sysop can change it to be anywhere between 1 and 255 seconds,
though.   In my experience, 120 seconds is sufficient time for trying
between 20-30 logon attempts while hand-hacking & a much higher amount
when using a hacking program.

USERS
The various users are identified by their user id (A123) & password.
Users are also identified by their group. Each group consists of 100
users. For example, A000 through A099 is a group, A100 through A199 is
another group, & Z900 through Z999 is the last possible group.   The
first user id in each group is designated as the Group Master & he has
certain privileges. For example, A000, A100,...H200..., & Z900 are
all Group Masters. The user id A000 is known as the System Master &
he has the most privileges (besides the hardwired sysop terminal).
The library associated with user Z999 can be used to store a HELLO
program which is executed each time someone logs on.
So, the best thing to hack on an HP2000 system is the System Master
(A000) account. It is also the only user id that MUST be on the
system. He logs on by typing: HEL-A000,PASSWD. You just have to hack
out his password. If you decide to hack Z999, you can create or change
the HELLO program to give every user your own personal message every
time he logs on! This is about all you can do with Z999 though since
it is otherwise a non-privileged account.

BRARY ORGANIZATION
ch user has access to 3 levels of libraries: his own private
brary, a group library, and the system library. To see what is in
ese libraries you would type: CATalog, GROup, & LIBrary
spectively (all commands can be abbreviated to the first 3 letters).
e individual user is responsible for his own library and maintaning
l the files. If a program is in your CATALOG, then you can change
.

roup Masters]
oup Masters (GM) are responsible for controling all programs in the
oup libraries. Only members of the group can use these programs.
ese are viewed by typing GROUP. For example, user S500 controls all
ograms in the Group library of all users beginning with id S5xx.
her users in the group CANNOT modify these programs. All programs
 the group library are also in the Group Masters private library
ATALOG), therefore he can modify them! The Group Master also has
cess to 2 privileged commands. They are: PROtect & UNProtect. With
OTECT, the Group Master can render a program so it cannot be LISTed,
Ved, CSAved, PUNched to paper tape, or XPUNched. For example, if
e GM typed PRO-WUMPUS, other users in the group would be able to RUN
MPUS but they would not be able to list it. The GM can remove these
strictions with the UNProtect command.
ystem Master]
ere is exactly one System Master (SM) and his user id is A000. He
n PROTECT & UNPROTECT programs in the System Library. All users
ve access to these files by typing LIBRARY to view them. Only the
stem Master can modify these files since his private library & group
brary constitute the System Library. The SM also has access to
her privileged commands such as:
RECTORY: this command will printout all files and programs stored
 the system according to users. DIR will print out the entire
        directory. DIR-S500 will start listing the directory with
        user S500.
ample:
IR BOCES ED 1   053/84   1243

ID	NAME	DATE		LENGTH	DISC
00	ALPHA	043/84		00498	001384
	BCKGMN	053/84		04564	001526
	FPRINT	053/84		00567	002077
	STOCK	038/84		04332	002753
	TFILE	020/83	F	00028	002804
	WUMPUS	053/84	P	02636	003142
51	BLJACK	316/75		03088	011887
	GOLF	316/75		02773	011911
00	GIS	050/84	C	03120	019061
	GISCL4	050/84	F	03741	022299
99	HELLO	021/84		00058	011863

 this example, the system name is BOCES ED 1. The date of the
rintout is the 53rd day of 1984 (053/84) and the time is 12:43
24-hr). The files appearing under A000 are those in the System
ibrary. The DATE associated with the program is the date it was last
eferenced. The LENGTH is how long it is in words. DISC refers
 its storage block location on one of the hard drives. DRUM refers to
ts location on the drum storage unit. Only sanctified programs are
tored on a drum to increase their access time. The letters after the
ate refer to F if it is a file, P means it is protected, and C means
he program is compiled. In the example the system program, WUMPUS,
as last used on the 53rd day of 1984 (2-22-84); it is currently

unlistable (PROtected) and it occupies 2636 words of memory starting
at disc block 3142. The command SDIrectory will print out programs
that are only stored on drum. Most system directories are usually
longer than the example. The above example is an abridged version of
 43 page directory! The <BREAK> key will STOP the listing if
necessary.

REPORT
The REPORT command will show the USER id, how much terminal TIME they
have used since the last billing period (in minutes), and how much
disc SPACE they are using.
example:
REPORT
     BOCES ED 1 055/84   1905

ID	TIME	SPACE	ID	TIME	SPACE	ID	TIME	SPACE
A000	01150	12625	B451	00003	05861	B864	00000	00000
A500	00235	06861	S543	00421	00000	Z999	00000	00058

The advantage of hacking the A000 password first is that you can use
the privileged commands to see which which user id's exist and what
programs are stored where so that you can further penetrate the
system.

PORT
This command tells the character size and baud rate at which each of
the 32 ports are configured. It is in the format c-bbb, where
c=character size & bbb=baud rate. It is set up in columns of 8. The
first row corresponds to ports 0-7, the second row corresponds to
8-15, etc. This is generally useless in my opinion. Also, the ports
are usually only configured separately if the terminals are all
hard-wired.

STATUS
This command allows the SM to view information concerning the
mass-storage devices. It gives current locations of the ID table,
user swap areas, line printer status, etc. It tends to hold alot of
info if it is read correctly. Unfortunately, I don't have the room to
fully discuss it here.
Since all logins & logouts are printed at the system console along
with other pertinent information, I would strongly suggest that you
avoid extensive use of an A000 password if you find one.
The System Operator has access to alot of other commands.
Unfortunately, he is situated at the System Console which is
hard-wired to the computer. If anyone figures out a way to give a
remote user Sysop privileges, let me know & I can help you with his
commands.

NON-PRIVILEGED COMMANDS
LIBRARY - lists the system programs.   There is only 1 system library &
any user can access it.
example:
LIBRARY

NAME	LENGTH	NAME	LENGTH	NAME	LENGTH	NAME	LENGTH
LPHA	498	BCKGMN	4564	FPRINT	567	STOCK	4332
FILE F	28	WUMPUS P	2636				

This uses the same notation as the privileged DIRECTORY command.
To retrieve a program from the system library, you would type:
     GET-$NAME   (To load the STOCK program, you would type
                  GET-$STOCK)

u can then RUN or LIST it. If you attempted to LIST WUMPUS which is
OTECTed (P), it would say RUN ONLY.
UP - lists all files in your group. It is in the same format as
    the LIBRARY command.
 retrieve a program from your group library, you would type:
   GET-*NAME
TALOG - lists all files in your personal library. It is also in the
       same format as the LIBRARY command.
 retrive a program in your personal library, you would type:
   GET-NAME
her commands you can use with your personal files (or system files
 logged on as A000) include:

N	runs the program in the user swap area (memory)
ST	lists the program in the user swap area
VE-NAME	NAME may be upto 6 characters
VE-NAME	save in compiled form
ME-NAME	assign a name to it
LL-NAME	deletes a file from your library
NCH	punches a program onto paper tape
PE	input a paper tape
PEND-NAME	attaches the file NAME to current program in memory
ENGTH	tells the current length of program in memory
RINTER	designates the line printer as user output device
PEN	creates a file [OPEN-FILE,# of records, (record
engths)]	
ENUMBER	renumbers statements
	[REN-(1st statement #),(interval between statements),(# to start renumbering at),(# to end renumbering)]

OTE: All commands can be abbreviated to the first 3 digits. The
ain command is separated from the first parameter by a dash (-), the
irst parameter is separated by the second parameter by a comma (,),
nd all further parameters are separated by commas. Eg, HEL-A000,^C
 did actually find a system where the SM password was ^C).
THER USEFUL COMMANDS

YE	logs user off
CHO-ON	half-duplex
-OFF	full-duplex (default)
SRATCH	clears users swap area (NEW)
EY	transfers control to keyboard
IME	informs user of total connect time & console time
ESSAGE	sends a message to sysop console [MES-(text upto 68
hars)]	

B 2000
he programming of the system is above the scope of this tutorial. If
ou do manage to get into the A000 or Z999 accounts, there is
ufficient info provided in this text to help you manipulate the data.
he BASIC is rather extensive. The file commands are excellent & you
an mask files so that NOBODY can read them without the proper mask (I
ave already cracked this code, though!). Briefly, it is similar to
ost other BASIC's. If you want, order their programming manual. It
s called 20854A Timeshared BASIC/2000, Level F
art # 02000-90073).
OTE: There are different levels (versions) of TSB/2000. This
rticle is based primarily on Level F. Most of the levels are similar
n their commands so the differences should not affect the hacker.
lso, some systems are customized. Eg, one system I know doesn't have

the MESSAGE command because they don't want the operator bothered wit
messages. Another system says ??? instead of PLEASE LOG IN and ILLEGA
instead of ILLEGAL ACCESS. These are only trivial problems, though.

PROGRAMS
Hewlett-Packard often supplies programs from their TSB Library for th
systems. Utilities such as ASCII*, FPRINT, & others are almost
inevitably found on every system. Standard games such as WUMPUS,
STOCK, LUNAR, & many others are also a "system must." Other companie
offer very large programs for the HP2000 also. GIS (Guidance
Information Systems) is a database to help guidance counselors help
students to select colleges, jobs, financial aid, etc. GIS is usually
found in the S5xx group library (anyone with an S5xx password can use
it). Unfortunately, sometimes these programs are set so that a
certain password will automatically RUN them. In some cases you can
abort by pressing the <BREAK> key. There is a BASIC function
[X=BRK(0)] that disables the <BREAK> key. In this case, only the
sysop or the program can throw you into BASIC.
There are many alleged bugs on the HP2000 that allow users to do all
sorts of things. If you run across any of these be sure to let me
know. I have seen one system that consisted of 2 HP2000's running
together. In this case, the multiplexer would first ask the user

SYSTEM 1 OR SYSTEM 2? before logging in. You would then type SYS1 or
SYS2.
Most of the HP2000 systems are used by schools, school districts,
and various businesses. This was an ideal system for schools
before micro- computers existed. The HP2000 system has been in
existance since around 1973. It has been replaced by the HP3000 but
there are still many HP2000 systems in existance & I believe that the
will stay there for awhile.

If you need help with anything on an HP2000 or find other HP2000
ystems, feel free to ask me. Any comments, corrections, and/or
hreats are also welcome. Yours Truly,
*****BIOC
=$=*Agent
****003
s, corrections, and/or
hreats are also welcome. Yours Truly,
*****BIOC
=$=*Agent
****003

Hacking the Networks

In 1982, two Los Angeles hackers, still in their teens, devised one
of the most sensational hacks so far, running all over the
Pentagon's ARPA data exchange network. ARPAnet was and is
the definitive packet-switched network – more about these in the
next chapter; it has been running for twenty years, cost more than
$500 million and links together over 300 computers across the

United States and beyond. Reputedly it has 5,000 legitimate customers, among them NORAD, North American Air Defence Headquarters at Omaha, Nebraska. Ronald Austin and Kevin Poulsen were determined to explore it.

Their weapons were an old TRS-80 and a VIC-20, nothing complicated, and their first attempts relied on password-guessing. The fourth try, UCB, the obvious initials of the University of California at Berkeley, got them in. The password in fact was little used by its legitimate owner and in the end, it was to be their downfall.

Aspects of ARPAnet have been extensively written up in the textbooks simply because it has so many features which were first tried there and have since become 'standard' on all data networks. From the bookshop at UCLA, the hackers purchased the manual for Unix, the multi-tasking, multi-user operating system devised by Bell Laboratories, the experimental arm of ATT, the USA's biggest telephone company. At the heart of Unix is a small kernel containing system primitives; Unix instructions are enclosed in a series of shells and very complicated procedures can be called in a small number of text lines simply by defining a few pipes linking shells. Unix also contains a large library of routines which are what you tend to find inside the shells. Directories of files are arranged in a tree-like fashion, with master or root directories leading to other directories, and so on. One of the most important utilities available in the Unix system is *uucp*, which allows separate Unix machines to be linked together; using the correct commands, you can sit at one machine and be in complete control of another. Of course, if each Unix machine is set up carefully, the system manager can prevent this happening, but often they do not.

Ron and Kevin needed to become system 'super-users' with extra privileges, if they were to explore the system properly; 'UCB' was merely an ordinary user. Armed with their knowledge of Unix, they set out to find the files containing legitimate users' passwords and names. Associated with each password was a Unix shell which defined the level of privilege. Ron wrote a routine which captured the privilege shell associated with a known super-user at the point when that user signed on and then dumped it into the shell associated with a little-used identity they had decided to adopt for their own explorations. They became 'Jim Miller'; the original super-user lost his network status. Other IDs were added. Captured privilege shells were hidden away in a small computer called Shasta at Stanford, at the heart of California's Silicon Valley.

Ron and Kevin were now super-users. They dropped into SRI, Stanford Research Institute, one of the world's great centres of scientific research; into the Rand Corporation, known equally for its extensive futurological forecasting and its 'thinking about the unthinkable', the processes of escalation to nuclear war; into the National Research Laboratory in Washington; into two private research firms back in California and two defence contractors on the East Coast; and across the Atlantic to the Norwegian Telecommunications Agency which, among other things, is widely believed to have a special role in watching Soviet Baltic activity. And, of course, NORAD.

Their running about had not gone unnoticed; ARPAnet and its constituent computers keep logs of activity as one form of security (see the section below, pp. 114 – 115) and officials both at UCLA (where they were puzzled to see an upsurge in activity by 'UCB') and in one of the defence contractors sounded an alarm. The KGB were suspected, the FBI alerted.

One person asked to act as sleuth was Brian Reid, a professor of electrical engineering at Stanford. He and his associates set up a series of system trips inside a Unix shell to notify them when certain IDs entered an ARPAnet computer. His first results seemed to indicate that the source of the hacking was Purdue, Indiana, but the strange IDs seemed to enter ARPAnet from all over the place. Eventually, his researches led him to the Shasta computer and he had identified 'Miller' as the identity he had to nail. He closed off entry to Shasta from ARPAnet. 'Miller' reappeared; apparently via a gateway from another Stanford computer, Navajo.

Reid, who in his sleuthing role had extremely high privileges, sought to wipe 'Miller' out of Navajo. A few minutes after 'Miller' had vanished from his screen, he re-appeared from yet another local computer, Diablo. The concentration of hacking effort in the Stanford area led him to suppose that the origin of the trouble was local. The most effective way to catch the miscreant was by telephone trace. Accordingly, he prepared some tantalizing, apparently private, files.

This was the bait, designed to keep 'Miller' online as long as possible while the FBI organized a telephone trace. 'Miller' duly appeared, the FBI went into action – and arrested an innocent businessman.

But, back at UCLA, they were still puzzling about 'UCB'. In one of his earliest sessions, Ron had answered a registration questionnaire with his own address, and things began to fall into place.

In one of his last computer 'chats' before arrest, Kevin, then only 17 and only beginning to think that he and his friend might have someone on their trail, is supposed to have signed off: 'Got to go now, the FBI is knocking at my door.' A few hours later, that is exactly what happened. Ron Austin was eventually convicted on twelve felony counts and imprisoned; after a few months he was released to perform 600 hours of community service work.

Several years after, late in 1986, a group of West German hackers pulled off an even more spectacular coup. They broke into SPAN – Space Physics Analysis Network, a worldwide network connecting NASA to over 1,500 scientific research centres in the UK, Germany, France, Switzerland and Japan. It is believed that as many as 135 separate computers were 'visited'. Unlike many of the hacks described in this book, the German Data Travellers included insiders, and indeed their feat would have been impossible without such help. The main technique appears to have been that old trusty, the keystroke capture program which waits for a legitimate user to log on and then writes all his or her keystrokes into a text file which can then be examined later for passwords and other interesting material. Whilst the technique was not new, what shocked security experts was that it had been carried out on a computer family and operating system thought to be secure – DEC's VAX VMS. Indeed, the US government had given this precise set-up clearance for secure applications. The Data Travellers had access to the operating system manuals, had spotted and developed flaws and had managed to get them mounted onto one system. From there they were able to plant their keyboard capture programs – in effect a form of Trojan Horse – on a number of other machines, using the first as a gateway into all the others. In effect, SPAN had at least two weaknesses: first the flawed operating system, but more crucially, an obvious lack of administrative supervision: in secure operating system environments, it should be impossible for *any* new program or modification to be introduced without formal 'acceptance' and 'signing-off' procedures. These procedures should cover both the introduction of software via a terminal or physical mounting via a floppy disc or tape. One of the functions of a secure operating system is to make clandestine unauthorized additions much more difficult – but *all* computer security devices work only if they are used and managed effectively.

Once care hacking material had been extracted by means of the Trojans, other hackers were able to use the information thus gained to explore SPAN using home computers via dial-up ports.

When DEC became aware of the security weakness, they issued a mandatory patch to VMS to block off the loophole which the Trojan had exploited. For some time the hack remained a closely guarded secret until a security manager decided to publish the names of the perpetrators in order, he hoped, to punish them. It is believed that the intelligence authorities would have preferred that the events had remained concealed from the public.

As with other hacks described in this book, the closer one examines the claims and rebuttals issued by hacker and hackee, the muddier the details become. The Data Travellers let the Hamburg Computer Chaos Club – these people also re-appear in Chapter 8 – handle much of their propaganda and many of the press accounts that appeared as the story unfolded in autumn 1987 clearly included 'interpretations' from those not directly involved. In the end, the actual achievements of the Data Travellers must remain a matter of conjecture: NASA stated; 'We know of no classified information which can be accessed through our network.' The Computer Chaos Club said it had a 200-page print-out of the Data Travellers' activities which, however, as an act of public responsibility, it was not prepared to publish.

Computer Security Methods

There is now a profession of computer security experts and they have had some successes. The first thing such consultants do is to attempt to divide responsibility within a computer establishment as much as possible. Only operators are allowed physical access to the installation, only programmers can use the operating system (and under some of these, such as VM, may be only part of the operating system), only system managers are permitted to validate passwords, and only the various classes of users are given access to the appropriate applications programs.

Next, if the operating system permits (it usually does), all accesses are logged; surveillance programs carry out an audit, which gives a historic record, and also, sometimes, perform monitoring, which is real-time surveillance.

In addition, separate programs may be in existence, the sole purpose of which is 'threat monitoring': they test the system to see if anyone is trying repeatedly to log on without apparent success (say by using a program to try out various likely passwords), they assess if any one port or terminal is getting more than usual usage, or if IDs other than a regular small list start using a particular terminal – as when a hacker obtains a legitimate ID but one that normally operates from only one terminal within close proximity to the main installation whereas the hacker is calling from outside.

Increasingly, in newer mainframe installations, security is built into the operating system at hardware level. In older models this was not done, partly because the need was not perceived but also because each such 'unnecessary' hardware call tended to slow the whole machine down. (If a computer must encrypt and decrypt every process before it is executed, if activity journals must be constantly written to, regular calculations and data accesses take much longer.) However the world's largest manufacturers now seem to have found viable solutions for this problem.

Yet the existence of computer security facilities does not mean that they are used properly. Time and again, hackers and indeed fraudsters have been successful, not because the resources to prevent them have been absent, but because they weren't being used – the equivalent of buying an expensive lock and then leaving it open. Readers who wish to discover more should read my *DataTheft* which is intended for a readership of owners and managers of businesses that depend on computers.

7 Networks

Until ten or twelve years ago, the telecommunications and computer industries were almost entirely separate. Shortly they will be almost completely fused. Most of today's hackers operate largely in ignorance of what goes on in the lines and switching centres between the computer they own and the computer they wish to access. Increasingly, dedicated hackers are having to acquire knowledge and experience of data networks, a task made more interesting, but not easier, by the fact that the world's leading telecommunications organizations are pushing through an unprecedented rate of innovation, both technical and commercial.

Apart from purely local, low-speed working, computer communications are now almost exclusively found on separate high-speed data networks, separate that is, from the two traditional telecommunications systems – telegraphy and telephone. Telex lines operate typically at 50 or 75 bits/s with an upper limit of 110 bits/s. The highest efficient speed for telephone-line-based data is 2400 bits/s. All of these are pitifully slow compared with the internal speed of even the most sluggish computer.

When system designers first came to evaluate what sort of facilities and performance would be needed for data communications, it became obvious that relatively few lessons would be drawn from the solutions already worked out in voice communications.

Analogue Networks
In voice-grade networks, the challenge had been to squeeze as many *analogue* signals down limited-size cables as possible. One of the earlier solutions, still very widely used, is frequency division multiplexing (FDM): each of the original speech paths is modulated onto one of a specific series of radio frequency carrier waves; each such RF wave is then suppressed at the transmitting source and re-inserted close to the receiving position so that only one of the side–bands (the lower), the part that actually contains

116

the intelligence of the transmission, is actually sent over the main data path. This is similar to SSB transmission in radio.

The entire series of suppressed carrier waves, are then modulated onto a further carrier wave which then becomes the main vehicle for taking the bundle of channels from one end of a line to the other. Typically a small co-axial cable can handle 60 to 120 channels in this way, but large cables, the type dropped on the beds of oceans and employing several stages of modulation, can carry 2700 analogue channels. Changing audio channels (as it leaves the telephone instrument and enters the local exchange) into RF channels, as well as making frequency division multiplexing possible, also brings benefits in that, over long circuits, it is easier to amplify RF signals to overcome losses in the cable.

Just before World War II the first theoretical work was carried out to find further ways of economizing on cable usage. What was then described is called Pulse Code Modulation – PCM. There are several stages. In the first, an analogue signal is sampled at specific intervals to produce a series of pulses – this is called Pulse Amplitude Modulation and takes advantage of the characteristic of the human ear that if such pulses are sent down a line with only a very small interval between them, the brain smooths over the gaps and reconstitutes the entire original signal. In the second stage the levels of amplitude are sampled and translated into a binary code. The process of dividing an analogue signal into digital form and then re-assembling it in analogue form is called quantization. Most PCM systems use 128 quantizing levels, each pulse being coded into 7 binary digits, with an eighth added for supervisory purposes.

By interleaving coded characters in a high-speed digital stream it is possible to send several separate voice channels along one physical link. This process is called Time Division Multiplexing (TDM) and together with FDM still forms the basis of most of the globe's voice-grade communications.

Digital Networks
Elegant though these solutions are – though they are rapidly being replaced by total digital schemes – they are very wasteful when all that is being transmitted are the discrete audio tones of the output of a modem. In a speech circuit, the technology has to be able to 'hear' – receive, digitize and re-assemble – the entire audio spectrum between 100 Hz and 3000 Hz, which is the usual pass-band of what we have come to expect from the audio quality

of the telephone. Moreover the technology must also be sensitive to a wide range of amplitude – speech is made up of pitch and associated loudness. In a digital network, however, all one really wants to transmit are the digits, and it doesn't matter whether they are signified by audio tones, radio frequency values, voltage conditions, or light pulses, just so long as there is circuitry at either end which can encode and decode.

There are other problems with voice transmission: once two parties have made a connection with each other (by the one dialling a number and the other lifting a handset), good sense has suggested that it was desirable to keep a total physical path open between them, it not being practical to close down the path during silences and re-open it when someone speaks. In any case the electromechanical nature of most of today's phone exchanges would make such turning off and on very cumbersome and noisy. But with a purely digital transmission, routing of a 'call' doesn't have to be physical – individual blocks merely have to bear an electronic label of their originating and destination addresses, such addresses being 'read' in digital switching exchanges using chips rather than electromechanical ones. Two benefits are thus simultaneously obtained: the valuable physical path (the cable or satellite link) is only in use when some intelligence is actually being transmitted and is not in use during 'silence'; secondly, switching can be much faster and more reliable.

Packet Switching
These ideas were synthesized into creating what has now become packet switching. The methods were first described in the mid-1960s, but it was not until a decade later that suitable cheap technology existed to create a viable commercial public service. The principal British Telecom product is called Packet Switch-Stream (PSS) and notable comparable US services are Compunet,Telenet and Tymnet. PSS in the UK now offers several services. Many other countries have their own services and international packet switching is entirely possible – the UK service is called, unsurprisingly, IPSS.

In essence the service operates at 48 kbits/s full duplex (both directions simultaneously) and uses an extension of time division multiplexing. Transmission streams are separated in convenient-sized blocks or packets, each one of which contains a head and tail signifying origination and destination. The packets are assembled, either by the originating computer, or by a special

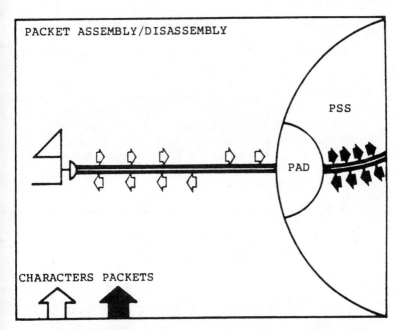

PACKET ASSEMBLY/DISASSEMBLY

PSS

PAD

CHARACTERS PACKETS

facility supplied by the packet switch system. The packets in a single transmission stream may all follow the same physical path or may use alternate routes depending on congestion. The packets from one 'conversation' are very likely to be interleaved with packets from many other 'conversations'. The originating and receiving computers see none of this. At the receiving end, the various packets are stripped of their routing information, and re-assembled in the correct order before presentation to the computer's VDU or applications program.

All public data networks using packet switching seek to be compatible with each other, at least to a considerable degree. The international standard they have to implement is called CCITT X.25. This is a multi-layered protocol covering (potentially) everything from electrical connections to the user interface.

The levels work like this:

7	*Application*	User interface
6	*Presentation*	Data formatting and code conversion
5	*Session*	Coordination between processes
4	*Transport*	Control of quality service
3	*Network*	Set up and maintenance of connections

2 *Data link*   Reliable transfer between terminal and network
1 *Physical*   Transfer of bitstream between terminal and network

At the moment international agreement has only been reached on the lowest three levels, Physical, Data Link and Network. Above that, there is a huge galactic battle in progress between IBM, which has solutions to the problems under the name SNA (Systems Network Architecture) and most of the remainder of the principal mainframe manufacturers, whose solution is called OSI (Open Systems Interconnection).

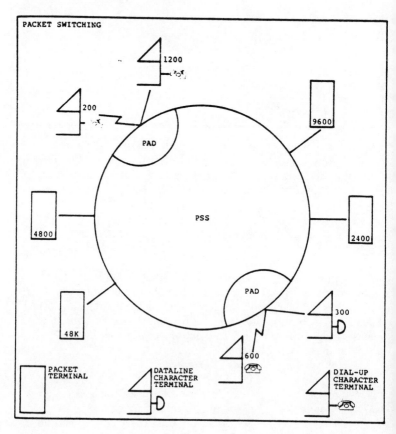

Packet Switching and the Single User

So much for the background explanation. How does this affect the user?

Single users can access packet switching in one of two principal ways: either they use a special terminal directly able to create the data packets in an appropriate form – these are called packet terminals in the jargon – and these sit on the packet switch circuit accessing it via the nearest PSS exchange, using a permanent dataline and modems operating at speeds of 2400, 4800, 9600 or 48 kbits/s, depending on level of traffic. You can buy X.25 boards for the IBM PC, for example. Alternatively, the customer can use an ordinary asynchronous terminal, without packet-creating capabilities and connect into a special PSS facility which handles the packet assembly for him. Such devices are called packet assembler/disassemblers, or PADs. In the jargon, such users are said to have character terminals. PADs are accessed either via leased line at 300 or 1200, or via dial-up at those speeds, but also at 1200/75.

Most readers of this book, if they have used packet switching at all, will have done so using their own computers as character terminals and by dialling into a PAD.

The phone numbers of UK PADs can be found in the PSS directory, published by Telecom National Networks.

In order to use PSS, you as an individual need a network user identity (NUI) which is registered at your local packet switch exchange (PSE). The PAD at the PSE will throw you off if you don't give it a recognizable NUI. If you subscribe to some information services, rather than expecting you to secure your own NUI, they supply you with one of their own – and incorporate the costs in their own overall charges. The UK NUI for Dialog, for example, is *NDIALOG0006OSQ*. PADs are extremely flexible devices, they will configure their ports to suit your equipment – both as to speed and screen addressing – rather like a bulletin board (though to be accurate, it is the bulletin board which mimics the PAD).

If you are using an ordinary dumb terminal, you must send $\langle cr \rangle$ $\langle cr \rangle\langle A2 \rangle\langle cr \rangle$ to tell the PAD what to expect. If you are using a commercial VDU, the command is $\langle cr \rangle$ $\langle cr \rangle$ D1 $\langle cr \rangle$. PAD ports are available at 300 bits/s, 75/1200 and 1200/1200 full duplex. If you are using a remote information retrieval service the most economical mode is 75/1200: the host sends you far more information than you send it, so high speed *from* the host is desirable; after all, you get four times as much information back in the same time as at 300/300 and this is important on those services that charge by time connected. If you are sending equal amounts of information, then, unless you can afford a 1200/1200 full duplex modem (V.22), 300/300 will have to do. Do not use a viewdata emulator at 75/1200 unless you want awkward line breaks!

The first thing that happens after dialling a PAD number and sending it details of the sort of VDU you have is that the PAD responds by transmitting to you the details of the packet switch exchange and the number of the specific port to which your computer is attached.

You then send your NUI. This is always twelve characters long. The PAD responds by echoing back the first six of these – in the case of the Dialog NUI above, you would see on your screen: NDIALOG.

The PAD then responds 'ADD?'. It wants the network user address (NUA) of the host you are calling. These are also available from the same directory: Cambridge University Computing Services's NUA is 234 222339399, BLAISE is 234 219200222, Istel is 234 252724241, and so on. The first four numbers are known as the DNIC, data network indentification code; the first three are the country, 234' is the UK identifier, and the last one the specific service in that country,' 2' signifying PSS.

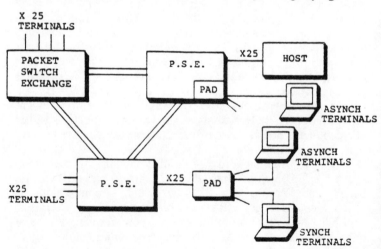

You can also get into Prestel via PSS, though for UK purposes it is an academic exercise: A9 234 1100 2018 gives you Prestel without the graphics (A9 indicates to the system that you have a teletype terminal). Confirmation of connection comes when the full NUA is returned thus: '234222339399+COM'.

Once you have been routed to the host computer of your choice, then it is exactly as if you were entering by direct dial, your password and so on will be requested.

Costs of using PSS are governed by number of packets exchanged rather than the distance between two computers or the actual time of the call. A typical PSS session will thus contain the following running costs: local phone call to PAD (on regular phone bill, time–related), PSS charges (dependent on number of packets sent) and host computer bills (which could be time-related or be per record accessed or on fixed subscription).

PSS, in the form described above, is not particularly friendly to the naive user, even if some of the logging on procedures can be installed on keyboard macros. There is one other problem: although packet switching uses error correction over its high-speed links, none used to be available between PAD and character terminal. If there was a bad line – well, tough. Accordingly, new features were introduced in 1985 under the name MultiStream. MultiStream makes it possible for a PAD to present a user with a simple menu of choices of database and/or destination. The PAD needs to be set up only once for each user. There is an option to let the user into the unfriendly world of NUAs, if necessary.

So much for the user-hostility problem. Error correction is now available under the name EPAD – and it is yet another new standard to add to Xmodem, Kermit and all the existing commercial alternatives. EPAD is hardware-based, and so requires a special modem. Finally, in recognition of the number of Prestel-compatible terminals to be found in the UK, there is a viewdata formatter called VPAD which means that owners of private videotex systems (see Chapter 8) can use PSS as a national data network. However, Prestel itself doesn't use PSS.

There are also a number of private packet switched networks, a few of which are limited to one large company or serve universities and research facilities but some of which compete directly with PSS: Istel's Infotrac and ADP's Network services are two examples. Valued added networks (VANs) are basic telecoms networks or facilities to which some additional service –

NETWORK RESPONSES AND ERROR MESSAGES

MESSAGE	MEANING
NUA + COM	A datacall to this NUA is established
NUA + INC	An incoming call to a Dataline terminal
CLR DTE	Datacall cleared by the host (probably at the request of the terminal)
CLR CONF	Datacall cleared by the PAD at the request of the terminal
CLR OCC	The called number is occupied
CLR NC	Network congestion prevents connection
CLR INV	Invalid facility requested
CLR NA	Access not permitted (e.g. closed user group)
CLR ERR	Invalid request from the terminal
CLR RPE	Host computer procedure error
CLR NP	Called number not assigned
CLR DER	Called number out of order (e.g. host computer down or disconnected)
CLR PAD	The host was instructed the PAD to clear
CLR NRC	The host does not subscribe to transfer charging
RESET DTE	Reset at request of the host computer
RESET ERR	Procedure error reset
RESET NC	Network congestion reset
ERROR	Incorrect command from the terminal
INV	Invalid parameter reference or value
FREE or ENGAGED	Status of the datacall

data processing or hosting of publishing ventures, for example –
has been added.

BT also provides a number of digital communication products
for large organizations outside the packet switch system. It is up
to the users of these point-to-point links to decide which
protocols to use. In practice, packet switch techniques offer the
best usage of a circuit's capacity. BT's services are marketed
under the name KiloStream (data rates at 2400, 4800, 9600, 48k,
56k – for international circuits, and 64 kbits/s) and MegaStream
(even higher data rates). If you come across references to other
xxxStream services, they could be: VideoStream for Videocon-
ferencing, SatStream (guess) and InterStream which provides
some rather interesting gateways between services: InterStream 1
links PSS and telex, 2 links PSS and the new high-speed telex
variant teletex, 3 links teletex and telex.

Public packet switching, by offering easier and cheaper access,
is a boon to the hacker. No longer does the hacker have to worry
about the protocols that the host computer normally expects to
see from its users. The X.25 protocol and the adaptability of the
PAD mean that the hacker with even lowest quality asynchronous comms can talk to anything on the network. The tariff
structure, favouring packets exchanged and not distance, means
that any computer anywhere in the world can be a target. The
networks are fascinating in themselves. Like most large computer
installations they have their imperfections which can be explored
and exploited. And like many systems in the process of growing
to meet new challenges and markets, there are often unan-
nounced experiments, openly available to be played with at no
cost.

Austin and Poulsen, the ARPAnet hackers, made dramatic use
of a private packet switched net; the Milwaukee 414s ran around
GTE's Telenet service, one of the biggest public systems in the
US. Their self-adopted name comes from the telephone area code
for Milwaukee, a state chiefly known hitherto as the centre of the
US beer industry.

During the spring and summer of 1983, using publicly
published directories, and the usual guessing games about pass-
numbers and pass-words, the 414s dropped into the Security
Pacific Bank in Los Angeles, the Sloan-Kettering Cancer Clinic in
New York (it is unlikely they actually altered patients' records but
merely looked at them, despite the fevered newspaper reporting
of the time), a Canadian cement company and the Los Alamos

research laboratory in New Mexico, home of the atomic bomb, and where work on nuclear weapons continues to this day. It is believed that they saw there 'sensitive' but not 'classified' files.

Commenting about their activities, one prominent computer security consultant, Joseph Coates, said:

> The Milwaukee babies are great, the kind of kids anyone would like their own to be... There's nothing wrong with those kids. The problem is with the idiots who sold the system and the ignorant people who bought it. Nobody should buy a computer without knowing how much security is built in.... You have the timid dealing with the foolish.

During the first couple of months of 1984 British hackers carried out a thorough exploration of SERCNET, the private packet-switched network sponsored by the Science and Engineering Research Council and centred on the Rutherford Appleton Laboratory in Cambridge. It links together all the science and technology universities and polytechnics in the United Kingdom and has gateways to PSS and CERN (European Nuclear Research). Almost every type of mainframe and large mini-computer can be discovered hanging on to the system, IBM 3032 and 370 at Rutherford itself, Prime 400s, 550s and 750s all over the place, VAX 11/780s at Oxford, Daresbury, other VAXs at Durham, Cambridge, York, East Anglia and Newcastle, large numbers of GEC 4000 family members, and the odd PDP11 running Unix.

Penetration was first achieved when a telephone number appeared on a popular hobbyist bulletin board, together with the suggestion that the instruction 'CALL 40' might give results. It was soon discovered that, if when asked for name and establishment the hacker typed DEMO, things started to happen.

For several days hackers left each other messages on the hobbyist bulletin board, reporting progress, or the lack of it.

Eventually, it became obvious that DEMO was supposed, as its name suggests, to be a limited facilities demonstration for casual users, but that it had been insecurely set up.

I can remember the night I pulled down the system manual, which had been left in an electronic file, watching page after page scroll down my VDU at 300 bits/s. All I had had to do was type the word 'GUIDE'. I remember also fetching down lists of addresses and mnemonics of SERCNET members. Included in the manual were extensive descriptions of the network protocols and their relation to 'standard' PSS-style networks.

Certain forms of access to SERCNET have since been shut off but hacker exploration continues. Another group of university-based hackers has found a similar network, JANET, rather interesting.

JANET, the UK Joint Academic Network, consists of a series of local and wide area networks and links together all British universities, research institutes, computer-based libraries and polytechnics. It is more extensive in ambition than SERCNET but shares many facilities and is also run from the Rutherford Appleton Laboratory. It is an extremely hybrid system, consisting of many different types of computer and with a variety of local facilities, although the basis of the interconnection is the X.25 packet-switching protocol. JANET has been 'raped' (not my choice of term, but one that has now had widish usage) on a number of occasions, but never so extensively as in early 1984, probably at around the same time as the SERCNET penetrations described above but in fact quite independently.

A couple of students at a university in the south of England developed a familiarity in PRIMOS, the operating system for Prime computers. There was a fundamental weakness in the way in which the operating system had been set up. From time to time it was desirable to permit users to load additional material in the form of magnetic tape onto one of the university's Primes. To do this successfully, you had to have access to the entire filestore and, among other things, you could explore the MFD – the Master File Directory. From here it became possible to gain access to some valid user identities.

As the students continued their exploration, they discovered an on-line HELP facility which explained the mechanism for CALLing a remote machine. They started to issue CALLs in sequence, starting from 01, and recorded what they discovered. By combining the knowledge they had accumulated, they were now able to start serious exploration. Hunting around in the filestore of a Prime in an adjacent university, they discovered they had access to the sensitive RMAN directory which contained a file (LOGIN.CPL) which, in turn, led to the unmasking of the password for the RMAN user (in effect, the system manager). This gave them almost total control over that computer but, since many of the passwords were common to other computers on the network, they had mastery of them as well. They could add attributes (the right to carry out certain functions), authorize new users, delete existing ones. By using the CPL language they were able to capture new passwords as users logged on. After a while, the authorities became aware of what was happening, but for a long time the students were able to keep ahead because they were able to watch everything the authorities tried.

In the end it was carelessness as much as anything that allowed the hackers to be caught. One of them decided to make a clean breast of things and agreed to assist the authorities in patching the system so that the hack could not be repeated.

Both the JANET and SERCNET networks are rather 'loose' in their structure as they were never intended for use by the naive. Gateways and interconnections appear to have been added in a very *ad hoc* fashion, perhaps to support particular sets of (non-computer) experimental work going on at several different centres, the results of which needed to be shared among several computer systems. Advanced hackers derive much pleasure from discovering anomalies in the networks.

Some of the best hacker stories do not have a definite ending. I offer some brief extracts from captured SERCNET sessions.

```
@3E0PBaae NODE 3.
Which Service?
PAD
COM
PAD>CALL 40
Welcome to SERCNET-PSS Gateway. Type HELP for help.

Gatewx c'nkging in
user HELP
ID last used Wednesday, 18 January 1984 16:53
Started - Wed 18 Jan 1984 17:07:58
Please enter your name and establishment DEMO
Due to a local FTP problem, messages entered via the HELP system
during the last month have been lost. Please resubmit if problem/question
is still outstanding  9/1/84

No authorisation is required for calls which do not incur charges at the
Gateway.  There is now special support for TELEX.  A TELEX service
may be announced shortly.

Copies of the PSS Guide issue 4 are available on request to Program
Advisory Office at RAL, telephone 0235 44 6111 (direct dial in) or
0235 21900 Ext 6111.  Requests for copies should no longer be placed
in this help system.

The following options are available:
```

```
NOTES  GUIDE  TITLES  ERRORS  EXAMPLES  HELP  QUIT
Which option do you require? GUIDE
The program 'VIEW' is used to display the Gateway guide
Commands available are:
<CR> or N          next page
P                  previous page
n                  list page n
+n or -n           go forward or back n pages
S                  first page
E                  last page
L/string           find line containing string
F/string           find line beginning string
Q                  exit from VIEW


VIEW Vn 6> Q
The following options are available:

NOTES  GUIDE  TITLES  ERRORS  EXAMPLES  HELP  QUIT
Which option do you require? HELP
NOTES    replies to user quries & other notes
GUIDE    is the complete Gateway user guide (including the Appendices)
TITLES   is a list of SERCNET & PSS addresses & mnemonics (Guide Appendix 1)
ERRORS   List of error codes you may receive
EXAMPLES are some examples of use of the Gateway (Guide Appendix 2)
HELP     is this
QUIT     exits from this session
The following options are available:

NOTES  GUIDE  TITLES  ERRORS  EXAMPLES  HELP  QUIT
Which option do you require? TITLES


VIEW Vn 6>

If you have any comments, please type them now, terminate with E
on a line on its own. Otherwise just type <cr>

CPU used: 2 ieu, Elapsed: 14 mins, IO: 2380 units, Breaks: 114
Budgets: this period = 32.000 AUs, used = 0.015 AUs, left = 29.161 AUs
User HELP   terminal  2 logged out  Wed 18 Jan 1984 17:21:59


 84/01/18. 18.47.00.
 I.C.C.C. NETWORK OPERATING SYSTEM.       NOS 1.1-430.20A
USER NUMBER:
PASSWORD
████████
IMPROPER LOG IN, TRY AGAIN.
USER NUMBER:
PASSWORD
>
>
>SCIENCE AND ENGINEERING RESEARCH COUNCIL
>
>RUTHERFORD APPLETON LABORATORY
>COMPUTING DIVISION
>
>
>                        The SERCNET - PSS Gateway
>
>                            User's Guide
>
>
>                                                          A S Dunn
>                                                     16 February 1983
>Issue 4
>
>
>
>
>Introduction
>
```

Frm   1; Next>
>The SERCNET-PSS Gateway provides access from SERCNET to PSS and PSS to
>SERCNET. It functions as a 'straight through' connection between the
>networks, ie it is protocol transparent. It operates as a Transport Level
>gateway, in accordance with the 'Yellow Book' Transport Service. However
>the present implementation does not have a full Transport Service, and
>therefore there are some limitations in the service provided. For X29 which
>is incompatible with the Yellow Book Transport Service, special facilities
>are provided for the input of user identification and addresses.
>
>No protocol conversion facilities are provided by the Gateway - protocol
>conversion facilities (eg X29 - TS29) can be provided by calling through a
>third party machine (usually on SERCNET).
>
>The Transport Service addressing has been extended to include authorisation
>fields, so that users can be billed for any charges they incur.
>
>The Gateway also provides facilities for users to inspect their accounts and
>change their passwords, and also a limited HELP facility.
>
>User Interface
>
>The interface which the user sees will depend on the local equipment to
Frm   2; Next>
>which he is attached. This may be a PAD in which case he will probably be
>using the X29 protocol, or a HOST (DTE) in which case he might be using FTP
>for example. The local equipment must have some way of generating a
>Transport Service Called Address for the Gateway, which also includes an
>authorisation field - the format of this is described below. The
>documentation for the local system must therefore be consulted in order to
>find out how to generate the Transport Service Called Address. Some
>examples are given in Appendix 2.
>
>A facility is provided for the benefit of users without access to the 'Fast
>Select' facility, eg BT PAD users, (but available to all X29 terminal users)
>whereby either a minimal address can be included in the Call User Data Field
>or an X25 subaddress can be used and the Call User Data Field left absent.
>   - 1 -
>
>The authorisation and address can then be entered when prompted by the
>Gateway.
>
>
>Unauthorised Use
Frm   3; Next>
>.
>No unauthorised use of the Gateway is allowed regardless of whether charges
>are incurred at the Gateway or not.
>
>However, there is an account DEMO (password will be supplied on request)
>with a small allocation which is available for users to try out the Gateway,
>but it should be noted that excessive use of this account will soon exhaust
>the allocation, thus depriving others of its use.
>
>Prospective users of the Gateway should first contact User Interface Group
>in the Computing Division of the Rutherford Appleton Laboratory.
>
>
>Addressing
>
>To connect a call through the Gateway, the following information is required
>in the Transport Service Called Address:
>
>1)   The name of the called network
>2)   Authorisation, consisting of a USERID, PASSWORD and ACCOUNT, and
>   optionally, a reverse charging request
>3)   The address of the target host on the called network
Frm   4; Next>
>
>The format is as follows:
>
><netname>(<authorisation>).<host address>
>
>
>1)   <Netname> is one of the following:

```
>SERCNET              to connect to the SERC network
>PSS                  to connect to PSS
>S                    an alias for SERCNET
>69                   another alias for SERCNET
>
>
>2)        <Authorisation> is a list of positional or keyword  parameters  or
>booleans as follows:
:
:Keyword              Meaning
:
>US                   User identifier
 PW                   User's password
 AC                   the account - not used at present - taken to be same as US
Frm    5; Next>
 RP                   'reply paid' request (see below)
 R                    reverse charging indicator (boolean)

 Keywords are separated from their values by '='.
-Keyword-value pairs, positional parameters and booleans are  separated  from
 each other by ','. The whole string is enclosed in parentheses: ().


                                 - 2 -

 Examples:

: (FRED,XYZ,R)
: (US=FRED,PW=XYZ,R)
: (R,PW=XYZ,US=FRED)

>All the above have exactly the same meaning.  The first  form  is  the  most
>usual.

 When using positionals, the order is: US,PW,AC,RP,R

Frm     6; Next>

>3)        <Host address> is the address of the machine being called  on  the
 target network.  It may be a compound address, giving the service within the
 target machine to be used.  It may begin with a mnemonic instead of  a  full
>DTE  address.  A list of current mnemonics for both SERCNET and PSS is given
>in Appendix 1.

 A restriction of using the Gateway is that where a Transport Service address
>(service  name) is required by the target machine to identify the service to
:be used, then this must be included explicitly by the user in the  Transport
 Service Called Address, and not assumed from the mnemonic, since the Gateway
 cannot know from the mnemonic, which protocol is being used.

 Examples:

 RLGB.FTP
>4.FTP

 Both the above would refer to the FTP service on  the  GEC  'B'  machine  at
>Rutherford.

>RLGB alone would in fact connect to the X29 server, since no service name is
Frm    7; Next>
 required for X29.


:In order  to  enable  subaddresses  to  be  entered  more  easily  with  PSS
:addresses,  the  delimiter  '-'  can be used to delimit a mnemonic. When the
:mnemonic is translated to an address the delimiting '-' is deleted  so  that
>the following string is combined with the address. Eg:

 SERC-99 is translated to 23422351919199


 Putting the abovementioned  three  components  together,  a  full  Transport
 Service Called Address might look like:

 S(FRED,XYZ,R).RLGB.FTP
```

>Of course a request for reverse charging on SERCNET is meaningless, but not
>illegal.

Reply Paid Facility   (Omit at first reading)
>
—In many circumstances it is necessary for temporary authorisation to be
>passed to a third party. For example, the recipient of network MAIL may not
>himself be authorised to use the Gateway, and therefore the sender may wish
>to grant him temporary authorisation in order to reply. With the Job
>Transfer and Maniplulation protocol, there is a requirement to return
>output documents from jobs which have been executed on a remote site.
>
>The reply paid facility is invoked by including the RP keyword in the
>authorisation. It can be used either as a boolean or as a keyword-value
>pair. When used as a boolean, a default value of 1 is assumed.

The value of the RP parameter indicates the number of reply paid calls which
>are to be authorised. All calls which use the reply paid authorisation will
>be charged to the account of the user who initiated the reply paid
>authorisation.
Frm   9: Next>

The reply paid authorisation parameters are transmitted to the destination
>address of a call as a temporary user name and password in the Transport
>Service Calling Address. The temporary user name and password are in a form
>available for use by automatic systems in setting up a reply to the address
>which initiated the original call.

Each time a successful call is completed using the temporary user name and
>password, the number of reply paid authorisations is reduced by 1, until
>there are none left, when no further replies are allowed. In addition there
>is an expiry date of 1 week, after which the authorisations are cancelled.

>In the event of call failures and error situations, it is important that the
>effects are clearly defined. In the following definitions, the term 'fail'
>is used to refer to any call which terminates with either a non-zero
>clearing cause or diagnostic code or both, regardless of whether data has
>been communicated or not. The rules are defined as follows:
>
>1)   If a call which has requested reply paid authorisation fails for any
>   reason, then the reply paid authorisation is not set up.
>
>2)   If the Gateway is unable to set up the reply paid authorisation for
Frm   10: Next>
>   any reason (eg insufficient space), then the call requesting the
>   authorisation will be refused.
>
>3)   A call which is using reply paid authorisation may not create another
>   reply paid authorisation.
>
>4)   If a call which is using reply paid authorisation fails due to a
>   network error (clearing cause non zero) then the reply paid count is
>   not reduced.
>
>5)   If a call which is using reply paid authorisation fails due to a host
>   clearing (clearing cause zero, diagnostic code non-zero) then the
>   reply paid count is reduced, except where the total number of segments
>   transferred on the call is zero (ie call setup was never completed).
>
Frm   11: Next>
>
>X29 Terminal Protocol
>
>There is a problem in that X29 is incompatible with the Transport Service.
>For this reason, it is possible that some PAD implementations will be unable
>to generate the Transport Service Called Address. Also some PAD's, eg the
>British Telecom PAD, may be unable to generate Fast Select calls - this
>means that the Call User Data Field is only 12 bytes long - insufficient to
>hold the Transport Service Address.
>
>If a PAD is able to insert a text string into the Call User Data Field,
>beginning at the fifth byte, but is restricted to 12 characters because of
>inability to generate Fast Select calls, then a partial address can be
>included, consisting of either the network name being called, or the network
>name plus authorisation.

>
>The first character is treated as a delimiter, and should be entered as the
>character '∂'. This is followed by the name of the called network - SERCNET,
>S or PSS.
>
>Alternatively, if the PAD is incapable of generating a Call User Data Field,
>then the network name can be entered as an X25 subaddress. The mechanism
Frm   12; Next>
>employed by the Gateway is to transcribe the X25 subaddress to the beginning
>of the Transport Service Called Address, converting the digits of the
>subaddress into ASCII characters in the process. Note that this means only
>SERCNET can be called with this method at present by using subaddress 69.
>
>
>The response from the Gateway will be the following message:
>
>Please enter your authorisation and address required in form:
>(user,password).address
>>
>
>Reply with the appropriate response eg:
>
>(FRED,XYZ).RLGB
>
>There is a timeout of between 3 and 4 minutes for this response, after which
>the call will be cleared. There is no limit to the number of attempts which
>may be made within this time limit - if the authorisation or address entered
>is invalid, the Gateway will request it again. To abandon the attempt, the
>call should be cleared from the local PAD.
>
Frm   13; Next>
>A restriction of this method of use of the Gateway is that a call must be
>correctly authorised by the Gateway before charging can begin, thus reverse
>charge calls from PSS which do not contain authorisation in the Call Request
>packet will be refused. However it is possible to include the authorisation
>but not the address in the Call Request packet. The authorisation must then
>be entered again together with the address when requested by the Gateway.
>
>The above also applies when using a subaddress to identify the called
>network. In this case the Call User Data Field will contain only the
>authorisation in parentheses (preceded by the delimiter '∂')
>

- 5 -

>Due to the lack of a Transport Service ACCEPT primitive in X29, it will be
>found, on some PADs, that a 'call connected' message will appear on the
>terminal as soon as the call has been connected to the Gateway. The 'call
>connected' message should not be taken to imply that contact has been made
>with the ultimate destination. The Gateway will output a message 'Call
>connected to remote address' when the connection has been established.

Frm   14; Next

ITP Terminal Protocol

The terminal protocol ITP is used extensively on SERCNET, and some hosts
support only this terminal protocol. Thus it will not be possible to make
calls directly between these hosts on SERCNET and addresses on FSS which
support only X29 or TS29. In these cases it will be necessary to go through
─ an intermediate machine on SERCNET which supports both X29 and ITP or TS29
and ITP, such as a GEC MUM. This is done by first making a call to the GEC
MUM, and then making an outgoing call from there to the desired destination.

TS29 Terminal Protocol

This is the ideal protocol to use through the Gateway, since there should be
no problem about entering the Transport Service address. However, it is
advisable first to ascertain that the machine to be called will support
TS29.

When using this protocol, the service name of the TS29 server should be
entered explicitly, eg:

```
Frm   15; Next>
>S(FRED,XYZ).RLGB.TS29
>
>
>Restrictions
>
>Due to the present lack of a full Transport Service  in  the  Gateway,  some
>primitives are not fully supported.
>
>In particular, the ADDRESS, DISCONNECT and RESET primitives  are  not  fully
>supported.   However  this  should  not  present serious problems, since the
>ADDRESS and RESET  primitives  are  not  widely  used,  and  the  DISCONNECT
>primitive can be carried in a Clear Request packet.
>
>
>IPSS
>
>Access to IPSS is through PSS.  Just enter the IPSS address in place of  the
>PSS address.
>
>
```

...............and on and on for 17 pages........

8   Videotex Systems

Viewdata, or videotex as I am proposing to call it in this chapter, has had a curious history. At one stage, in the late 1970s, it was possible to believe that it was about to take over the world, giving computer power to the masses via their domestic television sets. It was revolutionary in the time it was developed, around 1975, in research laboratories owned by what was then called the Post Office but which is now British Telecom. It had a colour-and-graphics display, a user-friendly means of talking to it at a time when most computers needed precise grunts to make them work, and the ordinary layperson could learn how to use it in five minutes. The essence of videotex is that information is always presented on a 'page' or screen basis – 40 characters by 24 lines – instead of in the scrolling mode of conventional teletypewriters and VDUs. Each page always begins with a 'clear screen' command. Pages are identified by numbers rather than words and, in its original Prestel-like format, all commands use numbers only.

The videotex revolution never happened, because Prestel, its most public incarnation, was mismarketed by its owners, British Telecom, and because, in its original version, it is simply too clumsy and limited to handle more sophisticated applications. Since the information is held on electronic file cards which can easily be either too big or too small for a particular answer and the only way you can obtain the desired information is by keying numbers, trundling down endless indices, certain sorts of information cannot be conveniently fitted on to a videotex system without causing user fatigue. In the early days of Prestel, most of what you got was indices, not substantive information. By the time that videotex sets were supposed to exist in their hundreds of thousands, home computers, not predicted at all when videotex first appeared in the mid-1970s, had already sold into the millionth British home.

Yet private videotex, mini-computers configured to look like Prestel and to use the same special terminals, has been a modest success. By mid 1985 there were over 500 significant installations in the UK, though there has been little substantial growth since then. You can even set up videotex hosts on desk-top micros. They have been set up partly to serve the needs of individual companies, but also to help particular trades, industries and professions. The falling cost of videotex terminals has made private systems attractive to the travel trade, to retail stores, the motor trade, to some local authorities and to the financial world. What is curious about all this is that increasingly many professional customers are using not dedicated videotex terminals but PCs with terminal emulators – the emulators reduce the number of characters displayed from 80 – the norm for the IBM sort of machine to 40 and, graphics apart, make the machine less efficient as a display device!

The hacker, armed with a dumb videotex set, or with a software 'fix' for his micro, can go ahead and explore these services. At the beginning of this book, I said my first hack was of a videotex service, Viditel, the Dutch system. It is astonishing how many British hackers have had a similar experience. Indeed, the habit of videotex hacking has spread throughout Europe also: the wonderfully named Chaos Computer Club of Hamburg, later to gain even more notoriety through its association with the SPAN Data Travellers, had some well-publicized fun with Bildschirmtext, the West German Prestel equivalent colloquially named Btx.

What they appear to have done was to acquire the password of the Hamburger Sparkasse, the country's biggest savings bank group. Whereas telebanking is a relatively modest part of Prestel – the service is called Homelink – the West German banks have been a powerful presence on Btx since its earliest days. In fact, another Hamburg bank, the Verbraucher Bank, was responsible for the world's first videotex Gateway (see page 140), for once in this technology, showing the British the way. The 25-member Computer Chaos Club probably acquired the password as a result of the carelessness of a bank employee. Having done so, they set about accessing the bank's own, rather high priced, pages, some of which cost almost DM10 (£2.70). In a deliberate demonstration, the Club then set a computer to call the pages systematically over and over again, achieving a re-access rate of one page every 20 seconds. During a weekend in mid-November 1984, they made more than 13,000 accesses and ran up a notional bill of DM135,000 (£36,000). Information providers, of course, are not charged for looking at their own pages, so no bill was payable and the real cost of the hack was embarrassment.

In hacking terms, the Hamburg hack was relatively trivial – simple password acquisition. Much more sophisticated hacks have been perpetrated by British enthusiasts.

Videotex hacking has three aspects: to break into systems and become user, editor or system manager thereof; to discover hidden parts of systems to which you have been legitimately admitted; and to uncover new services.

Videotex Software Structures

An understanding of how a videotex database is set up is a great aid in learning to discover what might be hidden away.

Remember, there are always two ways to each page: by following the internal indexes, or by direct keying using **nnn#*. Some systems, including Prestel, now have keyword access, but this is very much a bolt-on facility and does not disturb the basic numeric page structure.

In typical videotex software, each electronic file card or 'page' exists on an overall tree-like structure:

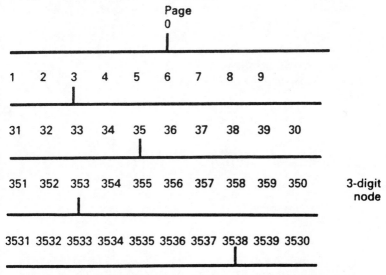

Top pages are called parents; lower pages filials. Thus page 3538 needs parent pages 353, 35, 3 and 0 to support it, i.e. these pages must exist on the system. On Prestel, the parents owned by

Information Providers (the electronic publishers) are 3 digits long (3-digit nodes). Single and double-digit pages (0 to 99) are owned by the 'system manager' (and so are any pages beginning with the sequences 100nn–199nn and any beginning with a 9nnn).

When a page is set up by an information provider (the process of going into 'edit' mode varies from software package to package; on Prestel, you call up page 910) two processes are necessary. The overt page (i.e. the display the user sees) must be written using a screen editor. Then the IP must select a series of options – for example, whether the page is for gathering a response from the user or is just to furnish information, whether the page is to be open for viewing by all, by a closed user group, or just by the IP (this facility is used while a large database is being written and so that users don't access part of it by mistake), the price (if any) the page will bear – and the 'routing instructions'. When you look at a videotex page and it says 'Key 8 for more information on ABC', it is the routing table that is constructed during edit that tells the videotex computer: 'If a user on this page keys 8, take him through to the following next page.' Thus, page 353880 may say 'More information on ABC ... KEY 8.' The information on ABC is actually held on page 3537891. The routing table on page 353880 will say: '8=3537891'.

In the above example you will see that 3537891 is not a true filial of 353880 – this does not matter; however, in order for 3537891 to exist on the system, *its* parents must exist, i.e. there must be pages 353789, 35378, 3537, etc etc.

```
P R E S T E L
PRESTEL EDITING SYSTEM
 Input Details -

          Update option   o
Pageno    4190100           Frame-Id    a

User CUG                 User access    y

Frame type  i            Frame price       2p

          Choice type    s
Choices
 0-   *                  1-    4196121
 2-   4196118            3-    4196120
 4-   4196112            5-    4196119
 6-   4196110            7-    *
 8-   4190101            9-    4199
```

Prestel Editing. This is the 'choices' page which sets up the frame before the overt page – the one the user sees – is prepared.

These quirky features of videotex software can help the hacker search out hidden databases:

1 Using a published directory, you can draw up a list of 'nodes' and who occupies them. You can then list out apparent 'unoccupied' nodes and see if they contain anything interesting. It was when a hacker spotted that an 'obvious' Prestel node, 456, had been unused for a while, that news first got out early in 1984 about the Prestel Microcomputing service, several weeks ahead of the official announcement.

2 If you look at the front page of a service, you can follow the routings of the main index – are all the obvious immediate filials used? If not, can you get at them by direct keying?

3 Do any services start lower down a tree than you might expect (i.e. more digits in a page number than you might have thought)? In that case, try accessing the parents and see what happens.

4 Remember that you can get a message 'no such page' for two reasons: because the page really doesn't exist, or because the information provider has put it on 'no user access'. In the latter case, check to see whether this has been done consistently – look at the immediate possible filials. To go back to when Prestel launched its Prestel Microcomputing service, using page 456 as a main node, 456 itself was closed off until the formal opening, but page 45600 was open. In fact, there are no less than three different 'no such page' messages. The first is 'MISTAKE? TRY AGAIN OR TELL US ON *36#'. The second is 'PRIVATE PAGE – FOR EXPLANATION *37#' – this indicates a page is in a closed user group. The third gives you a full-page display 'UNAVAILABLE PAGE'.

Prestel Special Features
In general, this book has avoided giving specific hints about individual services, but Prestel is so widely available in the UK and so extensive in its coverage, that a few generalized notes seem worthwhile:

1 Not all Prestel's databases may be found via the main index or in the printed directories; even some that are on open

access are unadvertised. Occasionally equipment manufacturers offer experimental services as well: I have found high-res graphics and even instruction codes for digitized full video lurking around.

2 In theory, what you find on one Prestel computer you will find on all the others. In practice this has never been true as it has always been possible to edit individually on each computer as well as on the main updating machine which is supposed to broadcast to all the others. The differences in what is held in each machine will become greater over time.

3 Gateway is a means of linking non-videotex external computers to the Prestel system. It enables on-screen buying and booking, complete with validation and confirmation. It even permits telebanking. Most 'live' forms of gateway are very secure, with several layers of password and security. However, gateways require testing before they can be offered to the public; in the past, hackers have been able to secure free rides out of Prestel.

4 Careful second-guessing of the routings on the databases including telesoftware* have given users free programs while the telesoftware was still being tested and before actual public release.

5 Prestel's special functions are accessible on pages *9nn#. What you can use depends on who you are. IPs, as opposed to ordinary users get the following:

---

*Telesoftware is a technique for making regular computer programs available via videotex: the program lines are compressed according to a simple set of rules and set up on a series of videotex frames. Each frame contains a modest error-checking code. To receive a program, the user's computer, under the control of a 'download' routine, calls the first program page down from the videotex host, runs the error check on it, demands a retransmission if the check gives a 'false' or if it gives a 'true', unsqueezes the program lines and then dumps them into the computer's main memory or disc store. It then requests the next videotex page until the whole program is collected. You then have a text file which must be converted into program instructions. Depending on what model of micro you have, and which telesoftware package, you can either run the program immediately or 'exec' it. Personally I found the telesoftware experience interesting the first time I tried it and quite useless in terms of speed, reliability and quality ever since.

91   Edit facilities menu – contains facilities to frame fill response pages and convert ordinary pages into gateway frames

910   Edit Page

911   CUG membership validation/devalidation

912   Page interrogate – to count up accesses

913   (Private)

914   Change edit password

92   Your Prestel bill

920   Change personal password

921   Thank you for changing your password

924   Programming your Prestel set (remote facility)

93   Prestel mailbox menu

930   Display new messages

931   Display stored messages

932   Display new messages

934   Display stored messages

940   Intermediate frame leading to your welcome frame

942   Message to IPs about changes to edit passwords

970   (Private)

6 Since early 1987, it has been possible to type in words as well as numbers. Keyword access on Prestel – and most other videotex services – is, however, a more limited facility than you get with an on-line retrieval database. The numeric system of identifying videotex pages is still paramount; what the system manager (or sometimes the information provider) can do is to associate a single keyword with a single videotex page. Keywording saves the user all the trouble of exploring down endless indexes by taking him or her straight to a suitable index page highly specific to the nature of the enquiry from which, with luck, the desired information can be obtained with only one or two further keystrokes. Thus, the Prestel user wanting news about microcomputers, instead of falling back on a printed directory or starting grimly at page 1, can type '*M NEWS#' which, at the time of writing takes him straight to Prestel page *40111#, from where there are direct routes to two or three suitable services and various computer club areas. Prestel have also introduced a short-form page-call-up facility, but since you can achieve the same with keyboard macros in most videotex terminal emulator software, I don't expect it will be widely used.

Prestel, so far as the ordinary user is concerned, is a very secure system – it uses fourteen-digit passwords and disconnects after three unsuccessful tries. For most purposes, the only way of hacking into Prestel is to acquire a legitimate user's password, perhaps because they have copied it down and left it prominently displayed. Most commercial videotex sets allow the owner to store the first ten digits in the set (some even permit the full fourteen), thus making the casual hacker's task easier.

However, Prestel was sensationally hacked at the end of October 1984, the whole system lying at the feet of a team of four West London hackers. Their success was the result of persistence and good luck on their side and poor security and bad luck on the part of BT. Two of the hackers ended up in court charged under the Forgery and Counterfeiting Act, 1981, were convicted but then were able to make a successful appeal. Because an important point of law is involved, the case is scheduled to end up in the House of Lords. The first edition of this book had an almost accurate account of how the hack was accomplished; this was removed from the second edition as many of the issues were then *sub judice*. This present description additionally relies on what was revealed in court.

The public Prestel service in 1984 consisted of a network of computers, mostly for access by ordinary users, but with two special-purpose machines: Duke, for IPs to update their information into, and Pandora, to handle Mailboxes (Prestel's variant on electronic mail). The computers were linked by non-public packet-switched lines. The present system is slightly different and is being upgraded and has extra facilities. Ordinary Prestel users are registered (usually) onto two or three computers local to them which they can access with the simple three-digit telephone number 618 or 918. In most parts of the UK, these two number will return a Prestel whistle. (BT Prestel have installed a large number of local telephone nodes and leased lines to transport users to their nearest machine at local call rates, even though in some cases that machine may be 200 miles away.) Every Prestel machine also has several regular phone numbers associated with it, for IPs and engineers. Most of these numbers confer no extra privileges on callers: if you are registered to a particular computer and get in via a 'back-door' phone number you will pay Prestel and IPs exactly the same as if you had dialled 618 or 918. If you are not registered, you will be thrown off after three tries.

In addition to the public Prestel computers there were a

number of other BT machines, not on the network, which looked like Prestel and indeed carried versions of the Prestel database. These machines, left over from an earlier stage of Prestel's development, were (and to an extent still are) used for testing and development of new Prestel features. The old Hogarth computer, originally used for international access, became 'Gateway Test' and, as its name implies, was used by IPs to try out the interconnections of their computers with those of Prestel prior to public release.

Some hackers first became aware of the existence of these 'extra' machines because some of them used the same phone numbers that they had had when they were part of the older Prestel network; the numbers were posted up on at least one Hacker's bulletin board. However, Robert Schifreen, the leading hacker in this exercise, discovered them quite independently: he tried various 'obvious' log-in pass-numbers on a public Prestel computer and with 2222222222 1234 found himself logged on as a Prestel official and with authorization for a BT internal closed user group which contained lists of phone numbers for the development computers. He made his discovery in early spring 1984.

At this first stage Schifreen and those whom he told had no passwords; they could simply call up the log-in page. Not being registered on that computer, they were given the usual three tries before the line was disconnected. For a while the existence of these log-in pages was a matter of mild curiosity. Then, one day, early in the following October, one of the log-in pages looked different: it contained what appeared to be a valid password, and one with system manager status, no less. A satisfactory explanation for the appearance of this password imprinted on a log-in page has not so far been forthcoming. Perhaps it was carelessness on the part of a BT engineer who thought that, as the phone number was unlisted, no unauthorized individual would ever see it. The pass-number was tried and admission secured. After a short period of exploration of the database, which appeared to be a 'snapshot' of Prestel rather than a live version of it – thus showing that particular computer was not receiving constant updates from Duke – Schifreen and co. decided to explore the benefits of System Manager status.

Since they had between them some freelance experience of editing on Prestel, they knew that all Prestel special features pages are in the *9nn# range: 910 for editing; 920 to change personal passwords; 930 for mailbox messages and so on ... what would pages 940, 950, 960 and so on do? It became obvious that these pages would reveal details of users together with account numbers (systelnos), passwords and personal passwords. There were facilities to register and deregister users.

However, all this was taking place on a non-public computer. Would the same passwords on a 'live' Prestel machine give the same benefits? Amazingly enough, the passwords gave access to every computer on the Prestel network. It was now time to examine the user registration details of real users as opposed to the BT employees who were on the development machine.

The hackers were able to assume any personality they wished and could thus enter any closed user group, simply by picking the right name. Among the CUG services they swooped into were high-priced ones providing investment advice, for clients of the stockbroker Hoare Govett, and commentary on international currency markets supplied by correspondents of the *Financial Times*. They were also able to penetrate the pages of Homelink, a telebanking service run by the Nottingham Building Society. They were not able to divert sums of money, however, as Homelink uses a series of security checks which are independent of the Prestel system.

Another benefit of being able to become whom they wished was the ability to read Prestel mailboxes, both messages in transit that had not yet been picked up by the intended recipient and those that had been stored on the system once they had been read. Among the mailboxes read was the one belonging to Prince Philip. Later, with a newspaper reporter as witness, one hacker sent a Mailbox, allegedly from Prince Philip, to the Prestel system manager:

> I do so enjoy puzzles and games. Ta ta. Pip! Pip!
> HRH Hacker

Newspaper reports also claimed that the hackers were able to gain editing passwords belonging to IPs, enabling them to alter pages and indeed the *Daily Mail* of 2 November carried a photograph of a Prestel page from the *Financial Times International Financial Alert* saying:

FT NEWSFLASH!!!   £1 EQUALS $50

The FT maintained that, whatever might theoretically have been possible, in fact they had no record of their pages actually being so altered and hazarded the suggestion that the hacker, having broken into their CUG and accessed the page, had 'fetched it back' onto his own micro and then edited there, long enough for the *Daily Mail's* photographer to snap it for his paper, but without actually retransmitting the false page back to Prestel.

Some time before the *Daily Mail* was contacted, however, Schifreen and co. tried to inform Prestel of the extent of the breach. Using an intermediary at Micronet, the information provider that supplies computer hobbyist material to the Prestel database, Prestel were told what to look for. Prestel appears to have told Micronet that everything was 'under control' twenty-fours later. At this point Prestel lost the opportunity to resolve the breach in private. They only seemed to take real notice after the press story had appeared. They were convinced of the extent of the breach when asked to view page 1, the main index page, which bore the deliberate mis-spelling: Idnex. Such a change theoretically could only have been made by a Prestel employee with the highest internal security clearance. Within 30 minutes, the system manager password had been changed on all computers, public and research. Every one of the 50,000 Prestel users signing on immediately after 2 November was told to change their personal password without delay on every computer to which they were registered. And every IP received, by special delivery, a complete set of new user and editing passwords.

Prestel's problems were far from over: three weeks after the story broke, the *Daily Mail* thought it had found yet another Prestel hack and ran the following page 1 headline: 'Royal codebuster spies in new raid on Prestel', a wondrous collection of headline writer's buzzwords to capture the attention of the sleepy reader. This time an information provider was claiming that, even after new passwords had been distributed, further security breaches had occurred and that there was a 'mole' within Prestel itself. That evening, Independent Television News ran a feature much enjoyed by cognoscenti: although the story was about the Prestel service, half the film footage used to illustrate it was wrong: they showed pictures of the Oracle (teletext) editing facility and of someone using a keypad that could only have belonged to a TOPIC set, as used for the Stock Exchange's private service. The following day, BBC-TV's breakfast show ran an item on the impossibility of keeping Prestel secure.

All this was too much for British Telecom who, after much grim activity, put up the following system notice to all its users:

P R E S T E L   5832a   0p
****
PRESTEL SECURITY
****

Over the past two days Timefame International, an Information Provider on
Prestel, has made specific allegations
that there was unauthorised use of
their security codes made during the
early hours of Sunday 4th November,
1984. Furthermore as a consequence of
this alleged security breach, Timefame
claimed that a 'mole' – within
Prestel's own staff – was responsible
for the release of the security codes
which would have allowed such unauthor–
ised access.

We have informed Timefame that we have
evidence to show that there was no such
unauthorised use of the system......
************ Please key # to continue..

P R E S T E L   5832b   0p
****
PRESTEL SECURITY
****

.... and have offered them the
opportunity to retract their
allegations. As their allegations
have not been retracted we have terminated our agreement with Timefame &
removed their facility to use the
Prestel system.
    Timefame did correct their earlier
assertion that Homelink could be less
than secure & confirmed that Homelink
control their own additional security
measures. So-called 'hackers' have

been portrayed as harmless, fun-loving
hobbyists but their use of the system
is fraudulent & they could be more
accurately described as electronic
shoplifters.
************ key 0 for main index

Almost certainly, there was no 'Timefame' hack, but Prestel had not succeeded in sealing the breach effectively: Schifreen appeared in silhouette on television to say he could still get in and demonstrated VAMPIRE, an internal BT facility which showed the port status of the Prestel computers – no outsider should have been allowed anywhere near that. British Telecom's priority appears to have been to 'get' the hackers.

On the day the story appeared, a call-logger was installed on Schifreen's phone. This identified numbers dialled and the duration of each call, but not the content. Four days afterwards a data-logger was also attached; this machine captures the contents of any data messages, but omits any conventional voice traffic.* A call-logger was attached to the phone of Steve Gold, one of the others, a few days later still with a data-logger following shortly afterwards. Little attempt seems to have been made to ensure that the substantive security loophole had been closed. By the third week of March 1985 BT had accumulated enough evidence as a result of the taps provided by the call-loggers and data-loggers to assemble charges of forgery against the two; a 'heavy mob' raid was organized and Schifreen and Gold, but not the others involved, were arrested and eventually charged with 'uttering' a forgery.

A number of court appearances followed whilst evidence continued to be accumulated and assessed. There was a committal at a magistrates' court. On each of these occasions, there was considerable press interest and, no doubt, BT told themselves that the message that was coming over was 'Hackers Beware.' Equally strongly another message was being broadcast: 'Prestel has terrible security.' Eventually the case came to a full trial and Schifreen and Gold were found guilty. On appeal, the judgment

---

* Doubts have been expressed whether the use of what was in effect a telephone tap without a properly issued warrant was quite legal; however the events took place before the coming into force of the Interception of Communications Act 1985.

was overturned, on the grounds that 'forgery' requires that an 'instrument' must be forged – for example a document, identity card or mag-stripe card. Merely inputting numbers into a computer which instantly accepts them is not, according to the Court of Appeal, creating an instrument. The point of law will eventually be reviewed by the House of Lords.

It is unlikely that penetration of Prestel to that extent will ever happen again, though where hacking is concerned, nothing is impossible.

There is one, relatively uncommented-upon vulnerability in the present Prestel set-up: the information on Prestel is most easily altered via the bulk update protocols used by information providers, where there is a remarkable lack of security. All the system presently requires is a four-character editing password and the IP's systel number, which is usually the same as his mailbox number (obtainable from the on-system mailbox directory on page *7#) which in turn is very likely to be derived from a phone number. This loophole should soon be closed.

Other Videotex Services
Large numbers of other videotex services exist: in addition to the Stock Exchange's TOPIC and the other videotex based services mentioned in Chapter 4, the travel trade has really clutched the technology to its bosom: the typical high street agent not only accesses Prestel but several other services – in some cases as many as eleven – which give up-to-date information on the take-up of holidays, announce price changes and allow confirmed airline and holiday bookings.

Several of the UK's biggest car manufacturers have a stock locator system for their dealers: if you want a British Leyland model with a specific range of accessories and in the colour combinations of your choice, the chances are that your local dealer will not have it in stock. He can, however, use the stock locator to tell him with which other dealer such a machine may be found. Other motor vehicle systems are run by BMW, Fiat, Ford, General Motors (Vauxhall-Opel), Mazda, Talbot (the system is called VITAL), Volvo, VW-Audi (VAG Dialog) and Yamaha runs a videotex service for its motorcycle dealers. Secondhand dealers can use Gladiator to check up on prices – it is based on the well-known *Glass's Guide*, FACT to discover recent car auction prices and Viewtrade for inter-dealer trading.

Stock control and management information is used by retail

chains using, in the main, a package developed by a subsidiary of Debenhams. Debenhams had been early enthusiasts of Prestel in the days when it was still being pitched at a mass consumer audience – its service was called Debtel which wags suggested was for people who owed money. Later it formed DISC to link together its retail outlets and this was hacked in 1983. The store denied that anything much had happened, but the hacker appeared (in shadow) on a TV program together with a quite convincing demonstration of his control over the system. Rumbelows and BHS are also videotex enthusiasts, Littlewoods have ShopTV on Prestel – a gateway ordering service and Tesco have been running a home-ordering facility for the housebound in the Gateshead area for some time.

The Press Association provides a news digest called Newsfile. It is mostly used by the public relations industry and has an economics digest service called Esmark. Audience research data is despatched in videotex mode to advertising agencies and broadcasting stations by AGB market research.

Local authorities in the UK have also clasped videotex to their bosoms. As well as the umbrella bureau service, Laser, the following are all owners of private videotex systems of various sizes: Basildon, Berkshire, Birmingham, Gateshead, Gloucestershire, Hackney, Herts (the pioneer and the first private system I hacked into – see Chapter 6), Kent, Kingston-on-Thames (it's called Kingtel, I'm afraid), Milton Keynes (Milton Skreens, ugh), Northamptonshire, North Herts, Oxfordshire and Suffolk. There are a number of other experiments, some of them using nothing more extensive than BBC micros running CommunItel software – a package much favoured by the ITECs, incidentally.

There are also databases, often using CommunItel, which are halfway between commercial services and bulletin boards. Some are used simply to record out-of-hours requests for mail-order houses but some, like that run by the Radio Society of Great Britain for radio amateurs, carries substantive news and features.

Beyond this, there are alternate videotex networks rivalling that owned by Prestel, the most important of which is, at the time of writing, the one run by Istel and headquartered at Redditch in the Midlands. This service, called Viewshare, sits on Istel's Infotrac network and claims to be the world's largest videotex service, larger than Prestel. It transports several different trade and professional services as well as the internal data of BL, of which Istel was a subsidiary. The company that launched

Timefame on Prestel eventually withdrew its services and is setting up a rival system; at the time of writing, it is still in 'trial' mode.

A videotex *front-end processor* is a minicomputer package which sits between a conventionally structured database and its ports which look into the phone-lines. Its purpose is to allow users with videotex sets to search the main database without the need to purchase an additional conventional dumb terminal. Some videotex front-end processors (FEPs) expect the user to have a full alphabetic keyboard and merely transform the data into videotex pages 40 characters by 24 lines in the usual colours. More sophisticated FEPs go further and allow users with only numeric keypads to retrieve information as well. By using FEPs a database publisher or system provider can reach a larger population of users. FEPs have been known to have a lower standard of security protection than the conventional systems to which they were attached.

Many of the private viewdata services described above are run on FEPs rather than Prestel-like software packages. As a result, they are likely to have such un-Prestel-like features as keyword access – try typing *HELP# which is nearly always in any keyword thesaurus. ICC (InterCompany Comparisons) have a very slick videotex service – see Chapter 4 – which is easier to use and cheaper than the same database on Dialog. A particularly impressive service comes from the credit agency CCN – again Chapter 4 has the details.

The careful videotex hacker soon gets to recognize the dominant software packages used on mainframes from the format of the sign-on page to the differences in page header design and 'command pages'. Prestel-like services, as noted, used *90# to logoff; others use *04# or some such. The packages you'll see over and over again are Aregon's IVS series, Computex, ICL Bulletin, and Mistel. Each has its own characteristic command set to access editing and system manager functions. See if they work even if they are not clearly listed on the main menus of the service.

Videotex Standards
The UK videotex standard – the particular graphics set and method of transmitting frames – is adopted in many other European countries and in former UK imperial possessions. Numbers and passwords to access these services occasionally appear on bulletin boards and the systems are particularly

interesting to enter while they are still on trial. As a result of a quirk of Austrian law, anyone can legitimately enter their service without a password; though one is needed if you are to extract valuable information. However, important variants to the UK standards exist: the French (inevitably) have a system that is remarkably similar in outline but incompatible.

Minitel, the French system, is now by far the world's largest videotex service. From the beginning, it was a state-sponsored exercise, part of a long-overdue essential upgrade of French public telecommunications. Minitel was conceived primarily as a device for the answering of telephone directory enquiries which had been carried out by humans with printed books before then. The other, commercial, information services were then hung onto the basic system. Minitels were given away to the French by the million, thus giving it the send-off and commercial impetus that Prestel never had. French videotex terminals thus have full alpha-keyboards instead of the numbers-only versions common in other countries. You can get Minitel-emulators for the PC. The service suffered its first serious hack late in 1984 when a journalist on the political/satirical weekly *Le Canard Enchaîné* claimed to have penetrated the Atomic Energy Commission's computer files accessible via Teletel and uncovered details of laser projects, nuclear tests in the South Pacific and an experimental nuclear reactor.

In North America the emerging standard which was originally put together by the Canadians for their Telidon service but which has now, with modifications, been promoted by Ma Bell, has high resolution graphics because, instead of building up images from block graphics, it uses picture description techniques (e.g. draw line, draw arc, fill-in, etc.) of the sort relatively familiar to most users of modern home micros. Implementations of NALPS (as the US standard is called) are available for the IBM PC. US videotex has not really taken off; the ASCII-based services are too well established and the drawbacks of videotex by now too obvious.

Countries vary considerably in their use of videotex technology: the German and Dutch systems consist almost entirely of gateways to third-party computers; the Finnish public service uses software which can handle nearly all videotex formats, including a near-photographic mode. Software similar to that used in the Finnish public service – Mistel – can be found on some private systems.

Videotex: the Future

Videotex grew up at a time when the idea of mass computer ownership was a fantasy, when the idea that private individuals could store and process data locally was considered far-fetched and when there were fears that the general public would have difficulties in tackling anything more complicated than a numbers-only key-pad. These failures of prediction have led to the limitations and clumsiness of present-day videotex. Nevertheless the energy and success of the hardware salesmen plus the reluctance of companies and organizations to change their existing set-ups will ensure that, for some time to come, new private videotex systems will continue to be introduced.

9 Radio Computer Data

Vast quantities of data traffic are transmitted daily over the radio frequency spectrum; hacking is simply a matter of hooking up a good-quality radio receiver and a computer through a suitable interface. On offer are news services from the world's great press agencies, commercial and maritime messages, meteorological data, and plenty of heavily encrypted diplomatic and military traffic. The press agency material is a back-up for land-line based services or for those going through satellites. A variety of systems, protocols and transmission methods are in use and the hacker jaded by land-line communication (and perhaps for the moment put off by the cost of phone calls) will find plenty of fun on the airwaves. High quality radio receivers covering a wide range of the radio frequency spectrum are falling in price and new services are beginning to appear, interleaved with conventional broadcasting material in the form of datacasting.

Many of the techniques of radio hacking are similar to those necessary for computer hacking. Data transmission over the airwaves usually uses either a series of audio tones to indicate binary 0 and 1 which are modulated on transmit and demodulated on receive or alternatively frequency-shift keying which involves the sending of one of two slightly different radio frequency carriers, corresponding to binary 0 or binary 1. The two methods of transmission sound identical on a communications receiver (see below) and both are treated the same for decoding purposes. The tones are different from those used on land-lines – 'space' is nearly always 1275 Hz and 'mark' can be one of three tones – 1445 Hz (170 Hz shift – quite often used by amateurs and with certain technical advantages); 1725 Hz (450 Hz shift – the one most commonly used by commercial and news services) and 2125 Hz (850 Hz shift – also used commercially).

There are other radio transmissions which use tones, but not in this way. These include the piccolo system which uses 32 tones and another, much favoured for UK military long-haul work, which uses up to twenty-four tones. Such transmissions, which are parallel rather than serial, require ultra-stable receivers even before you attempt to work out what is really going on!

The commonest two-tone protocol uses the 5-bit Baudot code rather than 7-bit or 8-bit ASCII. The asynchronous, start/stop mode is the most common. Transmission speeds include: 45 bits/s (60 words/minute), 50 bits/s (66 words/minute), 75 bits/s (100 words/minute). 50 bits/s is the most common. However, many interesting variants can be heard – special versions of Baudot, for non-European languages, and error correction protocols.

The material of greatest interest is to be found in the high-frequency or 'short-wave' part of the radio spectrum, which goes from 2 MHz, just above the top of the medium-wave broadcast band, through to 30 MHz, which is the far end of the 10 meter amateur band which itself is just above the well-known Citizens' Band at 27 MHz.

The reason this section of the spectrum is so interesting is that, unique among radio waves, it has the capacity for worldwide propagation, without the use of satellites, the radio signals being bounced back, in varying degrees, by the ionosphere. This special quality means that *everyone* wants to use HF (high frequency) transmission – not only international broadcasters, the propaganda efforts of which are the most familiar uses of HF. Data transmission certainly occurs on all parts of the radio spectrum, from VLF (very low frequency, the portion below the long wave broadcast band which is used for submarine communication), through the commercial and military VHF and UHF bands, beyond SHF (super high frequency, just above 1000 MHz) right to the microwave bands. But HF is the most rewarding in terms of range of material available, content of messages and effort required to access it.

Before going any further, hackers should be aware that in a number of countries even *receiving* radio traffic for which you are not licensed is an offence; in nearly all countries *making use* of information so received is also an offence and, in the case of news agency material, breach of copyright may also present a problem. However, owning the equipment required is usually not illegal and, since few countries require a special licence to *listen* to amateur radio traffic (as opposed to transmitting, where a licence is needed) and since amateurs transmit in a variety of data modes as well, hackers can set about acquiring the necessary capability without fear.

Equipment
The equipment required consists of a communications receiver, an antenna, an interface unit/software and a computer.

Communications receiver   This is the name given to a good-quality high frequency receiver. Suitable models can be obtained, second-hand, at around £100; new receivers cost upwards of £175. There is no point is buying a radio simply designed to pick up short-wave broadcasts – they will lack the sensitivity, selectivity and resolution necessary. A minimum specification would be:

Coverage	100 kHz – 30 MHz
Resolution	better than 100 Hz
Modes	AM, upper side band, lower side band, CW (Morse)

Tuning would be either by two knobs, one for MHz, one for kHz, or by keypad. On more expensive models it is possible to vary the bandwidth of the receiver so that it can be widened for musical fidelity and narrowed when listening to bands with many signals close to one another.

Broadcast stations transmit using AM – amplitude modulation – but in the person-to-person contacts of the aeronautical, maritime and amateur world, single-sideband suppressed-carrier techniques are used – the receiver will feature a switch marked AM, USB, LSB, CW, etc. Sideband transmission uses less frequency space and so allows more simultaneous conversations to take place and is also more efficient in its use of the power available at the transmitter. The chief disadvantage is that equipment for receiving is more expensive and must be more accurately tuned. Upper sideband is used on the whole for voice traffic and lower sideband for data traffic. (Radio amateurs are an exception: they also use lower sideband for voice transmissions below 10 MHz.)

A number of the big manufacturers for the consumer market have produced compact, high-quality short-wave receivers which can be operated from a keypad. The Sony 7600D is one example: it is paperback book-sized and also covers the VHF broadcast band. Although it is designed for the travelling businessman, the availability of an external antenna socket, single sideband and a fine-tune facility means that it can give surprisingly good results for picking up data signals.

Suitable sources of supply for communications receivers are amateur radio dealers, whose addresses may be found in specialist magazines like *Practical Wireless, Amateur Radio, Ham Radio Today*.

Antenna   Antennas are crucial to good short-wave reception – the sort of short 'whip' aerial found on portable radios is quite insufficient if you are to capture transmissions from across the globe. When using a computer close to a radio you must also take considerable care to ensure that interference from the CPU and monitor don't squash the signal you are trying to receive. The sort of antenna I recommend is the 'active dipole' which has the twin advantages of being small and of requiring little operational attention. It consists of a couple of 1-meter lengths of wire tied parallel to the ground and meeting in a small plastic box. This is mounted as high as possible, away from interference, and is the 'active' part. From the plastic box descends coaxial cable which is brought down to a small power supply next to the receiver and from there the signal is fed into the receiver itself. The plastic box contains special low-noise transistors.

It is possible to use simple lengths of wire but these usually operate well only on a limited range of frequencies and you will need to cover the entire HF spectrum.

Active antennas can be obtained by mail order from suppliers advertising in amateur radio magazines – the Datong is highly recommended.

Interface   The 'interface' is the equivalent of the modem in land-line communications; indeed, advertisements of newer products actually refer to radio modems. Radio teletype, or RTTY, as it is called, is traditionally received on a modified teleprinter or telex machine and the early interfaces or terminal units (TUs) simply converted the received audio tones into 'mark' and 'space' to act as the equivalent of the electrical line conditions of a telex circuit.

Since the arrival of the microcomputer, however, the design has changed dramatically and the interface now has to perform the following functions:

1 Detect the designated audio tones.
2 Convert them into electrical logic states.

3 Strip the start/stop bits, convert the Baudot code into ASCII equivalents, reinsert start/stop bits.
4 Deliver the new signal into an appropriate port on the computer. (If RS232C is not available, then any other port – e.g. user interface or game – that is.)

A large number of designs exist: some consist of hardware interfaces plus a cassette, disc or ROM for the software; others contain both the hardware for signal acquisition and firmware for its decoding in one box. In selecting a design, pay particular attention to the supplied tuning device; at the very least you should have two LEDs to indicate 'mark' and 'space'. More advanced devices feature a LED bargraph; top-notch professional boxes have a small cathode ray tube display.

Costs vary enormously and do not always appear to be related to quality of result. The kit-builder with a ZX Spectrum can have a complete set-up for under £40; semi-professional models, including keyboards and screen can cost in excess of £1000.

Until recently, the kit I used was based on the Apple II (because of that model's great popularity in the USA, much hardware and software exists); the interface talks into the game port and I have several items of software to present Baudot, ASCII or Morse at will. There is even some interesting software for the Apple which needs no extra hardware – the audio from the receiver is fed direct into the cassette port of the Apple, but this method is difficult to replicate on other machines because of the Apple's unique method of reading data from cassette. The BBC Model B also has a rich collection of appropriate software written for it, some of it available as a ROM.

Excellent inexpensive hard/firmware is available for many Tandy computers and also for the VIC20/Commodore 64. On the whole US suppliers seem better than those in the UK or Japan – products are advertised in the US magazines *QST* and *73*. In the UK you should look in the same amateur radio magazines as for receivers. *RadCom*, the magazine of the Radio Society of Great Britain (RSGB), often has interesting software in the classified section at the back as it is a good source of secondhand equipment.

I now use a full-feature radio modem (exactly the same size as my principal phone modem, as it happens) which contains a sophisticated firmware set. I simply feed audio tones into it and 7-bit ASCII at 300 baud at RS-232C levels comes out. I can command it with the same software package I use down the phone lines. The firmware copes with Baudot and Morse at all reasonable speeds, ASCII transmissions and the error correcting protocol, AMTOR, of which more later. Used in association with a transmitter, it will also originate radio data as well. Second-hand, it cost less than £200.

Setting Up

Particular attention should be paid to linking all the equipment together; there are special problems about using sensitive radio-receiving equipment in close proximity to computers and VDUs. Computer logic blocks, power supplies and the synchronizing pulses on VDUs are all excellent sources or radio interference (RFI). RFI appears not only as individual signals at specific points on the radio dial but also as a generalized hash which can blank out all but the strongest signals. Interference can escape not only from poorly packaged hardware but also from unshielded cables which act as aerials.

The remedy is simple to describe: encase and shield everything, connecting all shields to a good earth, preferably one separate from the mains earth.* In practice, much attention must be paid to the detail of the interconnections and the relative placing of items of equipment. In particular, the radio's aerial should use coaxial feeder with a properly earthed outer braid so that the actual wires that pluck the signals from the ether are well clear of computer-created RFI. It is always a good idea to provide a communications receiver with a proper earth, though they will work without one: if used with a computer, it is essential. Plastic-cased computers cause particular problems – get a metal case or line the inside with cooking foil; if you do the latter, be careful to avoid short-circuits and watch out you don't deny the circuit board air circulation, or your computer will overheat!

Do not let these paragraphs put you off; with care excellent results can be obtained. And bear in mind my own first experience: ever eager to try out some new kit, I banged everything together with great speed – ribbon cable, poor solder joints, an antenna taped quickly to a window in a metal frame less than two meters from the communications receiver – and all I

* Particular care must be used in those houses where mains earth and an actual RF earth may be at different voltage potentials.

could hear from 500 kHz to 30 MHz, wherever I tuned, was a great howl and whine of protest.

Where to Listen
Scanning through the bands on a good communications receiver, you realize just how crowded the radio spectrum is. The table in Appendix VII gives you an outline of the sandwich-like fashion in which the bands are organized.

The 'fixed' bands are the ones of interest; more particularly, the following ones are where you could expect to locate news agency transmissions (in kHz):

3155– 3400	14350–14990
3500– 3900	15600–16360
3950– 4063	17410–17550
4438– 4650	18030–18068
4750– 4995	18168–18780
5005– 5480	18900–19680
5730– 5950	19800–19990
6765– 7000	20010–21000
7300– 8195	21850–21870
9040– 9500	22855–23200
9900– 9995	23350–24890
10100–11175	25010–25070
11400–11650	25210–25550
12050–12330	26175–28000
13360–13600	29700–30005
13800–14000	

In addition, amateurs tend to congregate around certain spots on the frequency map: the following frequency points are used for RTTY transmissions: 3950, 14090, 21090, 28090; and at VHF/UHF: 144.600, 145.300, 432.600, 433.300.

Radio stations do not always observe band plans, unfortunately. For the last few years, propagation conditions on the HF bands have been poor. What has been happening is that the ionosphere has temporarily lost some of its capacity to reflect back radio waves – we have been in the trough of the eleven-year sunspot cycle. As a result, the higher frequencies have been useless for international radio communication and everyone, *all* users of the HF spectrum, have crowded into the few available megahertz.

Some of the bulletin boards cover radio material; you could find propagation reports and, in the hacking sections, details of individual frequencies.

Many of the more important radio services transmit on more than one frequency simultaneously (the same is true of international broadcasts). This is to maximize their chance of being heard, even in poor propagation conditions. Professional receivers listen on two or more frequencies simultaneously and a 'black box' picks the strongest signal out from moment to moment – this is called diversity reception.

The generally received opinion in the UK is that it is unwise to publish frequency lists, though UK-published lists, with obviously restricted coverage are beginning to be available from amateur radio retailers. However useful overseas publications can be obtained by mail order or in some amateur radio outlets. The best-known US titles are the Gilfer *Guide to RTTY Frequencies* and *Confidential Frequency List*, but they cover what can be heard in North America, as opposed to Europe. In many US electronics stores you will also find directories of local VHF and UHF 'utility' services – police, ambulance, paramedic, forestry, customs, dispatch services, etc. These are for use with VHF/UHF scanners; don't buy them by mistake. The best openly available frequency lists are produced by a one-man firm called Klingenfuss. He produces an annual *Utility Guide* as well as subsidiary books covering the various variants on standard Baudot – third shift Amharic and Thai, two versions of Cyrillic RTTY, Arabic and Japanese formats, and the special codes used in meteological services. Klingenfuss is expensive but worth while. His address is Panoramastrasse 81, D-7400 Tuebingen, Federal Republic of Germany.

Tuning In

Radio Teletype signals have a characteristic two–tone warble sound which you will only hear properly if your receiver is operating in SSB (single-sideband) mode. There are other digital tone-based signals to be heard, FAX (facsimile), Helschrieber (which uses a technique similar to dot-matrix printers and is used for Chinese and related pictogram-style alphabets), SSTV (slow-scan television which can take up to 8 seconds to send a low-definition picture), piccolo, and others.

But with practice, the particular sound of RTTY can easily be recognized. More experienced listeners can also identify shifts and speeds by ear.

You should tune into the signal watching the indicators on your terminal unit to see that the tones are being properly captured – typically this involves getting two LEDs to flicker simultaneously. The software will now try to decode the signal and it will be up to you to set the speed and 'sense'. The first speed to try is 66/7 words per minute, which corresponds to 50 bits/s, as this is the most common. On the amateur bands, the usual speed is 60 words per minute (45 bits/s); thereafter, if the rate sounds unusually fast you try 100 words per minute (approximately 75 bits/s). By 'sense' or 'phase' is meant whether the higher tone corresponds to logical 1 or logical 0. Services can use either format; indeed the same transmission channel may use one 'sense' on one occasion and the reverse 'sense' on another. Your software or firmware can usually cope with this. If it can't, all is not lost: you retune your receiver to the opposite sideband and the phase will thereby be reversed. So, if you are listening on the lower sideband (LSB), usually the conventional way to receive, you simply switch over to USB (upper sideband), retune the signal into the terminal unit, and the 'sense' will have been reversed.

Many news agency stations try to keep their channels open even if they have no news to put out: usually they do this by sending test messages like: 'The quick brown fox...' or sequences like 'RYRYRYRYRYRY...' such signals are useful for testing purposes, even if, after a while, they are a little dull to watch scrolling up the VDU screen.

You will discover many signals that you can't decode: the commonest reason is that the transmissions do not use European alphabets and that all the elements in the Baudot code has been re-assigned – some versions of Baudot use not two shifts, but three, to give the required range of characters. Klingenfuss describes ways in which you can use conventional Baudot software to work out which language is being used and to guess what the transmission is about. Straightforward encrypted messages are usually recognizable as coming in groups of five letters, but the encryption can also operate at the bit – as well as the character-level – in that case, too, you will get gobbledegook.

A limited amount of ASCII code as opposed to Baudot is to be found, but mostly on the amateur bands.

Finally, an error-correction protocol, called SITOR, is increasingly to be found on the maritime bands, with AMTOR, an amateur variant in the amateur bands. SITOR has various modes of operation but, in its fullest implementation, messages are sent in blocks which must be formally acknowledged by the recipient before the next one is dispatched. The transmitter keeps trying until an acknowledgement is received. The process is very similar to that used in Xmodem.

Other Radio Data Modes
Increasingly, you will come across, on the amateur bands, packet radio, which has many of the features of packet switching on digital land lines. This is one of the latest enthusiasms among radio amateurs and has taken off by leaps and bounds since the beginning of 1986 with at least two different protocols in relatively wide use. The one more likely to succeed is called, for obvious reasons, AX.25. Each radio amateur has to purchase or build a device called a terminal node controller, or TNC. This enables the amateur's station to act as part of a wide network, switching messages from one destination to another. As with X.25, messages are broken up into a series of packets which contain, not only the part of the text of the entire message but also 'address' information. The TNC software thus receives all the data on the network and retransmits it, retaining only those packets labelled with its unique address, which is then displayed to the station's owner.

AX.25 networks can be much more extensive and reliable than conventional pure radio-based networks because they are less reliant on the quality of the direct propagation path between the originator and the recipient; provided that there are TNC stations located in between the originator and recipient, the message will get through. TNCs are usually implemented as external hardware and used together with PCs and transceivers. You can get radio modems that include Baudot, ASCII, Amtor and Packet all in one box. In the UK the best place to look for packet radio traffic is at 144.650 MHz in the 2-meter band. Data-rate is 1200 baud. Packet can also be heard in the HF amateur bands near the RTTY frequencies at 300 baud. In both cases, the packetized nature of transmission is quite distinctive even to the casual listener. For more information, the reader is referred to BARTG, the British Amateur Radio Teletype Group, and its magazine *Datacom* for further information. You do not need to be a licensed radio amateur to join.

Operational problems of radio hacking are covered at the end of Appendix I, the Baudot code is given Appendix IV and an outline frequency plan is to be found in Appendix VI.

Computer Control of Radios

The latest generation of receivers for the amateur market feature computer interfaces: frequency and mode selection can be executed from a remote computer. A radio service could be called up by name, as opposed to by frequency. Where a transmission occurs on several frequencies simultaneously, the program could check which was being received best, or could calculate which frequency was *likely* to be best, based on predictions about propagation conditions. As home micros become able to support multi-tasking, I expect to see programs which both command radios and decode their traffic – an amateur GCHQ or NSA!

The material that follows represents some of the types of common transmissions: news services, test slips (essentially devices for keeping a radio channel open), and amateur. The corruption in places is due either to poor radio propagation conditions or to the presence of interfering signals.

```
REVUE DE LA PRESSE ITALIENNE DU VENDREDI 28 DECEMBR
E 1984
;;;;;;;;;;;;;;;;;;;;;;;;;;;;;;;;;;;;;;;;;;;;;;;;;;;;;;;;;;;

   LE PROCES AUX ASSASSINS DE L-\\3 POIELUSZKO, LA VISITE DE
M. SPADOLINI A ISRAEL, LA SITUATION AU CAMBODGE ET LA GUER-
ILLA AU MOZAMBIQUE FONT LES TITES DES PAGES POLITIQUES



        MOBILISATION TO WORK FOR THE ACCOUNT OF 1985

                - AT THE ENVER HOXHA AUTOMOBILE AND
                TRACTOR COMBINE IN TIRANA 2


   TIRANA, JANUARY XATA/. - THE WORKING PEOPLE OF THE ENVER HOXH
AUTOMOBILE AND TRACTOR COMBINE BEGAN THEIR WORK WITH VIGOUR
AND MOBILISATION FOR THE ACCOUNT OF 1985. THE WORK IN THIS
IMPROVOWNT CENTER FQR MECHANICAL INDUSTRY WAS NOT INTERRUPTED
FOR ONE MOMENT AND THE WORKING PEOPLE 83$ ONE ANOTHER FOR
FRESHER GREATER VICTORIES UNDER THE LEADERSHIP OF THE PARTY
WITH ENVER HOXHA AT THE HEAD, DURING THE SHIFTS, NEAR
THE FURNANCES, PRESSES ETC.. JUST LIKE SCORES OF WORKING COLLE-
CTIVES OF THE COUNTRY WHICH WERE NOT AT HOME DURING THE NEW
YEAR B
A
IN THE FRONTS OF WORK FOR THE BENEFITS OF THE SOCI-
ALIST CONSTRUCTION OF THE COUNTRY.
```

PUTTING INTO LIFE THE TEACHINGS OF THE PARTY AND THE INSTRU-
CTIONS OF COMRADE ENVER HOXHA, THE WORKING COLLECTIVE OF THIS
COMBINE SCORED FRESH SUCCESSES DURING 1984 TO REALIZE THE
INDICES OF THE STATE PLAN BY RASING THE ECEONOMIC EFFECTIVE-
NESS. THE WORKING PEOPLE SUCCESSFULLY REALIZED AND OVERFUL
FILLED THE OBJECTIVE OF THE REVOLUTIONARY DRIVE ON THE HIGHER
EFFECTIOVENESS OF PRODUCTION, UNDERTAKEN IN KLAIDQAULSK SO,
WITHIN 1984 THE PLANNED PRODUCTIVITY, ACCORDING TO THE INDEX
OF THE FIVE YEAR PLAN, WAS OVERFULFILLED BY 2 PER CENT.
MOREOVER, THE FIVE YEAR PLAN FOR THE GMWERING OF THE COST OF
PRODUCTION WAS RAISED 2 MONTHS AHEAD OF TIME, ONE FIVE YEAR
PLAN FOR THE PRODUCTION OF MACHINERIES LAND EQUIPMENT AND
THE PRODUCTION OF THE TRACTORS WAS OVER-
FULFILLED. THE NET INCOME OF THE FIVE YEAR PLAN WAS REALIZED
WITHIN 4 YEARS. ETCM

RYRYRYRYRYRYRYRYRYRYRYRYRYRYRYRYRYRYRYRYRYRYRYRYRYRYRYRYRYRYRYRY
YRYRYRYRYRYRYRYRYRYRYRYRYRYRYRYRYRYRYRYRYRYRYRYRYRYRYRYRYRYRYRYR
RYRYRYRYRYRYRYRYRYRYRYRYRYRYRYRYRYRYRYRYRYRYRYRYRYRYRYRYRYRYRYRY
RYRYRYRYRYRYRYRYRYRYRYRYRYRYRYRYRYRYRYRYRYRYRYRYRYRYRYRYRYRYRYRY
RYRYRYRYRYRYRYRYRYRYRYRYRYRYRYRYRYRYRYRYRYRYRYRYRYRYRYRYRYD DE GJ4YAD
GJ4YAD GJ4YAD DE G4DF G4DF
SOME QRM BUT MOST OK. THE SHIFT IS NORMAL...SHIFT IS NORMAL.
FB ON YOUR RIG AND NICE TO MEET YOU IN RTTY. THE WEATHER HERE
TODAY IS FINE AND BEEN SUNNY BUT C9LD. I HAVE BEEN IN THIS MODE
BEFORE BUT NOT FOR A FEW YEARS HI HI.

GJ4YAD GJ4YAD DE G4DF G4DF
PSE KKK

G4EJE G4EJE DE G3IMS G3IMS
TNX FOR COMING BACK. RIG HERE IS ICOM 720A BUT I AM SENDING
AFSK NOT FSK. I USED TO HAVE A CREED BUT CHUCKED IT OUT IT WAS

TOO NOISY AND NOW HAVE VIC20 SYSTEM AND SOME US KIT MY SON
BROUGHT ME HE TRAVELS A LOT.
HAD LOTS OF TROUBLE WITH RFI AND HAVE NOT YET CURED IT. VERTY B
QRM AT MOMENT. CAN GET NOTHING ABOVE 10 MEGS AND NOT MUCH EX-G
80. HI HI. SUNSPOT COUNT IS REALLY LOW.

G4EJE G4EJE DE G3IMS G3IMS
KKKKKKKKKKK
RYRYRYRYRYRYRYRYRYR
KKKKKKKKKKK

```
G3IMS G3IMS DE G4EJE G4EJE
FB OM. QRM IS GETTING WORSE. I HAVE ALWAYS LIKED ICOM RIGS BUT
THEY ARE EXEPENSIVE. CAN YOU RUN FULL 100 PER CENT DUTY CYCLE ON
RTTY OR DO YOU HAVE TO RUN AROUND 50 PER CENT. I GET OVER-HEATING
ON THIS OLD YAESU 101. WHAT SORT OF ANTENNA SYSTEM DO YOU USE.
HERE IS A TRAPPED VERTICAL WITH 80 METERS TUNED TO RTTY SPOT AT
3590.
I STILL USE CREED 7 THOUGH AM GETTING FED UP WITH MECHANICAL
BREAK-DOWN AND NOISE BUT I HAVE HEARD ABOUT RFI AND HOME
COMPUTERS. MY NEPHEW HAS A SPECTRUM, CAN YOU GET RTTY SOFTWARE
FOR THAT/.

G3IMS G3IMS DE G4EJE G4EJE
PSE KKK
```

Satellites

With rather different receiving equipment and a rather different antenna system, it is possible to eavesdrop on data traffic carried on satellites. There are three types which can be easily heard: amateur satellites, educational satellites and weather satellites. From these last, you can hack weather pictures.

Satellites don't often use the HF (short-wave) spectrum because, in the case of objects circulating the earth, you want to be sure that the radio waves *won't* be reflected back by the ionosphere. Although satellites carrying worldwide television pictures use microwave frequencies (2 GigaHertz and above), many satellites operate in the VHF and UHF portions of the radio frequency spectrum – 30 MHz to 1 GHz, and these present manageable problems in terms of reception. For a receiver, you can either use a special purpose machine which simply hears the radio traffic of interest and nothing else – it will probably be crystal controlled – or a general purpose 'scanner' which allows you to type in the frequency of interest on a calculator-type keyboard.

Such scanners pick up a huge variety of commercial, emergency, marine and aeronautical services. Costs are from £200 and up, depending on frequency range covered and additional facilities like memories and interfaces. Scanners can be purchased without licence, though in most countries their *use* is restricted. The more expensive scanners give you continuous coverage from about 25 MHz to 2000 MHz, that is 2 GHz, but most of them have gaps, usually corresponding to areas used by the military or for conventional radio and television broadcasts. The frequencies you will need are:

Amateur and educational	144–146 MHz
	430–440 MHz
Weather satellites	136–138 MHz
	1690 MHz*
Navigation satellites	159–151 MHz

Aerials suitable for these frequencies look like a horizontal-plane X in lightweight metal tubing. They are low-cost and obtainable by mail order out of amateur radio magazines. You need different sizes for different frequencies as they need to be 'tuned' for the service you are hunting for. More ambitious satellite hunters use steerable antennas. These look a little like TV aerials (the design is called Yagi) but they are controlled by rotators for both azimuth and elevation. Most of the satellites you look for are not geo-stationary; in other words they do not stay in the same part of the sky with respect to a fixed earth location, so you have to track them. The simple antennas will receive signals from anything reasonably high in the sky, but at low signal strength; the more sophisticated steerable antennas are directional in design and, if correctly aimed, will bring in a far better signal.

On the amateur bands you will hear RTTY and ASCII transmissions of the sort already described. The educational satellites, Uosat 1 and Uosat 2, which are controlled from the University of Surrey, use a set of compressed protocols to relay data about the earth and its atmosphere. Details of both from AMSAT-UK, London E12 5EQ.

There are two sorts of weather satellite. The one that relays the pictures most familiar from television forecasts belongs to a family called Meteosat. Meteosats are geostationary but transmit, in the European area, at 1691.0 MHz and 1694.5 MHz, which are in the low (S-band) microwave region. Reception equipment is expensive for the individual. The information comes down in a format called WEFAX and modules to decode it are available for both the BBC and IBM PC micros. Meteosats transmit global pictures, while the second type of weather satellite, called 'polar orbiting', transmit smaller portions of the world; they operate in the part of the radio spectrum between the civil VHF aircraft and commercial VHF, 136–137 MHz. US

---

*Most VHF/UHF scanners do not go as high as this and special down-converters are necessary.

satellites can be heard at 137.5 and 137.62 MHz and Russian satellites are at 137.3, 137.4 and 137.62 MHz. There are a large number of other, non-weather, satellites, in the same frequency band. The data format is called automatic picture transmission (APT) and software packages to decode it and resolve pictures are available for a number of micros. Again, amateur radio magazines are a good source of advertisements.

Hacking Teletext
Teletext was pioneered in Britain in the early 1970s originally to provide a means of supplying subtitles for deaf television viewers. It took advantage of the fact that of the 625 lines used for UK-standard television (525 lines are used in those parts of the world that have followed US-type TV standards), not all are used for the transmitting of the TV image. In fact there is a field-blanking interval of 25 lines. Although some of the apparently unused lines have other purposes, lines 7 through 22 and, on the interlace, 320 through 335, are spare. The broadcast authorities use some of them for internal purposes and to assist in the running of outside broadcasts, but that still leavès a number of lines that are 'spare'.

Teletext works by using these lines as carriers of data. The signalling rate is 6.9375 Mbits/s and each line contains 40 characters which, in conventional teletext, are eventually display-able, plus codes to synchronize the transmission with the receiver and 'address' information. The idea of a subtitles-only service was rapidly abandoned, and by the time the first Broadcast Teletext Specification was published in 1976, the idea of a page-orientated text service for the general viewer had been thoroughly and become established.

The conventional teletext page consists of 24 displayed lines, each line holding a maximum of 40 characters across. The page itself is held in a small memory bank within the teletext-television. (The display standards were later shared with the UK viewdata standard, so that Prestel and the BBC's Ceefax and IBA's Oracle all have a very similar appearance.) The viewer is able to call up a teletext page by using a keypad and inputting a three-digit number. The teletext circuitry then watches the teletext lines being transmitted and holds on to those lines with the appropriate addresses; one displayed teletext line corresponds to one TV line; however the signalling rate is so fast, that a teletext page, once captured, seems to appear on screen all at once, rather than bit by bit, as with telephone-based videotex. The way broadcast teletext is managed is that groups of pages, 100 at a time, are arranged in magazines. *All* the pages are constantly being transmitted in a cycle, all of the time, so that whenever a viewer selects a page, within a very short period of time the relevant addresses will flash by the viewer's decoder, be captured by it, and the page displayed.

After a slow start, the various public teletext services took off and today most medium-sized colour TVs sold in the UK and many European countries have teletext decoders. From quite early on experiments were carried out to see if teletext could be given more 'intelligence'; indeed telesoftware (see the previous chapter) was initially developed for teletext and not viewdata. Many of these experiments came to very little, but telesoftware is now available on some teletext services; you need a special adapter – they are mostly for the BBC/Acorn machines – and the results are, to my mind, rather unexciting for all the effort and cost involved.

Conventional teletext, however, still does not use all the capacity available from the spare lines. In addition, because all data is sent in a cycle every 60 to 90 seconds or so, the existing capacity is not used very efficiently. By the mid-1980s, therefore, technicians and commercial planners alike were trying to identify new applications for the spare capacity, while still retaining the existing public-broadcast services. On a technical level they knew that teletext circuitry had become cheaper and more compact and that PCs were available which could provide masses of additional intelligence and storage capacity. An effective service could be run without the need for all that constant re–transmission. The conventional TV-based teletext set might have the capacity to hold only a single page at a time; a PC, or a box based on it, could hold hundreds and hundreds. You could run a teletext-based service simply by sending *updates* of information and not the whole of the information. You wouldn't have send the 24 or so lines of the whole page, just the single line containing the information that had been updated.

So the idea of subscription or closed user teletext was born. What the BBC (and to an extent the licensees of the IBA) sells to would-be publishers is *capacity* on a data-stream. It undertakes to insert among all the datalines of the broadcast service, datalines for services that are intended for a small, paying group of people. The codes that are sent along these private lines do not need to conform to conventional broadcast teletext standards; indeed, they must ensure that they don't interfere. Users of their services already include the Stock Exchange and chains of bookmakers.

How can the hacker eavesdrop? Well, for a start, it can't be done with a conventional teletext receiver. However, modern teletext adapters for PCs can be set up to look for unusual address codes (i.e. any that fall outside the groups of address codes associated with broadcast services). Once you have identified these, you can capture them and see if they make any sense. They will, however, only be updates, and may include all sorts of strange instructions. To become a teletext hacker, you need to get hold of the published teletext specifications to see how the codes are set up. I await the news of the first teletext hack with interest: this is one of the areas for really creative and inventive hackers who wish to accomplish more than repeating the feats of others.

Also emerging could be a form of teletext based on FM radio. The conventional FM radio signal consists of two elements in order to create a stereo signal. The 'right' and 'left' of ordinary stereo is encoded before transmission in order to give 'sum' and 'difference' signals. The 'sum' signal is broadcast on the main carrier and that is the only signal you will hear if you have a mono FM radio receiver. The 'difference' signal is transmitted on a sub-carrier of the main radio frequency carrier (in fact at 38 kHz). In a stereo radio receiver the 'difference' signal is picked up and decoded, so that 'right' and 'left' re-appear. However, there can be more than one sub-carrier – the FM signal could carry another at around 57 KHz without spoiling the stereo signal. It would not be a very broad carrier and so could not handle hi-fidelity sound, but it could have some uses. In the USA it has been used for the transmission of MUZAK to the stores, hotels and elevators that use MUZAK to soothe their customers. But, more effectively, it can be used for data.

For some time engineers in Europe have been developing an appropriate specification: one application was thought to be radio programme labelling. The data carrier would contain information telling a suitably equipped radio receiver which broadcast radio service it was carrying, and what type – news, pop music, classical music, and so on. The largest customers for this were thought to be users of car radios: as the vehicle moves from the transmission area of one radio station the signal fades and the owner needs to re-tune to find another station with the same or similar material. Programme labelling could make the process automatic. However, the data-stream could, like TV-teletext, be used for anything. In New York and Chicago it has been used for shares and commodities information – to reach dealers away from their desks. Experiments to do the same in London have already taken place. The data-rate is just under 1200 bits/s.

10   Hacking – the Future

When the present spate of publicity about hacking began in 1983 the computer security industry welcomed it with garlands of flowers. *Transactional Data Report* wrote:

> Why, then, should computer operators be thankful to the hackers? The answer is very simple. They demonstrate what security specialists for more than ten years have been unable to present to a greater audience than a handful of security and software specialists: the vulnerability of modern computer systems, especially once they are linked with communications systems. This is the very point: the spoofs the hackers demonstrate night after night are only the very tip of the iceberg...

> In other words, as long as the user is not aware of the risks he runs by using a computer system, the market will not recognize a demand for security. The hackers now create this market... They hope that users will notice their spoofs. However there is another active group which seeks certain information or to cause trouble to computers but doesn't want to disclose any sign of penetration. Computer fraud and espionage are their business.

The newsletter *Computer Security* said more or less the same thing:

> The summer of 1983 may prove to be the watershed period for data security. The movie *WarGames* together with the well-publicized activities of the so-called '414 gang' from Milwaukee have given more credibility to data security concerns in the eyes of the general public than a decade of hypothesising and doom-saying by data security professionals. This may be a sad commentary on our profession, but it clearly indicates that an appeal to the emotions can be more effective than reasoned, rational argument.

The celebrations of these computer professionals was rather premature: there *is* a great deal more awareness about computer security, but the awareness is still not particularly well informed: far too many computer owners and far too many legislators and policemen believe that hacking is the most important and serious of computer crimes. Elsewhere* I have shown that whilst most statistics on computer crime are extremely unreliable, one clear message does emerge: overwhelmingly, the perpetrators are employees – supervisory and clerical – of the victim.

A moment's thought will show why this is so: a successful fraud of any kind requires that the criminal is able to transfer goods or cash from out of the control of the victim into a place where it is in the control of the perpetrator. To gain from industrial espionage, you must not only secure the information, you must know who will pay for it. In other words, it isn't enough merely to understand the computer system, you need to know a great deal about the commercial environment which it is serving. In the case of fraud: what do all the accounts represent? How do you transfer money from one account into your own? You can penetrate a computer to its very core and not find the answer. In the case of industrial espionage, most commercial secrets are only of interest to people within a specific industry. How can an outsider know what is important and what is not?

The computer-crime statistics also show something else: most computer crimes do not rely on particularly clever techniques; many of the perpetrators aren't even programmers or employed in data processing departments. Indeed, many computer crimes are ludicrously simple in methodology: the false or forged input (with the computer faithfully carrying out the misleading instructions) is easily the most frequent technique. Manipulated data files, viruses, worms, trojans, salamis – well, instances do exist, but they are relatively rare. Computer fraud shares with more conventional fraud a key attribute: there is very little linkage between the skill involved, the chances of success and the amount of money involved. What employees have – and hackers conspicuously lack – is opportunity and inside knowledge.

Although I have my doubts about many of the sets of statistics for computer-related crime and won't support any myself, I can quote those produced by other people. Donn Parker, a frequent writer and speaker on computer crime based at the Stanford Research Institute has put US computer fraud at $3000 million a year; although reported crimes amount to only $100 million annually. In June 1983 the *Daily Telegraph* claimed that British

* *DataTheft*, William Heinemann, 1987.

computer–related frauds could be anything between £500 million and £2.5 billion a year. Detective Inspector Ken McPherson, former head of the computer crime unit at the Metropolitan Police, was quoted in 1983 as saying that within fifteen years every fraud would involve a computer.

Here are two recent US assessments: Robert P Campbell of Advanced Information Management, formerly head of computer security in the US army, reckons that only 1 computer crime in 100 is detected; of those detected, 15 per cent or fewer are reported to the authorities, and of those reported, 1 in 33 is successfully prosecuted – a 'success' rate of 1 in 22,000.

Robert Courtney, a former security advisor at IBM produced a list of hazards to computers: 'The No 1 problem now and forever is errors and omissions.' Then there is crime by insiders, particularly non–technical people of three types: single women under 35; 'little old ladies' over 50 who want to give the money to charity; and older men who feel their careers have left them neglected. Next, natural disasters; sabotage by disgruntled employees; water damage. As for hackers and other outsiders who break in: he estimates it as less than 3 per cent of the total.

In the UK the National Computing Centre says that at least 90 per cent of computer crimes involve putting false information into a computer, as opposed to sophisticated logic techniques; such crimes are identical to conventional embezzlement – looking for weaknesses in an accounting system and taking advantage. In such cases the computer merely carries out the fraud with more thoroughness than a human and the print-out gives the accounts a spurious air of being correct. The *Computer Fraud Survey*, published in 1985 by the Audit Commission, came to similar conclusions. It received 943 replies to its general purpose survey and found 77 instances of fraud. Of these, 58 were frauds committed at inputting stage, 2 at the output stage and 17 involved misuse of resources by company employees. There was no instance of penetration by an outsider. The most quoted UK-figure for total losses is £40 million p.a., though the way in which this was actually calculated is rather elusive. No one really has any idea; everyone who collects data has different definitions of 'computer crime', differing reasons for wanting to collect the data, and differing methods of collection.

Hackers do have one outstanding feature, though. Media appeal. The reason is almost certainly that a section of the public regard the hacker as a weapon to fight back against the perceived encroachments of all-knowing computer systems. I am not all certain that the hacker can actually fulfil this role, but in terms of the assessing of news values – and that is what determines how headlines get written – the image is a potent one.

The result of all of this interest has been an over-rating of the successes of, and threats posed by, hackers. It has led both to unfortunate prosecutions and to law enforcement officers making fools of themselves. The hysteria reached an apogee with the Great Satellite Caper.

In July 1985 a prosecutor in New Jersey appeared in court to announce that he had discovered that a group of local hackers had been able to move satellites in space. The story made headlines all over the world and television news broadcasts produced elaborate graphics to show how it had been done. A detective had logged into a bulletin board called The Private Sector, had misunderstood the contents of a number of the files and decided he had uncovered a major conspiracy involving 630 people, of whom seven were ringleaders. Several months later, the authorities had still not found sufficient evidence to make a substantial case, the hardware was handed back, and the sysop pleaded guilty to a token offence of being in possession of a burglary tool – a small basic program for the Applecat modem.

I have copies of many of the files held by The Private Sector. The machine was the electronic expression of the phonephreak and hacker newsletter *2600*, named after the 2600 Hz tone that US phonephreaks send down the line to the exchange to tell it to accept the supervisory tones necessary for long-distance switching. Much of the material could be considered, I suppose, rather juvenile. There were extracts from a book called *The Poor Man's James Bond* which describes how to build what are alleged to be bombs and how to turn household equipment into lethal weapons. There's a tasteless set of instructions on how to blow up a seagull – apparently you use bait containing a large quantity of baking powder, if you are interested. Another file explains how to forge an identity card, or how to fake a credit card.

As with similar material that occasionally appears on UK bulletin boards, a detailed examination of these bits of advice shows them to be less useful than at first appears. In fact, and this is a conclusion the New Jersey courts appear eventually to have to come to, the Private Sector contained material which, whilst in places jejeune or ghoulish, was little different from the sort of books and magazines some teenagers (and those rather older) have been known to collect. No satellites were moved in their orbits. The existence of phone numbers to the Pentagon was not conclusive evidence that anyone had done more than stand outside its electronic front-door.

This is what Private Sector looked like after it came back on air:

```
/////+++++++/////////////////////////////
//                                     //
//            WELCOME TO THE           //
//          PRIVATE SECTOR BBS         //
//                                     //
//             300/1200 BAUD           //
//           24 HOURS / 7 DAYS         //
//                                     //
//          THE OFFICIAL BBS OF        //
//             2600 MAGAZINE           //
//                                     //
// SYSOPS:        PRIVATE SECTOR       //
//                KID & CO.            //
//                SHADOW 2600          //
//                                     //
/////////////////////////////////////////

ALL OLD ACCOUNTS HAVE BEEN PURGED

ACCOUNT NUMBER
:NEW

            ///////////////////////////
            //                       //
            //     WELCOME TO THE    //
            //    PRIVATE SECTOR BBS //
            //                       //
            ///////////////////////////


     I AM ASSUMING YOU ARE A SUBSCRIBER OF
2600 MAGAZINE.  IF YOU ARE NOT A SUB-
SCRIBER, CONSIDER BECOMING ONE.

     ALL USERS ARE GRANTED FULL ACCESS TO
THE BULLETIN BOARD REGARDLESS OF RACE,
COLOR, CREED OR EMPLOYMENT.  THERE ARE
NO >ELITE< BOARDS!!

     IN ORDER TO KEEP ORGANIZATIONS
LIKE THE FBI OR OTHER LAW ENFORCEMENT
AGENCIES FROM BREATHING DOWN MY NECK,
I WOULD LIKE THE USERS TO FOLLOW THESE
RULES!!
```

```
>>    IMPORTANT RULES!!

      O   THERE IS TO BE >NO< POSTING OF
          CODES TO LONG DISTANCE CARRIER
          SERVICES!!

      O   THERE IS TO BE >NO< POSTING OF
          CREDIT CARD NUMBERS!

      O   THERE IS TO BE >NO< POSTING OF
          MESSAGES HAVING TO DO WITH THE
          TRADE OF SOFTWARE

>>    SYSTEM RULES!!

      O   CALL NO MORE THAN TWO TIMES A
          DAY.

      O   DO NOT STAY ON THE SYSTEM FOR
          MORE THAN 20 MINUTES!

      O   ANYONE CAUGHT MAKING OPERATOR
          INTERRUPTS WILL BE THROWN OFF
          IMMEDIATELY.


    IF WE CAN ALL FOLLOW THESE SIMPLE
RULES, THE PRIVATE SECTOR WILL BE
AROUND FOR QUITE SOME TIME.....



ENTER THE FULL NAME THAT YOU WOULD LIKE
TO USE ON THIS SYSTEM:

VERIFYING NAME...

ENTER A PASS WORD THAT YOU WOULD LIKE
OR JUST PRESS RETURN IF YOU ONLY WANT
TO LOOK AROUND THE SYSTEM AND DO NOT
WANT A USER ID ASSIGNED:
C)   COMPUTER:     APPLE II
D)   LOWERCASE:    NO
E)   LINE LENGTH:  40
F)   LINE FEEDS:   YES
G)   NULLS:        0

ENTER 'Y' IF THIS IS ACCEPTABLE OR
ENTER THE LETTER OF THE PARAMETER TO
CHANGE:Y
```

```
SAVING INFORMATION...

    DATE ][ 03-29-86
    TIME ][ 00;52
    BAUD ][ 300  BAUD
    CALLER ][ 810


LAST CALLER ][ THE DEERHUNTER
   CALLED AT ][ 00;11
          BAUD ][ 300  BAUD
```

RULES OF THIS SYSTEM:

```
O    NO CREDIT CARD INFORMATION / NUMBER
O    NO SOFTWARE PIRACY
O    NO UNRELATED DISCUSSIONS
O    NO EXTENDER CODES
O    NO LONG DISTANCE ACCESS CODES
O    NO COMPUTER PASSWORDS
```

E-MAIL POLICY

E-MAIL IS COMPLETELY PRIVATE. ONLY
THE SENDER & RECIPIENT CAN READ SUCH
MAIL. THE USERS ARE FULLY RESPONSIBLE
FOR THE CONTENT OF THEIR E-MAIL.

THIS BULLETIN BOARD SYSTEM SUPPORTS
FREEDOM OF SPEECH AS GUARENTEED BY THE
1ST AMENDMENT. IN DEFENSE OF THIS
RIGHT THE PRIVATE SECTOR BBS WAS TAKEN
DOWN ON JULY 12, 1985. THE BOARD WAS
RETURNED UNDER COURT ORDER FEBRUARY 24,
1986 AS NO CRIMINAL ACTIVITY WAS
ASSOCIATED WITH THE BBS.

LATEST NEWS:

SYSTEM NEWS POSTED:
03-22-86
```
```

NEW STRUCTURE

   THE NEW STRUCTURE AND POLICIES FOR
PRIVATE SECTOR HAVE BEEN DECIDED AND
THE BOARDS HAVE BEEN SET UP. ALL OF
THE OLD MESSAGES HAVE BEEN REMOVED AND
WE CAN START OFF A NEW.

   IF YOU LEFT THE INFORMATION I HAD
REQUESTED YOU WILL HAVE ACCESS TO ALL
THE BOARDS THERE ARE. IF YOU DID NOT
LEAVE THE INFORMATION YOU WILL ONLY
HAVE ACCESS TO THE TELCOM DIGEST BOARD.

   IF YOU ENCOUNTER SOME PAUSES THEY ARE
BECAUSE OF SOME TROUBLE WITH A RAM CARD
THAT IS INSTALLED TO HELP RUN THIS
PROGRAM.

IF YOU HAVE ANY QUESTIONS OR SUGGESTIONS
PLEASE LEAVE FEEDBACK.

THANK YOU,
PRIVATE SECTOR
   IF YOU HAVE ANY INTERESTING ARTICLES
PLEASE SEND THEM TO 2600 VIA EMAIL TO
"2600 MAGAZINE" WE APPRECIATE ALL GOOD
AND INFORMATIVE ARTICLES.

DONATIONS:

IF YOU HAVE ANYTHING YOU WOULD LIKE TO
SEND US, PLEASE DO:

NEW MAILING ADDRESS

COMMANDS:

][][][][][][][- COMMANDS -][][][][][][][

]   [

```
2600 <=- INFORMATION ABOUT 2600
          MAGAZINE. THE TELCOM SOURCE
  BX <=- GO TO BOARD LEVEL AT BD X
  TP <=- G-PHILE SECTION...
  MS <=- SEND PERSONAL MAIL
  MR <=- READ PERSONAL MAIL
   S <=- YOUR SYSTEM STATUS
   P <=- VIEW OR CHANGE PARAMETERS
  PA <=- CHANGE YOUR PASSWORD
  RN <=- REREAD THE NEWS
   T <=- TIME INFORMATION
   U <=- READ NEW USER MESSAGE
   F <=- FEEDBACK FOR PRIVATE SECTOR
   I <=- INFO ON PRIVATE SECTOR
   C <=- CALL PRIVATE SECTOR TO CHAT
```

In Britain, the crest of the moral panic about hacking was the decision of British Telecom to prosecute Robert Schifreen and Steve Gold for the Prince Phillip Prestel Hack. The technical details of how they were able to take control of the system were described in Chapter 8. In fact, Prestel's software and hardware, *as delivered by the system's developers*, have perfectly adequate security, provided the facilities are properly used. The failures were all of poor administration and most of the losses incurred by Prestel were the result of clumsiness and arrogance. None of this should be read as condoning forgery but this case shows, with almost complete perfection, what happens when victims of hacking throw themselves into a sea of moral panic. It was not only BT that suffered; Gold lost his job and Schifreen decided it was better to resign his; both were fined and had to pay legal costs, and although their appeal was successful, there is to be a further hearing in the House of Lords. The warning to hackers must be: you cannot always expect victims to react rationally.

One reviewer of the first edition of this book suggested that the great days of hacking might already be over. This is palpable nonsense. Hacking already has a long history reaching back to the 1960s. Its antecedents in what I have called tech-freaking – lightly abusing technological artifacts to see what happens – go back even further. There's no reason to think that the intellectual curiosity which prompts people to undertake such activity has suddenly been snuffed out.

However, hacking has had a great deal of publicity lately. It has caught the fancy not only of participants but of the general public as well. Quite simply there's been rather a demand for spectacular hacking feats. But hacking doesn't happen to order. The big stories which have surfaced have two common features: there's always been a bright individual – or group of them – who liked the power of playing with big machines and making them misbehave in a controlled fashion; and there have been the opportunities offered by errors in security and design. The opportunities continue to come up, but not just because hackers want them to. So viewed at any one time, the golden age of hacking always seems to have been yesterday... until someone stumbles across a fresh opportunity.

What certainly has happened is that hackers are much less communicative and far less likely to shout their triumphs to the nearest journalist. There are two reasons for this: first, the authorities in both the UK and the USA are showing a greater tendency to attempt prosecution. As we have seen, these prosecutions are not always successful and can cause further harm to the victim. They are often born of the need to be 'doing something' about computer crime – chasing amateur hackers is much easier than tracking down professional computer fraudsters or getting involved in white-collar crime. The second reason is that hackers are beginning to realize that one of the areas where they can occasion real harm is in publicizing their feats. So the signs are, for the moment, that there will be less about hacking in the press for the next few years. It will be going on though; the challenges continue to beckon.

I am not certain how many more hacking prosecutions we will see; some victims certainly want to fight back, but the results from going to law are uncertain. As we saw right at the beginning, hacking itself is not a crime and the would-be prosecutor must find a crime to fit the particular circumstances of an event. In the UK, this is not easy.

What in fact is needed are new laws to cover computer-related crimes, as they actually occur and commensurate with the incidence of harm. Their object would be fraudsters, industrial spies and vandals rather than hackers. It seems to me that the emphasis purely on unauthorized access to a computer system or on technical thefts of electricity or CPU time misses the target. The West Germans in their law of 1986 appear to be along the right lines: there are three related offences: altering a computer record or program in order to gain a dishonest advantage for oneself or a third party, deleting or manipulating a computer record in order to cause harm to a computer or its owners, making unauthorized access to a computer for the purpose of acquiring commercial secrets. This would leave hackers, in the sense in which this book describes them, as occasional and very minor law-breakers.

For those computer operators who feel they must keep their machines completely secure, the news is that the task is in their own hands: and it demands a great deal less esoteric technology than is often thought; you can keep most hackers out simply by using properly the facilities you already have. If hackers can penetrate from outside, the conclusion must be accepted that your employees can wander where they shouldn't from inside.

But I also believe that it is about time that someone stood up to assert the benefits of hacking. Clearly such an argument can only be pushed so far and that all it can do is counterbalance the stories of juvenile behaviour shading into vandalism. At the beginning of this book I described hacking as an educational and recreational sport. The educational part should not be underestimated. Some of the most outstanding steps in the recent history of computing have emerged, not from the giant commercial firms or the large university-based research institutes. They came from maverick individuals, misfits and rebels. The desktop personal computer is the best example of this. It is important that such people are given the freedom to develop their ideas.

Again: the successive revolutions in the technologies of computer hardware and software are taking place at too great a rate for the conventional education process to cope. By the time the advisors and syllabus-writers have prepared for one development, the industry has moved further ahead. This means that individual computer enthusiasts have to be prepared for a considerable amount of self-training. Hacking, visiting advanced computers as a polite country rambler might walk across picturesque fields (to revert to my earlier analogy), is one pleasant way of keeping up with new developments.

Appendix I   Trouble Shooting

The assumption is that you are operating in the default mode of
300/300 bits/s asynchronous using CCITT tones, 7 bits, even
parity, one stop bit, full-duplex/echo off, originate. You have
dialled the remote number, seized the line and can hear a data
tone. Something is not working properly. This is a partial list of
possibilities.

The screen remains blank
- A physical link has failed. Check the cables between computer,
  modem and phone line.
- The remote modem needs waking up. Send a $\langle cr \rangle$ or failing
  that, a ENQ ($\langle ctrl \rangle$ E), character.
- The remote modem is operating at a different speed. Some
  modems can be brought up to speed by hitting successive
  $\langle cr \rangle$s; they usually begin at 110 bits/s and then go to 300, so
  two successive $\langle cr \rangle$s should do the trick.
- The remote modem is not working at V21 standards, either
  because it is a different CCITT standard, e.g. V.22, V.22 bis,
  V.23 etc., or operates on Bell (US) tones. Since different
  standards tend to have different 'wake-up' tones which are
  easily recognized with practice, you may be able to spot what
  is happening. It shouldn't need to be said that if you are calling
  a North American service you should assume Bell tones.
- Both your modem and that of the remote service are in answer
  or in originate and so cannot 'speak' to each other. Always
  assume you are in the originate mode.
- The remote service is not using ASCII/International Alphabet
  No. 5.

The screen fills with random characters
- Data format different from your defaults. Check 7- or 8-bit
  characters, even/odd parity, stop and start bits.
- Mismatch of characters owing to misdefined protocol. Check
  start/stop, try alternately EOB/ACK and XON/XOF.

- Remote computer operating at a different speed from you. Try, in order, 110, 300, 600, 1200, 75.
- Poor physical connection. If using an acoustic coupler check location of handset, if not, listen on line to see if it is noisy or crossed.
- The remote service is not using ASCII/International Alphabet No. 5.

Every character appears twice
- You are actually in half-duplex mode and the remote computer as well as your own are both sending characters to your screen. Switch to full-duplex/echo off.

All information appears on only one line, which is constantly overwritten
- The remote service is not sending carriage returns. If your terminal software has the facility, enable it to induce carriage returns when each display line is filled. Many on-line services and public dial-up ports let you configure the remote port to send carriage returns and vary line length. Your software may have a facility to show control characters, in which case you will see ⟨ ctrl ⟩ J if the remote service is sending carriage returns.

Wide spaces appear between display lines
- The remote service is sending carriage returns and your software is inducing another one simultaneously. Turn off your induced carriage return facility. In 'show control character' mode, you will see ⟨ ctrl ⟩ Js.

Display lines are broken awkwardly
- The remote service is expecting your screen to support more characters than it is able. Professional services tend to expect 80 characters across whilst many personal computers may have less than 40, so that they can be read on a TV screen. Check if your software can help, but you may have to live with it. Alternatively, the remote computer may let you reconfigure its character stream.

Most of the display makes sense, but every so often it becomes garbled
- You have intermittent line noise. Check if you can command the remote computer to send the same stream again and see if you get the garbling.

- The remote service is sending graphics instructions which your computer and software can't resolve.

The display contains recognizable characters in definite groupings, but otherwise makes no sense
- The data is intended for an intelligent terminal which will combine the transmitted data with a local program so that it makes sense.
- The data is intended for batch processing.
- The data is encrypted.

Although the stream of data appeared properly on my VDU, when I try to print it out, I get corruption and over-printing
- Most printers use a series of special control characters to enable various functions – line feeds, back-space, double-intensity, special graphics, etc. The remote service is sending a series of control characters which, though not displayed on your screen, are 'recognized' by your printer, though often in not very helpful ways. You may be able to correct the worst problems in software, e.g. by enabling line-feeds; alternatively many printers can be re-configured in hardware by appropriate settings of DIL switches internally.

When accessing a videotex service, the screen fills with squares
The square is the standard display default if your videotex terminal can't make sense of the data being sent to it. There could be several reasons:
- Check physical connections and listen for line noise.
- The videotex host does not work to UK videotex standards. French videotex uses parallel attributes and has a number of extra features. The CEPT standard for Europe contains features from both the UK and French systems and you may be able to recognize some of the display. North American videotex is alpha-geometric and sends line drawing instructions rather than characters.
- The videotex host has enhanced graphics features, perhaps for dynamically redefined character sets, alphageometric instructions, or alpha-photographic (full resolution) pictures. If the host has some UK standard-compatible features, you will be able to read them normally. If the cursor jumps about the screen, the host has dynamic graphics facilities. If the videotex protocol is anything at all like the UK standard, you

should see regular clear-screens as each new page comes up; however, advanced graphics features tend to work by suppressing clear-screens.

- The service you have dialled is not using videotex. PSS is accessible at 75/1200 as are one or two direct-dial services. In this case you should be seeing a conventional display or trying one of the other suggestions in this appendix. It is usual to assume that any subscriber dialling into a 75/1200 port has only a forty-character display.

I can't see what I am typing
- The remote computer is not echoing back to you. Switch to half-duplex. If the remote computer's messages now appear doubled; that would be unusual but not unique. You will have to toggle back to full-duplex for receive.

Data seems to come from the remote computer in jerky bursts rather than as a smooth stream
- If you are using PSS or a similar packet-switched service and it is near peak business hours either in your time zone or in that of the host you are accessing, the effect is due to heavy packet traffic. There is nothing you can do. Do not send extra commands to 'speed things up' as those commands will arrive at the host eventually and cause unexpected results.
- The host is pausing for a EOB/ACK or XON/XOF message. Check your protocol settings; try sending ⟨ctrl⟩Q or ⟨ctrl⟩F.

I am trying to download a file via a packet-switch service and am using a file tranfer protocol like Xmodem. It isn't working
- After each block is sent, the receiving computer has to send either an ACK or NAK character back to the transmitting computer to tell it what to do next. Packet switching itself, however, consists of bursts of blocks of data which, at peak times, may come unevenly over the link. If the host fails to get your ACKs or NAKs, or, if these characters get out of step with the Xmodem blocks they are supposed to relate to, the file protocol will fall over. The only thing you can do is to try later, when the PSS network is less congested.

I have an apparently valid password but it is not accepted
- You don't have a valid password, or you don't have all of it.

- The password has hidden control characters which don't display on the screen. Watch out for ⟨ctrl⟩ H – the back-space – which will overwrite an existing displayed character.
- The password contains characters which your computer doesn't normally generate. Check your terminal software and see if there is a way of sending them.

Most of the time everything works smoothly, but I can't get past certain prompts
- The remote service is looking for characters your computer doesn't normally generate. Check your terminal software and see if there is a way of sending them.

A list or file called up turns out to be boring – can I stop it?
- Try sending ⟨ctrl⟩ S; this may simply make the remote machine pause, until a ⟨ctrl Q is sent, and you may find the list resumes where it left off. On the other hand it may take you on to a menu.
- Send a BREAK signal (⟨ctrl⟩ 1). If one BREAK doesn't work, send another in quick succession

I wish to get into the operating system from an applications program
Don't we all? There is no standard way of doing this and indeed it might be almost impossible because the operating system can only be addressed by a few privileged terminals, of which yours (and its associated password) is not one. However, you could try the following:
- Immediately after signing on, send two BREAKs (⟨ctrl⟩ 1).
- Immediately after signing on, try combinations of ESC, CTRL and SHIFT. As a desperate measure, send two carriage returns before signing on – this has been known to work!
- At an options page, try requesting SYSTEM or some obvious contraction like SYS or X. If in the Basic language, depending on the dialect, SYSTEM or X in immediate mode should get you the operating system.

I am trying to capture data traffic from a short-wave radio and am having little success
- Your computer could be emitting so much radio noise itself that any signal you are attempting to hear is squashed. To test: tune your radio to a fairly quiet short-wave broadcast and then

experiment listening to the background hash with the computer switched first on, then off. If the noise level drops when you turn off the computer, then you need to arrange for more RF suppression and to move the computer and radio further apart. Another source of RF noise is the sync scan in a TV tube.

- If you can hear the two-tones of RTTY traffic but can't get letters resolved, check that your terminal unit is locking on to the signal (often indicated by LEDs). You should then at least get some response on your screen, if it doesn't make immediate sense.

- Once you have letters on screen, try altering the speed at which you are receiving (see Chapter 10); check also that you are reading in the right 'sense', i.e. that mark and space have not been reversed.

- In addition to signals sent with the conventional International Telegraphic Code No. 2 (Baudot), variants exist for foreign letter sets, like Cyrillic, which your software may not be able to resolve.

- There are other data-type services which sound a little like RTTY, but are not: they include FAX (facsimile) hellschreiber (a form of remote dot-matrix printing), SITOR (see Chapter 9) and special military/diplomatic systems like piccolo.

Appendix II   Eclectic Glossary

This glossary collects together the sort of name, word, abbreviation or phrase you could come across during your network adventures and for which you may not be able to find a precise meaning.

ACK   non-printing character used in some comms protocols to indicate that a block has been received and that more can be sent; used in association with EOB.

ANSI   American National Standards Institute – one of a number of standards organizations.

Answer mode   When a modem is set up to receive calls – the usual mode for a host. The user's computer will be in originate.

ARQ   Automatic repeat request – a method of error correction.

ASCII   American Standard Code for Information Interchange – alternate name for International Telegraph Alphabet No. 5, a 7-bit code to symbolize common characters and comms instructions, usually transmitted as 8-bit code to include a parity bit.

ASR   Automatic send receive – any keyboard terminal capable of generating a message into off-line storage for later transmission; includes paper-tape telex machines as well as microcomputers.

Asynchronous   Description of communications which rely on 'start' and 'stop' bits to synchronize originator and receiver of data – hence asynchronous protocols, channels, modems, terminals, etc.

Backward channel   Supervisory channel, not used as main channel of communication; in viewdata the 75 baud back from the user to the host.

Baseband   Modulation is direct on the comms line rather than using audio or radio frequencies. Used in some local area networks. A baseband or 'short-haul' modem can be used to link computers in adjacent offices, but not over telephone lines.

Baud   Measure of the signalling rate on a data channel, number of signalling elements per second; not the same as bits/sec.

Baudot   5-bit data code used in telegraphy, telex and RTTY;

also known as International Telegraph Alphabet No. 2.

Bell   (1) Non-printing character which sounds a bell or bleep, usually enabled by   ctrl   G.   (2) Common name for US phone company and, in this context, specifiers for a number of data standards and services, e.g. Bell 103a, 202a, 212a, etc. – see Appendix V.

Bit   Binary digit – value 0 or 1.

Bits/s   Bits per second – rate at which information is passed along a data channel; not the same as baud rate (q.v.).

Bisynchronous   IBM protocol involving synchronous transmission of binary coded data.

BLAISE   British Library Automated Information Service – substantial bibliographic on-line host.

BREAK   Non-printing character used in some data transmission protocols and found on some terminals; can sometimes be regenerated by using ⟨ctrl⟩1.

Broadband   Broadband data channels have a wider bandwidth than ordinary telephone circuits – twelve times in fact, to give a bandwidth of 48 kHz, over which many simultaneous high-speed data transfers can take place.

Broadcast service   Data service in which all users receive the same information simultaneously, without the opportunity to interrogate or query; e.g. news services like AP, Reuters News, UPI etc. Compare on-line services.

BSC   Binary synchronous communications – see bi-synchronous.

Byte   Group of bits (8) representing one data character.

Call accept   In packet-switching, the packet that confirms that the party is willing to proceed with the call.

Call redirection   In packet-switching, allows call to be automatically redirected from original address to another, nominated, address.

Call request   In packet-switching, packet sent to initiate a datacall.

CCITT   Comité Consultatif International Téléphonique et Télégraphique – committee of International Telecommunications Union which sets international comms standards. Only the USA fails to follow its recommendations in terms of modem tones, preferring 'Bell' tones. The CCITT also sets such standards as V.21, 24, X.25, etc.

CEPT   European communications standards organization. CEPT produces a number of standards, some of which are actually followed on a Europe-wide basis. The most important, as far as computer communications is concerned, is the CEPT videotex standard which reconciles the differences between UK and French basic protocols.

Character terminal In packet-switching, a terminal which can only access via a PAD.

Cluster When two or more terminals are connected to a data channel at a single point.

Common carrier A telecommunications resource providing facilities to the public.

Connect-time Length of time connected to a remote computer, often the measure of payment, contrast with CPU time or CPU units, which measures how much 'effort' the host put into the communication.

CPS Characters per second.

CPU Time In an on-line session, the amount of time the central processor actually spends on the interaction process, as opposed to connect-time; either can be used as the basis of tariffing.

CRC Cyclic redundancy check – error detection method.

CUG Closed user group – group of users/terminals who enjoy privacy with respect to a public service.

Datacall In packet-switching, an ordinary call, sometimes called a 'switched virtual call'.

Dataline In packet-switching, dedicated line between customer's terminal and packet-switch exchange (PSE).

Datel BT's name for its data services, covering both the equipment and the type of line, e.g. Datel 100 corresponds to telegraph circuits, Datel 200 is the usual 300/300 asynchronous service, Datel 400 is for one-way transmissions, e.g. monitoring of remote sites, Datel 600 is a two- or four-wire asynchronous service at up to 1200 baud, Datel 2400 typically uses a four-wire private circuit at 2400 baud synchronous, etc.

DCE Data circuit-terminating equipment – officialese for modems.

DES Data Encryption Standard – a US-approved method of encrypting data traffic, and somewhat controversial in its effectiveness.

Dialog Well-established on-line host available worldwide, covering an extensive range of scientific, bibliographic and news services. Also known as Lockheed Dialog.

Dial-up Call initiated via PTSN, no matter where it goes after that; as opposed to service available via permanent leased line.

DTE Data terminal equipment – officialese for computers.

Duplex Transmission in two directions simultaneously, sometimes called full-duplex; contrast half-duplex, in which alternate transmissions by either end are required. (NB this is terminology used in data communications over land-lines. Just to confuse matters radio technology refers to simplex, when only one party can transmit at a time and a single radio frequency is used, two-frequency-simplex or half-duplex when only one party can speak but two frequencies are used, as in repeater and remote base working, and full-duplex, when both parties can speak simultaneously and two radio frequencies are used, as in radio-telephones.)

EBCDIC Extended Binary Coded Decimal Interchange Code – IBM's alternative to ASCII, based on an 8-bit code, usually transmitted synchronously. 256 characters are available.

Echo (1) When a remote computer sends back to the terminal each letter as it is sent to it for confirming re-display locally. (2) Effect on long comms lines caused by successive amplifications. Echo-suppressors are introduced to prevent disturbance caused by this phenomenon, but in some data transmission the echo-suppressors must be switched off.

EIA Electronic Industries Association, US standards body.

Emulator Software/hardware set-up which makes one device mimic another, e.g. a personal computer may emulate an industry-standard intelligent terminal like the VT100. Compare with simulator which gives a device the attributes of another, but not necessarily in real time, e.g. when a large mini carries a program making it simulate another computer to develop software.

ENQ Non-printing character signifying 'who are you?' and often sent by hosts as they are dialled up. When the user's terminal receives ENQ it may be programmed to send out a password automatically. Corresponds to $\langle$esc$\rangle$ E.

EOB End of block – non-printing character used in some protocols, usually in association with ACK.

EPAD Variant on PSS PAD which gives error correction facilities between PAD and user's (character) terminal – see Chapter 7.

Equalization Method of compensation for distortion over long comms channels.

Euronet-Diane European direct access information network.

FDM Frequency division multiplexing – a wide-bandwidth transmission medium, e.g. coaxial cable, which supports several narrow bandwidth channels by differentiating by frequency. Compare with time division multiplexing.

FSK Frequency shift keying – a simple signalling method in which frequencies but not phase or amplitude are varied according to whether '1' or '0' is sent. Used in low-speed asynchronous comms both over land line and by radio.

Gateway Link between one large computer system and another; the usual arrangement is that the customer enters the first computer in the normal way and, when it is desired to obtain information or use a service available on the second, the first computer provides a supervised means of entry into the second. Most large mature videotex systems have their more sophisticated services available via gateways; many electronic mail services offer gateway links to online databases and travel ticket order computers.

Handshaking Hardware and software rules for remote devices to communicate with each other, supervisory signals such as 'wait', 'acknowledge', 'transmit', 'ready to receive', etc.

Hayes Protocols Set of de facto standard commands for intelligent modems often used by software packages.

HDLC In packet-switching, high level data link control procedure, an international standard which detects and corrects errors in the stream of data between the terminal and the exchange – and to provide flow control.

Host The 'big' computer holding the information the user wishes to retrieve.

Infoline Scientific on-line service from Pergamon.

ISB *See* sideband.

ISO International Standards Organization.

Kermit Error correction protocol widely installed on a large number of mainframes, minis and micros.

KSR Keyboard send receive – terminal with keyboard on which anything that is typed is immediately sent, no off-line preparation facility, e.g. teletypewriter, 'dumb' terminals.

LAN Local area network – normally using coaxial cable, this form of network operates at high speed over an office or works site, but no further. It may have inter-connect facility to PTSN or PSS.

LF Line feed – cursor moves active position down one line. Usual code is ⟨ctrl⟩ J; not the same as carriage return which merely sends cursor to left-hand side of line it already occupies. However in many protocols/terminals/set-ups, hitting the

⟨ret⟩ or ⟨enter⟩ button means both ⟨lf⟩ and ⟨cr⟩.

Logical channel Apparently continuous path from one terminal to another.

LSB *See* sideband.

Macro Software facility frequently found in comms programs which permits the preparation and sending of commonly used strings of information, particularly passwords and routing instructions.

Mark One of the two conditions on a data communications line, the other being 'space'; mark indicates idle and is used as a stop bit.

Message switching When a complete message is stored and then forwarded, as opposed to a packet of information. This technique is used in some electronic mail services, but not for general data transmission.

Modem Modulator–demodulator.

Multiplexer Device which divides a data channel into two or more independent channels.

Multistream BT variant on PSS to make it more user-friendly; includes EPAD and VPAD (q.v.).

MVS Multiple virtual storage – IBM operating system dating from the mid-70s.

NUA Network user address, number by which each terminal on a packet-switch network is identified (character terminals don't have them individually, because they use a PAD). In PSS, it's a twelve-digit number.

NUI Network user identity, used in PSS for dial-up access by each user.

Octet In packet-switching, eight consecutive bits of user a data, e.g. one character.

On-line service Interrogative or query service available for dial-up, examples include Lockheed Dialog, Blaise, Dow Jones News Retrieval, etc. Leased-line examples include Reuters Monitor, Telerate.

Originate mode Setting for a modem operated by a user about to call another computer.

OSI Open Systems Interconnect – intended world standard for digital network connections. Compare with SNA.

Packet-switching See Chapter 7.

Packet terminal Terminal capable of creating and disassembling packets, interacting with a packet-network. Compare with character terminal.

PAD   Packet assembly/disassembly device – permits 'ordinary' terminals to connect to packet switch services by providing addressing, headers (and removal), protocol conversion, etc.

Parity checking   Technique of error correction in which one bit is added to each data character so that the number of bits is always even (or always odd).

PDP 8 & 11   Large family of minis, commercially very successful, made by DEC. The PDP 8 was 12-bit, the PDP 11 is 16-bit. The LSI 11 have strong family connections to the PDP 11, as have some configurations of the desktop Rainbow.

Polling   Method of controlling terminals on a clustered data network where each is called in turn by the computer to see if it wishes to transmit or receive.

Protocol   Agreed set of rules.

PSE   Packet-switch exchange – enables packet-switching in a network.

PSTN   Public switched telephone network – the voice-grade telephone network dialled from a phone. Contrast with leased lines, digital networks, conditioned lines, etc.

PTT   Common term for the publicly owned telecommunications authority/utility.

PVC   Permanent virtual circuit – a connection in packet switching which is always open; no set-up required.

Redundancy checking   Method of error correction.

RS232C   EIA RS232C is the list of definitions for interchange circuit: the US term for CCITT V.24. See Appendix III.

RSX-11   Popular operating system for PDP/11 family.

RTTY   Radio teletype – method of sending telegraphy over radio waves.

RUBOUT   Back-space deleting character, using ⟨ctrl⟩ H.

Secondary channel   Data channel, usually used for supervision, using same physical path as main channel; in V.23 which is usually 600 or 1200 baud half-duplex, 75 baud traffic is supervisory but in viewdata is the channel back from the user to the host, thus giving low-cost full duplex.

Segment   Chargeable unit of volume on PSS.

Serial   Transmission one bit at a time, using a single pair of wires, as opposed to parallel transmission, in which several bits are sent simultaneously over a ribbon cable. A serial interface often uses many more than two wires between computer and modem or computer and printer, but only two wires carry the data traffic, the remainder being used for supervision, electrical power and earthing, or not at all.

Sideband   In radio the technique of suppressing the main carrier and limiting the transmission to the information-bearing sideband. To listen at the receiver, the carrier is re-created locally. The technique, which produces large economies in channel occupancy, is extensively used in professional, non-broadcast applications. The full name is *single sideband, suppressed carrier*. Each full carrier supports two sidebands, an *upper* and *lower*, USB and LSB respectively; in general, USB is used for speech, LSB for data, but this is only a convention – amateurs used LSB for speech below 10 MHz, for example. ISB, independent sideband, is when the one carrier supports two sidebands with separate information on them, usually speech on one and data on the other. If you listen to radio teletype on the 'wrong' sideband, 'mark' and 'space' values become reversed with a consequent loss of meaning.

SITOR   Error-correction protocol for sending data over a radio-path using frequent checks and acknowledgements. Used in the maritime service. The amateur equivalent is called AMTOR.

SNA   System Network Architecture – IBM proprietary networking protocol, the rival to OSI.

Space   One of two binary conditions in a data transmission channel, the other being 'mark'. Space is binary 0.

Spooling   Simultaneous peripheral operation on-line. More usually, the ability, while accessing a database, to store all fetched information in a local memory buffer, from which it may be recalled for later examination, or dumped to disc or printer.

Start/Stop   Asynchronous transmission; the 'start' and 'stop' bits bracket each data character.

Statistical multiplexer   A statmux is an advanced multiplexer which divides one physical link between several data channels, taking advantage of the fact that not all channels bear equal traffic loads.

STX   Start Text – non-printing character used in some protocols.

SVC   Switched virtual circuit; in packet switching, when connection between two computers or computer and terminal must be set up by a specific call.

SYN   Non-printing character often used in synchronous transmission to tell a remote device to start its local timing mechanism.

Synchronous   Data transmission in which timing information is superimposed on pure data. Under this method 'start/stop' techniques are not used and data exchange is more efficient, hence synchronous channel, modem, terminal, protocol, etc.

TDM Time division multiplexer, technique for sharing several data channels along one high-grade physical link. Not as efficient as statistical techniques.

Telenet US packet-switch common carrier.

Teletex High-speed replacement for telex, 2400 baud, as yet to find much commercial support.

Teletext Use of vertical blanking interval in broadcast television to transmit magazines of text information, e.g. BBC's Ceefax and IBA's Oracle.

Telex Public switched low-speed telegraph network.

Tempest Set of standards to reduce the opportunities of electronmagnetic eavesdropping on to VDUs, printers, etc. See Chapter 6.

TOPIC The Stock Exchange's market price display service; it comes down a leased line and has some of the qualities of both viewdata and teletext.

TOPS Operating system founds on DEC mainframes like the DEC-10 and -20.

Tymnet US packet-switch common carrier.

V-standards Set of recommendations by CCITT. See Appendix III.

VAX Super-mini family made by DEC; often uses VMS or Unix operating systems.

Videotex Technology allowing large numbers of users to access data easily on terminal based (originally) on modified TV sets. Information is presented in 'page' format rather than on a scrolling screen and the user issues all commands on a numbers-only keypad. Various standards exist of which the UK one is so far dominant; other include the European CEPT standard which is similar to the UK one, a French version and the US Presentation Level Protocol. Transmission speeds are usually 1200 baud from the host and 75 baud from the user. Previously referred to in the UK as *viewdata*.

Virtual In the present context, a virtual drive, store, machine, etc. is one which appears to the user to exist, but is merely an illusion generated on a computer; thus several users of IBM's VM operating system each think they have an entire separate computer, complete with drives, discs and other peripherals – in fact the one actual machine can support several lower-level operating systems simultaneously.

VPAD Variant on PSS PAD which allows videotex terminals to operate with full support. Part of BT's Multistream.

VT52/100 Industry-standard general purpose computer terminals with no storage capacity or processing power but with the ability to be locally programmed to accept a variety of asynchronous transmission protocols; manufactured by DEC. The series has developed since the VT100.

X standards Set of recommendations by CCITT. See Appendix III.

XON/XOF Pair of non-printing characters sometimes used in protocols to tell devices when to start or stop sending. XON often corresponds to ⟨ctrl⟩ Q and XOF TO ⟨ctrl⟩ S.

3101 IBM intelligent display terminal. Emulation sometimes included on asynchronous comms packages; has limited windowing capacity.

3270 IBM interactive bisynchronous terminal usually sitting direct on mainframes or connected via cluster controllers.

80–80 Type of circuit used for telex and telegraphy. Mark and space are indicated by conditions of – or + 80 volts. Also known in the UK as Tariff J. Usual telex speed is 50 baud, private wire telegraphy (news agencies, etc.) 75 baud.

Appendix III   Selected CCITT Recommendations

V series: Data Transmission over Telephone Circuits

V.1	Power levels for data transmission over telephone lines
V.3	International Alphabet No. 5 (ASCII)
V.4	General structure of signals of IA5 code for data transmission over public telephone network
V.5	Standardization of modulation rates and data signalling rates for synchronous transmission in general switched network
V.6	Ditto, on leased circuits
V.13	Answerback simulator
V.15	Use of acoustic coupling for data transmission
V.19	Modems for parallel data transmission using telephone signalling frequencies
V.20	Parallel data transmission modems standardized for universal use in the general switched telephone network
V.21	200 bits/s modem standardized
V.22	1200 bits/s full-duplex 2-wire modem for PTSN
V.22 bis	2400 bits/s full-duplex 2-wire modem for PTSN
V.23	600/1200 bits/s modem for PTSN
V.24	List of definitions for interchange circuits between data terminal equipment and data circuit-terminating equipment
V.25	Automatic calling and/or answering equipment on PTSN
V.26	2400 bits/s modem on 4-wire circuit
V.26 bis	2400/1200 bits/s modem for PTSN
V.27	4800 bits/s modem for leased circuits
V.27 bis	4800 bits/s modem (equalised) for leased circuits
V.27 ter	4800 bits/s modem for PTSN

V.29   9600 bits/s modem for leased circuits
V.35   Data transmission at 48 kbits/s using 60–108 kHz
        band circuits

X series: Recommendations Covering Data Networks
X.1   International user classes of services in public data
        networks
X.2   International user facilities in public data networks
X.3   Packet assembly/disassembly facility (PAD)
X.4   General structure of signals of IA5 code for
        transmission over public data networks
X.20   Interface between data terminal equipment and data
        circuit-terminating equipment for start-stop
        transmission services on public data networks
X.20   V.21-compatible interface
bis
X.21   Interface for synchronous operation
X.25   Interface between data terminal equipment and data
        circuit-terminating equipment for terminals
        operating in the packet-switch mode on public data
        networks
X.28   DTE/DCE interface for start/stop mode terminal
        equipment accessing a PAD on a public data
        network
X.29   Procedures for exchange of control information and
        user data between a packet mode DTE and a PAD
X.95   Network parameters in public data networks
X.96   Call progress signals in public data networks
X.121   International addressing scheme for PDNs
X.400   Standards for electronic mail, covering addressing and
        presentation

Appendix IV   Computer Alphabets

Four alphabets are in common use for computer communications: ASCII, also known as International Telegraphic Alphabet No 5; Baudot, used in telex and also known as International Telegraphic Alphabet No. 2; UK Standard videotex, a variant of ASCII; and EDCDIC, used by IBM.

ASCII
This is the standard, fully implemented character set. There are a number of national variants: # in the US variant is £ in the UK variant. Many micro keyboards cannot generate all the characters directly, particularly the non-printing characters used for control of transmission, effectors of format and information separators. The 'keyboard' column gives the usual method of providing them, but you should check the firmware/software manuals for your particular set-up. You should also know that many of the 'spare' control characters are often used to enable special features on printers. The IBM PC and its clones use ASCII, not EBCDIC; they display 'non-printing' characters as graphics so you can view the full 256-character set.

HEX	DEC	ASCII	Name	Keyboard	Notes
00	0	NUL	Null	ctrl @	
01	1	SOH	Start heading	ctrl A	
02	2	STX	Start text	ctrl B	
03	3	ETX	End text	ctrl C	
04	4	EOT	End transmission	ctrl D	
05	5	ENQ	Enquire	ctrl E	
06	6	ACK	Acknowledge	ctrl F	
07	7	BEL	Bell	ctrl G	
08	8	BS	Backspace	ctrl H	or special key
09	9	HT	Horizontal tab	ctrl I	or special key
0A	10	LF	Line feed	ctrl J	
0B	11	VT	Vertical tab	ctrl K	
0C	12	FF	Form feed	ctrl L	
0D	13	CR	Carriage return	ctrl M	or special key
0E	14	SO	Shift out	ctrl N	
0F	15	SI	Shift in	ctrl O	

10	16	DLE	Data link escape	ctrl P	
11	17	DC1	Device control 1	ctrl Q	also XON
12	18	DC2	Device control 2	ctrl R	
13	19	DC3	Device control 3	ctrl S	also XOF
14	20	DC4	Device control 4	ctrl T	
15	21	NAK	Negative acknowledge	ctrl U	
16	22	SYN	Synchronous Idle	ctrl V	
17	23	ETB	End trans. block	ctrl W	
18	24	CAN	Cancel	ctrl X	
19	25	EM	End medium	ctrl Y	
1A	26	SS	Special sequence	ctrl Z	spare
1B	27	ESC	Escape	check manuals to transmit	
1C	28	FS	File separator		
1D	29	GS	Group separator		
1E	30	RS	Record separator		
1F	31	US	Unit separator		
20	32	SP	Space		
21	33	!			
22	34	"			
23	35	#			£
24	36	$			
25	37	%			
26	38	&			
27	39	'	Apostrophe		
28	40	(			
29	41	)			
2A	42	*			
2B	43	+			
2C	44	,	Comma		
2D	45	–			
2E	46	.	Period		
2F	47	/	Slash		
30	48	0			
31	49	1			
32	50	2			
33	51	3			
34	52	4			
35	53	5			
36	54	6			
37	55	7			
38	56	8			
39	57	9			
3A	58	:	Colon		
3B	59	;	Semi-colon		
3C	60	<			
3D	61	=			
3E	62	>			
3F	63	?			
40	64	@			
41	65	A			
42	66	B			

43	67	C	
44	68	D	
45	69	E	
46	70	F	
47	71	G	
48	72	H	
49	73	I	
4A	74	J	
4B	75	K	
4C	76	L	
4D	77	M	
4E	78	N	
4F	79	O	
50	80	P	
51	81	Q	
52	82	R	
53	83	S	
54	84	T	
55	85	U	
56	86	V	
57	87	W	
58	88	X	
59	89	Y	
5A	90	Z	
5B	91	[	
5C	92	\	Backslash
5D	93	]	
5E	94	^	Circumflex
5F	95	_	Underscore
60	96	`	Grave accent
61	97	a	
62	98	b	
63	99	c	
64	100	d	
65	101	e	
66	102	f	
67	103	g	
68	104	h	
69	105	i	
6A	106	j	
6B	107	k	
6C	108	l	
6D	109	m	
6E	110	n	
6F	111	o	
70	112	p	
71	113	q	
72	114	r	
73	115	s	
74	116	t	
75	117	u	

76	118	v	
77	119	w	
78	120	x	
79	121	y	
7A	122	z	
7B	123 {		
7C	124			
7D	125 }		
7E	126 –		Tilde
7F	127	DEL	Delete

Baudot

This is the telex/telegraphy code known to the CCITT as International Alphabet No. 2. It is essentially a 5-bit code, bracketed by a start bit (space) and a stop bit (mark). Idling is shown by 'mark'. The code only supports capital letters, figures and two 'supervisory' codes: 'Bell' to warn the operator at the far end and 'WRU' – 'Who are you?' to interrogate the far end. 'Figures' changes all characters received after to their alternates, and 'Letters' switches back.

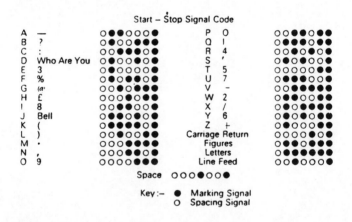

Videotext

This is the character set used by the UK system, which is the most widely used, worldwide. The character-set has many features in common with ASCII but also departs from it in significant ways, notably to provide various forms of graphics, colour controls, screen-clear (⟨ ctrl ⟩ L), etc. The set is shared with teletext which in itself requires further special codes, e.g. to enable subtitling to broadcast television, newsflash, etc. If you are using proper viewdata software, then everything will display properly; if you are using a conventional terminal emulator then the result may look confusing.

Each character consists of 10 bits:

Start	binary 0
7 bits of character code	
Parity bit	even
Stop	binary 1

ENQ ($\langle$ Ctrl $\rangle$ E) is sent by the host on log-on to initiate the auto-log-on from the user's terminal. If no response is obtained, the user is requested to input the password manually.

Each new page sequence opens with a 'clear screen' instruction ($\langle$ Ctrl $\rangle$ L, CHR$12) followed by a 'home' ($\langle$ Ctrl $\rangle$ M, CHR$14).

Some viewdata services are also available via standard asynchronous 300/300 ports (Prestel is, for example); in these cases, the graphics characters are stripped out and replaced by ****s; and the pages will scroll up the screen rather than present themselves in the frame-by-frame format.

If you wish to edit to a viewdata system using a normal keyboard, or view a viewdata stream as it comes from a host using 'control–show' facilities, the table below gives the usual equivalents. The normal default at the left-hand side of each line is alphanumerics white. Each subsequent 'attribute', i.e. if you wish to change to colour, or a variety of graphics, occupies a character space. Routing commands and signals to start and end edit depend on the software installed on the viewdata host computer: in Prestel compatible systems, the edit page is *910#, options must be entered in lower case letters and end edit is called by $\langle$ esc $\rangle$ K.

$\langle$ esc $\rangle$ A	alpha red	$\langle$ esc $\rangle$ Q	graphics red
$\langle$ esc $\rangle$ B	alpha green	$\langle$ esc $\rangle$ R	graphics green
$\langle$ esc $\rangle$ C	alpha yellow	$\langle$ esc $\rangle$ S	graphics yellow
$\langle$ esc $\rangle$ D	alpha blue	$\langle$ esc $\rangle$ T	graphics blue
$\langle$ esc $\rangle$ E	alpha magenta	$\langle$ esc $\rangle$ U	graphics magenta
$\langle$ esc $\rangle$ F	alpha cyan	$\langle$ esc $\rangle$ V	graphics cyan
$\langle$ esc $\rangle$ G	alpha white	$\langle$ esc $\rangle$ W	graphics white
$\langle$ esc $\rangle$ H	flash	$\langle$ esc $\rangle$ I	steady
$\langle$ esc $\rangle$ L	normal height	$\langle$ esc $\rangle$ M	double height

PRESTEL TRANSMISSION CODES

ROW	BITS (b4 b3 b2 b1)	Col 0	Col 1	Col 2	Col 3	Col 3b	Col 4	Col 4b	Col 5	Col 5L	Col 6	Col 7
0	0000	NUL		SP	0		@		P		—	p
1	0001		CURSOR ON	!	1	ALT VERIFY MODE (1)	A	ALPHANUMERIC RED	Q	MOSAIC RED	a	q
2	0010			"	2	ALT VERIFY MODE (2)	b	ALPHANUMERIC GREEN	R	MOSAIC GREEN	b	r
3	0011			#	3	SKIP BLOCK	C	ALPHANUMERIC YELLOW	S	MOSAIC YELLOW	c	s
4	0100		CURSOR OFF	$	4	ALT PROGRAMME MODE	D	ALPHANUMERIC BLUE	T	MOSAIC BLUE	d	t
5	0101	LINQ		%	5		E	ALPHANUMERIC MAGENTA	U	MOSAIC MAGENTA	e	u
6	0110			&	6		F	ALPHANUMERIC CYAN	V	MOSAIC CYAN	f	v
7	0111			'	7		G	ALPHANUMERIC WHITE	W	MOSAIC WHITE	g	w
8	1000	ACTIVE POSITION BACKWARD (APB)		(	8		H	FLASH	X	CONCEAL DISPLAY	h	x
9	1001	ACTIVE POSITION FORWARD (APF)		)	9		I	STEADY	Y	CONTIGUOUS MOSAICS	i	y
10	1010	ACTIVE POSITION DOWN (APD)		*	:		J		Z	SEPARATED MOSAICS	j	z
11	1011	ACTIVE POSITION UP (APU)	ESC	+	;		K				k	
12	1100	CLEAR SCREEN (CS)		,	<		L	NORMAL HEIGHT		BLACK BACKGROUND	l	
13	1101	ACTIVE POSITION RETURN (APR)		-	=		M	DOUBLE HEIGHT		NEW BACKGROUND	m	
14	1110		ACTIVE POSITION HOME (APH)	.	>		N			HOLD MOSAICS	n	
15	1111			/	?		O		#	RELEASE MOSAICS	o	

NOTE:

COLUMNS 0 AND 1 FORM THE CO CONTROL CHARACTER SET

COLUMNS 4B AND 5B FORM THE C1 SET OF DISPLAY ATTRIBUTE CONTROL CODES

COLUMNS 2,3,4,5,6, AND 7 FORM THE GO CHARACTER SET

COLUMNS 2A, 3A, 4,5, 6A AND 7A FORM THE MOSAIC CHARACTER SET.

THE SHADED AREA REPRESENTS FOREGROUND COLOUR.

<esc>Y	contiguous graphics	<esc>Z	separated graphics
<esc>ctrl D	black background	<esc-shift>M	new background (varies)
<esc>J	start edit	<esc>K	end edit

EBCDIC

The Extended Binary Coded Decimal Interchange Code is a 265-state 8-bit extended binary coded digit code employed by IBM – except for the PC family – for internal purposes and is the only important exception to ASCII. Not all 256 codes are utilised, being reserved for future expansion, and a number are specially identified for application-specific purposes. In transmission, it is usual to add a further digit for parity checking. Normally the transmission mode is synchronous, so there are no 'start' and 'stop' bits. The table shows how EBCDIC compares with ASCII of the same bit configuration.

IBM control characters:

EBCDIC	bits	Notes
NUL	0000 0000	Nul
SOH	0000 0001	Start of heading
STX	0000 0010	Start of text
ETX	0000 0011	End of text
PF	0000 0100	Punch off
HT	0000 0101	Horizontal tab
LC	0000 0110	Lower case
DEL	0000 0111	Delete
	0000 1000	
RLF	0000 1001	Reverse line feed
SMM	0000 1010	Start of manual message
VT	0000 1011	Vertical tab
FF	0000 1100	Form feed
CR	0000 1101	Carriage return
SO	0000 1110	Shift out
SI	0000 1111	Shift in
DLE	0001 0000	Data link exchange
DC1	0001 0001	Device control 1
DC2	0001 0010	Device control 2
TM	0001 0011	Tape mark
RES	0001 0100	Restore

NL	0001 0101	New line
BS	0001 0110	Back space
IL	0001 0111	Idle
CAN	0001 1000	Cancel
EM	0001 1001	End of medium
CC	0001 1010	Cursor control
CU1	0001 1011	Customer use 1
IFS	0001 1100	Interchange file separator
IGS	0001 1101	Interchange group separator
IRS	0001 1110	Interchange record separator
IUS	0001 1111	Interchange unit separator
DS	0010 0000	Digit select
SOS	0010 0001	Start of significance
FS	0010 0010	Field separator
	0010 0011	
BYP	0010 0100	Bypass
LF	0010 0101	Line feed
ETB	0010 0110	End of transmission block
ESC	0010 0111	Escape
	0010 1000	
	0010 1001	
SM	0010 1010	Set mode
CU2	0010 1011	Customer use 2
	0010 1100	
ENQ	0010 1101	Enquiry
ACK	0010 1110	Acknowledge
BEL	0010 1111	Bell
	0011 0000	
	0011 0001	
SYN	0011 0010	Synchronous idle
	0011 0011	
PN	0011 0100	Punch on
RS	0011 0101	Reader stop
UC	0011 0110	Upper case
EOT	0011 0111	End of transmission
	0011 1000	
	0011 1001	
	0011 1010	
CU3	0011 1011	Customer use 3
DC4	0011 1100	Device control 4

NAK	0011 1101	Negative acknowledge
	0011 1110	
SUB	0011 1111	Substitute
SP	0100 0000	Space
	0100 0001	

Appendix V   Modems and Services

The following table gives the standards and tones in common use. The V standards are those used in most of the world; Bell is confined largely to North America. V.22 and Bell 212A are more-or-less the same.

Service Designator	Speed	Duplex	Transmit 0	1	Receive 0	1	Answer
V.21 orig	300*	full	1180	980	1850	1650	–
V.21 ans	300*	full	1850	1650	1180	980	2100
V.23 (1)	600	half	1700	1300	1700	1300	2100
V.23 (2)	1200	f/h†	2100	1300	2100	1300	2100
V.23 back	75	f/h†	450	390	450	390	–
Bell 103 orig	300*	full	1070	1270	2025	2225	–
Bell 103 ans	300*	full	2025	2225	1070	1270	2225
Bell 202	1200	half	2200	1200	2200	1200	2025
V.22/212A	1200	full	see below				
V.22 bis	2400	full	see below				

* Any speed up to 300 bits/s, can also include 75 and 110 bits/s services.
† Service can either be half-duplex at 1200 bits/s or asymmetrical full duplex, with 75 bits/s originate and 1200 bits/s receive (commonly used as viewdata user) or 1200 transmit and 75 receive (viewdata host).

Transmission at higher speeds uses different signalling techniques from the simple on-and-off keying of pairs of tones used for low-speed working. Simple tone detection circuits cannot switch on and off sufficiently rapidly to be reliable so another method of detecting individual 'bits' has to be employed. The way it is done is by using *phase detection*. The rate of signalling doesn't go up – it stays at 600 baud – but each signal is modulated at origin by phase and then demodulated in the same way at the far end. Two channels are used, high and low so that you can achieve bi–directional or duplex communication.
   The tones are:

Originate (low channel)	1200 Hz
Answer (high channel)	2400 Hz

and they are the same for the European CCITT V.22 standard and for the Bell equivalent, Bell 212A. V.22 bis is the variant for 2400 bits/s full duplex transmission, there is no equivalent Bell term.

The speed differences are obtained in this way:

600 bits/s (V.22)   Each bit encoded as a phase change from the previous phase. There are two possible symbols which consist of one of two phase angles; each symbol conveys 1 bit of information.

1200 bits/s (V.22 and Bell 212A)   Differential phase shift keying is used to give 4 possible symbols which consist of one of four phase angles. Each symbol conveys 2 bits of information to enable a 600 baud signal rate to handle 1200 bits.

2400 bits/s (V.22 bis)   Quadrature amplitude modulation is used to give 16 possible symbols which consist of 12 phase angles and 3 levels of amplitude. Each symbol conveys 4 bits of information to enable a 600 baud signal rate to handle 2400 bits.

British Telecom markets the UK services under the name of Datel as follows (for simplicity the list covers only those services which use the PTSN or are otherwise easily accessible; 4-wire services, for example, are excluded):

Datel	Speed	Mode	Remarks
100(H)	50	async	Teleprinters, Baudot code
100(J)	75–110	async	News services, etc., Baudot code
	50	async	Telex service, Baudot code
200	300	async	Full duplex, ASCII
400	600 Hz	async	Out-station to in-station only
600	1200	async	Several versions exist: for 1200 half-duplex; 75/1200 for viewdata users; 1200/75 for viewdata hosts; and a rare 600 variant. The 75 speed is technically only for supervision but gives asymmetrical duplex

BT has supplied the following modems for the various services (the older ones are now available on the 'second-user' market):

Modem No.	Remarks
1	1200 half-duplex, massive
2	300 full-duplex, massive
11	4800 synchronous, older type
12	2400/1200 synchronous
13	300 full-duplex, plinth type
20(1)	1200 half-duplex, 'shoe-box' style
(2)	1200/75 asymetrical duplex, 'shoe-box' style
(3)	75/1200 asymetrical duplex, 'shoe-box' style
21	300 full-duplex, modern type
22	1200 half-duplex, modern type
24	4800 synchronous, modern type (made by Racal)
27A	1200 full duplex, sync or async (US-made and slightly modified from Bell 212A to CCITT tones)
27B	1200 full duplex, sync or async (UK-made)

You should note that some commercial 1200/1200 full duplex modems also contain firmware providing ARQ error-correction protocols; modems on both ends of the line must have the facilities, of course.

BT Line Connectors
Modems can be connected directly to the BT network ('hard-wired') simply by identifying the pair that comes into the building. Normally the pair you want are the two outer wires in a standard 4 × 2 BT junction box. (The other wires are the 'return' or to support a 'ringing' circuit.)

A variety of plugs and sockets have been used by BT. Until recently, the standard connector for a modem was a 4-ring jack, type 505, to go into a socket 95A. Prestel equipment was terminated into a similar jack, this time with 5 rings, which went into a socket type 96A.

However, now all phones, modems, viewdata sets, etc., are terminated in the identical modular jack, type 600. The corresponding sockets need special tools to insert the line cable into the appropriate receptacles. Whatever other interconnections you see behind a socket, the two wires of the twisted pair are the ones found in the centres of the two banks of receptacles.

North America also uses a modular jack and socket system,

but not one which is physically compatible with UK designs. Did you expect otherwise?

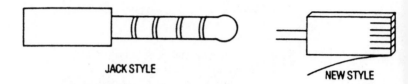

JACK STYLE

NEW STYLE

Hayes Protocols

The US firm of D. C. Hayes & Co. pioneered the idea of 'smart' or intelligent modems, ones which could be completely commanded from a computer keyboard or from within a program. The modems include an auto-dialler, auto-answer facilities and the ability to read the status of a telephone line and report back results. Hayes are not the only company to produce such models, but, because of their early dominance of the US market, first with the Apple II and then with the IBM PC, much comms software has been written with its command set in mind. As a result, other manufacturers have had to come into line.

Not all 'Hayes-compatible' modems feature all the Hayes commands – some are considered illegal in the UK, for example, because it is thought their use might tie up telephone lines for too long – repeated retrying of an engaged number is frowned on, for example. It does not seem to occur to BT officials that, even if a firmware feature is disabled, it can easily be rectified in software.

The following are the principal Hayes commands. They all begin with the characters AT and end with $\langle$ cr $\rangle$.

AT A	Answer phone
AT Dn	Dial phone number n
AT E0	Echo suppress characters
AT E1	Echo show characters
AT H0	Hang up
AT H1	Go online
AT O	Force online
AT Q	Enable/disable result codes
AT $	Set registers
AT ?	Read value of registers
AT =	Set register value

AT W0   Non-verbose result code format
AT W1   Verbose result code format
AT Z   Software re-set

The registers set such items as the number of rings before auto-answer is enabled or the length of time that a modem will wait to hear a remote carrier tone before disconnecting itself. The result codes are messages from the modem to the computer reporting such events as 'ringing', 'connected', 'disconnected', 'no carrier', etc.

Appendix VI RS232C and V.24

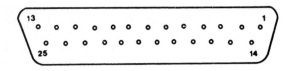

The RS232C or, to give its proper name outside the United States, CCITT Recommendation V.24, standard specifies a list of definitions for interchange circuits between data terminal equipment and data circuit-terminating equipment. More familiarly, it is the standard way of connecting a computer with a peripheral like a modem or printer where the data is passed serially, one bit at a time, rather than in parallel format, where several bits are passed simultaneously. The RS232 cable must be the only interconnecting cable ever to have a song written about it – the *Spitting Image* adult puppet show featured a skit on heavy metal rock with words that were a hymn of praise to RS232C. Clearly the writers were unaware of the many annoying variants to the standard which make life so difficult for computer buffs.

The only links essential to communication are transmit, receive, and signal ground. However, many micros and modems and popular comms software require other links to exist as well. The links are used to enable the computer to control the flow of data into and out from its buffer and to provide signals to the software which can trigger on-screen messages to the user like 'CONNECT' or 'CARRIER LOST'.

In its full implementation there are 25 lines and each may be referred to in no less than 4 ways, by pin number, by short-form name, by EIA (United States) code and by CCITT code (everywhere else). The table below is designed to help you identify a link by any of these systems:

Pin No.	Name	Direction	EIA	CCITT	Notes
1	FG		AA	101	Frame protective ground
2	TD ≫		BA	103	Transmitted data
3	RD ≪		BB	104	Received data
4	RTS ≫		CA	105	Request to send
5	CTS ≪		CB	106	Clear to send
6	DSR ≪		CC	107	Data set ready
7	SG		AB	102	Signal ground
8	DCD ≪		CF	109	Data carrier detect
9	≪				Testing + voltage
10	≪				Testing – voltage
11	≪		SA		Supervisory transmitted data – used in equalizing
12	SDCD ≪		SCF	122	Secondary received line Signal detect – used for high speed detect in multispeed modems
13	SCTS ≪		SCB	121	Secondary clear to send
14	STD ≫		SBA	118	Secondary transmitted data
15	TC ≪		DB	114	Transmitter clock (synchronous protocols)
16	SRD ≪		SBB	119	Secondary received data
17	RC ≪		DD	115	Receiver clock (synchronous protocols)
18					Unassigned
19	SSRTS ≫		SCA	120	Secondary request to send
20	DTR ≫		CD	108.2	Data terminal ready
21	SQ ≪		CG	110	Signal quality detector
22	RI ≪		CE	125	Ring indicator (for auto-answer)
23	≫		CH	111	Data rate selector
	≪		CI	112	ditto
24	ETC ≫		DA	113	External transmitter clock (synchronous protocols)
25	≫				Unassigned

*The third column shows the direction of data flow.

BT modems tend to use the CCITT nomenclature on their status lights; other manufacturers use almost anything: Tx and Rx are transmit and receive respectively; CD often means 'carrier detect' (i.e. line seized and appropriate remote modem tone being heard).

Many personal micros do not use the full RS232C implementation and, in particular, adopt different physical connectors. (Even the IBM AT now uses a 9-pin D connector instead of the 25-pin.)

Appendix VII   The Radio Spectrum

The table gives the allocation of the radio frequency spectrum up to 30 MHz. The bands in which radio-teletype and radio-data traffic are most common are those allocated to 'fixed' services, but data traffic is also found in the amateur and maritime bands. In the official publication (see below), 'Government' services include military traffic as well as those belonging to civilian government agencies. Aeronautical (R) means aircraft travelling along recognized civil aircraft routes; aeronautical (OR) means off-route aircraft – these are nearly always military. Do not expect to make much sense of non-civilian radio traffic!

VLF, MF, HF, Radio Frequency Spectrum Table

9	–	14	Radio navigation
14	–	19.95	Fixed/maritime mobile
20			Standard frequency and Time
20.05	–	70	Fixed and maritime mobile
70	–	90	Fixed/maritime mobile/radio navigation
90	–	110	Radio navigation
110	–	130	Fixed/maritime mobile/radio navigation
130	–	148.5	Maritime mobile/fixed
148.5	–	255	Broadcasting
255	–	283.5	Broadcasting/radio navigation (aero)
283.5	–	315	Maritime/aeronautical navigation
315	–	325	Aeronautical radio navigation/ maritime radio beacons
325	–	405	Aeronautical radio navigation
405	–	415	Radio navigation (410 = DF)
415	–	495	Aeronautical radio navigation/ maritime mobile
495	–	505	Mobile (distress and calling) >500: CW and RTTY

505	–	526.5	Maritime mobile/aeronautical navigation
526.5	–	1606.5	Broadcasting
1606.5	–	1625	Maritime mobile/fixed/land mobile
1625	–	1635	Radio location
1635	–	1800	Maritime mobile/fixed/land mobile
1800	–	1810	Radio location
1810	–	1850	Amateur
1850	–	2000	Fixed/mobile
2000	–	2045	Fixed/mobile
2045	–	2160	Maritime mobile/fixed/land mobile
2160	–	2170	Radio location
2170	–	2173.5	Maritime mobile
2173.5	–	2190.5	Mobile (distress and calling) >2182: voice
2190.5	–	2194	Maritime and mobile
2194	–	2300	Fixed and mobile
2300	–	2498	Fixed/mobile/broadcasting
2498	–	2502	Standard frequency and time
2502	–	2650	Maritime mobile/maritime radio navigation
2650	–	2850	Fixed/mobile
2850	–	3025	Aeronautical mobile (R)
3025	–	3155	Aeronautical mobile (OR)
3155	–	3200	Fixed/mobile/low power hearing aids
3200	–	3230	Fixed/mobile/broadcasting
3230	–	3400	Fixed/mobile/broadcasting
3400	–	3500	Aeronautical mobile (R)
3500	–	3800	Amateur/fixed/mobile
3800	–	3900	Fixed/aeronautical mobile (OR)
3900	–	3930	Aeronautical mobile (OR)
3930	–	4000	Fixed/broadcasting
4000	–	4063	Fixed/maritime mobile
4063	–	4438	Maritime mobile
4438	–	4650	Fixed/mobile
4650	–	4700	Aeronautical mobile (R)
4700	–	4750	Aeronautical mobile (OR)
4750	–	4850	Fixed/aeronautical mobile (OR)/land mobile/broadcasting
4850	–	4995	Fixed/land mobile/broadcasting
4995	–	5005	Standard frequency and time
5005	–	5060	Fixed/broadcasting

5060	– 5450	Fixed/mobile
5450	– 5480	Fixed/aeronautical mobile (OR)/land mobile
5480	– 5680	Aeronautical mobile (R)
5680	– 5730	Aeronautical mobile (OR)
5730	– 5950	Fixed/land mobile
5950	– 6200	Broadcasting
6200	– 6525	Maritime mobile
6525	– 6685	Aeronautical mobile (R)
6685	– 6765	Aeronautical mobile (OR)
6765	– 6795	Fixed/ISM
7000	– 7100	Amateur
7100	– 7300	Broadcasting
7300	– 8100	Maritime mobile
8100	– 8195	Fixed/maritime mobile
8195	– 8815	Maritime mobile
8815	– 8965	Aeronautical mobile (R)
8965	– 9040	Aeronautical mobile (OR)
9040	– 9500	Fixed
9500	– 9900	Broadcasting
9900	– 9995	Fixed
9995	– 10005	Standard frequency and Time
10005	– 10100	Aeronautical mobile (R)
10100	– 10150	Fixed/amateur(sec)
10150	– 11175	Fixed
11175	– 11275	Aeronautical mobile (OR)
11275	– 11400	Aeronautical mobile (R)
11400	– 11650	Fixed
11650	– 12050	Broadcasting
12050	– 12230	Fixed
12230	– 13200	Maritime mobile
13200	– 13260	Aeronautical mobile (OR)
13260	– 13360	Aeronautical mobile (R)
13360	– 13410	Fixed/radio astronomy
13410	– 13600	Fixed
13600	– 13800	Broadcasting
13800	– 14000	Fixed
14000	– 14350	Amateur
14350	– 14990	Fixed
14990	– 15010	Standard frequency and time
15010	– 15100	Aeronautical mobile (OR)
15100	– 15600	Broadcasting

15600	– 16360	Fixed
16360	– 17410	Maritime mobile
17410	– 17550	Fixed
17550	– 17900	Broadcasting
17900	– 17970	Aeronautical mobile (R)
17970	– 18030	Aeronautical mobile (OR)
18030	– 18052	Fixed
18052	– 18068	Fixed/space research
18068	– 18168	Amateur
18168	– 18780	Fixed
18780	– 18900	Maritime mobile
18900	– 19680	Fixed
19680	– 19800	Maritime mobile
19800	– 19990	Fixed
19990	– 20010	Standard frequency and time
20010	– 21000	Fixed
21000	– 21450	Amateur
21450	– 21850	Broadcasting
21850	– 21870	Fixed
21870	– 21924	Aeronautical fixed
21924	– 22000	Aeronautical (R)
22000	– 22855	Maritime mobile
22855	– 23200	Fixed
23200	– 23350	Aeronautical fixed and mobile (R)
23350	– 24000	Fixed/mobile
24000	– 24890	Fixed/Land mobile
24890	– 24990	Amateur
24990	– 25010	Standard frequency and time
25010	– 25070	Fixed/mobile
25070	– 25210	Maritime mobile
25210	– 25550	Fixed/mobile
25550	– 25670	Radio astronomy
25670	– 26100	Broadcasting
26100	– 26175	Maritime mobile
26175	– 27500	Fixed/mobile (CB) (26.975–27.2835 ISM)
27500	– 28000	Meteorological aids/fixed/mobile (CB)
28000	– 29700	Amateur
29700	– 30005	Fixed/mobile

Note These allocations are as they apply in Europe; slight variations occur in other regions of the globe. More information can be obtained from *The United Kingdom Table of Frequency Allocations*, HMSO for the Department of Trade and Industry Radio Regulatory Division.

Frequencies for specific services may be found in *Guide to RTTY Frequencies* and *Confidential Frequency List* both published by Gilfer Associates Inc, Po Box 239, 52 Park Avenue, Ridge, NJ 07656, USA, and *Klingenfuss Utility Guide*, available from Panoramastrasse 81, D-7400 Tuebingen, Federal Republic of Germany.

Appendix VIII   Port-Finder Flow Chart

This flow chart will enable owners of auto–diallers to carry out an automatic search of a range of telephone numbers to determine which of them have modems hanging off the back.

It's a flow chart and not a program listing, because the whole exercise is very hardware-dependent: you will have to determine what sort of instructions your auto-modem will accept, and in what form; you must also see what sort of signals it can send back to your computer so that your program can 'read' them.

You will also need to devise some ways of sensing the phone line, whether it has been seized, whether you are getting 'ringing', if there is an engaged tone, a voice, a number obtainable tone, or a modem whistle. Most 'smart' modems have these functions built in, but the command set required to make a program work varies from machine to machine (see Appendix V).

Line seizure detect, if not already available on your modem, is simply a question of reading the phone line voltage; the other conditions can be detected with simple tone decoder modules based on the 567 chip.

The lines from these detectors should then be brought to an A/D board which your computer software can scan and read.

Documentation for one such program, CAT-SCAN, appears on page 81.

PORT-FINDER FLOW CHART

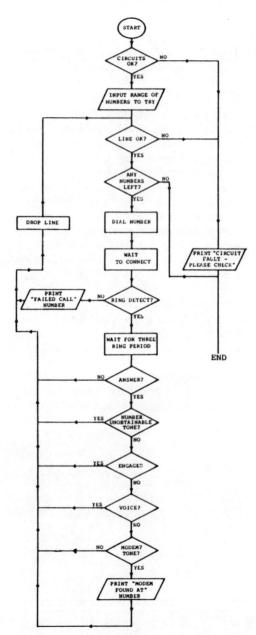

Appendix IX File Transfer Protocols

The purpose of a file transfer protocol is to ensure that data held on one computer is accurately received on another. The simplest form of transfer is to tell the transmitting computer to send a straightforward stream of characters to its serial port and simultaneously tell the receiving computer to stand by to store any characters received at *its* serial port. This transfer is limited in two respects: first, it is limited to text files and does not work for programs. Secondly, any error induced by the cabling and network apparatus between the two computers won't be recognized. The protocols described here are the ones most frequently implemented on micros; proprietary protocols, specific to just one software producer, have been omitted, as have been synchronous protocols for which considerable hardware support is needed.

Xmodem FIle Transfer Xmodem is a block-oriented error-checking protocol released into the public domain by its creator Ward Christensen. It is very popular on electronic bulletin board systems. Xmodem transfers only a single file at a time. The protocol uses two-way communications and either a checksum or cyclic redundancy check for error checking. Xmodem can handle text or executable files with over 99 per cent accuracy. Xmodem requires transfers to be performed with 8 data bits, 1 stop bit and no parity.

Modem7 File Transfers Modem7 is a variant of the Xmodem protocol adapted to 7-bit transmission for networks that can't handle 8-bit transmission. By sending the filename batch transfers (multiple files) can be accomplished. CRC and checksum are supported.

Ymodem File Transfers Ymodem is another Xmodem variant. Its main advantage is support for longer data blocks to speed transfer times. It exists both for single files and for batches of files.

Kermit File Transfer   Kermit is a packet–oriented protocol developed at Columbia University that is available for many different computer systems. By using a technique called 8th-bit quoting, Kermit is able to transfer binary files between 7- and 8-bit systems. In some implementations, Kermit supports multiple file transfers and other enhancements, such as data compression, file attributes, and sliding windows. The most significant of these features is sliding windows. A 'sliding window' protocol is a full duplex protocol that can transmit and receive data at the same time. The Xmodem family of protocols are half-duplex protocols. They must wait between each block of data for a reply from the other side. This wastes a lot of time. Full duplex protocols can send a continuous stream of data while receiving replies at the same time. This greatly increases file transfer efficiency.